On Hawthorne

The Best from *American Literature*

Edited by Edwin H. Cady and Louis J. Budd

Duke University Press   Durham and London 1990

© 1990 Duke University Press
All rights reserved
Printed in the United States of America
on acid-free paper ∞
Library of Congress Cataloging-in-Publication data
appear on the last page of this book.

Suggestions for Interpreting *The Marble Faun*
Dorothy Waples

PERHAPS *The Marble Faun* is a novel which needs to be seen in a certain light to be fully revealed. Although Hawthorne has always had his admirers and defenders among literary critics, this novel has sometimes been selected for unfavorable comparison. Henry James, who so frequently penetrated to the core of Hawthorne's thought, set *The Marble Faun* at comparatively slight value among its author's novels. The faun he granted to be charming, but he said: "I think it a pity that the author should not have made him more definitely modern, without reverting so much to his mythological properties and antecedents, which are very gracefully touched upon, but which belong to the region of picturesque conceits, much more than to that of real psychology."[1] James was regarding the romance in the light of cosmopolitan realistic novels, and under that light it did not show well. Granville Hicks has complained in *The Great Tradition* that Hawthorne wrote as if unaware of the stream of thought in his own day. But Hicks was regarding Hawthorne from a point of view which sees only that great literature cannot be written within our social framework; and examined for traces of socialism, the novel does not shine. Ludwig Lewisohn has called *The Marble Faun* a book "quite without bone or muscle, that is, acceptable intellectual or moral content." He was viewing it as the expression of a private, personal, unnaturally exaggerated sense of guilt in Hawthorne. So viewed, of course the novel is devoid of acceptable content—even of sense.

Now, Mr. Lewisohn tells us that Hawthorne's treatment of sin is different from a normal artist's treatment; and to define the difference, he uses a statement by Thomas Mann. "The difference between Hawthorne and the more normal artist is this," Mr. Lewisohn says, "that the latter dwells upon the process of creative justification of himself and, as Thomas Mann has pointed out, hence of

[1] *Nathaniel Hawthorne* (New York, n.d.), pp. 163-164.

The mature Hawthorne found that his early admiration for Scott had become limited with the passing years and his changing concept of the function of literature. He was aware of a certain lack of depth in Scott which perhaps he consciously contrasts with his own seriousness. In "P's Correspondence" (1845), Hawthorne makes "P" say of Scott: "Were he still a writer, and as brilliant a one as ever, he could no longer maintain anything like the same position in literature. The world, nowadays, requires a more earnest purpose, a deeper moral, and a closer and homelier truth than he was qualified to supply it with." In the same sketch is included a characterization of Abbotsford (long before Hawthorne had seen it) and a judgment of Scott: ". . . that splendid fantasy . . . which grew out of his brain and became a symbol of the great romancer's tastes, feelings, studies, prejudices, and modes of intellect. Whether in verse, prose, or architecture, he could achieve but one thing, although that one in infinite variety."[20] Some years later in his account of a visit to Abbotsford in the *English Notebooks,* Hawthorne, after a description of Scott's collection of curios, is led to reflect on the lack in Scott's character that Abbotsford typifies. What he writes seems to be partly an unconscious reminiscence of the passage just quoted:

On the whole, there is no simple and great impression left by Abbotsford; and I felt angry and dissatisfied with myself for not feeling something which I did not and could not feel. But it is just like going to a museum, if you look into particulars; and one learns from it, too, that Scott could not have been really a wise man, nor an earnest one, nor one that grasped the truth of life; he did but play, and the play grew very sad toward its close. In a certain way, however, I understand his romances the better for having seen his house; and his house the better for having read his romances. They throw light on one another.

Yet Hawthorne confesses "a sentiment of remorse" for having visited the home of Scott "with so cold a heart and in so critical a mood,— *his* dwelling-place . . . whom I had so admired and loved, and who had done so much for my happiness when I was young." He still cherishes Scott in "a warm place" and he anticipates rereading all his novels.[21] Hawthorne may indeed have cherished Scott, for much of his work is to be regarded as a development in an American tradition which nourished itself on Scott.

[20] Works, II, 415-416.   [21] *Works,* VIII, 273-274.

tition of the familiar plea for an American literature that will use the materials of American history. Hawthorne's review represents his dislike for the bombastic generalization in which Simms is fairly typical of middle nineteenth-century literary theory in America. But Hawthorne's most important stricture on Simms's book suggests his own position concerning the use of historical material. For Hawthorne, historical background relieves, and at the same time gives perspective to, an ethical or spiritual theme. He says of Simms's book:

... we cannot help feeling that the real treasures of his subject have escaped the author's notice. The themes suggested by him, viewed as he views them, would produce nothing but historical novels, cast in the same worn out mould that has been in use these thirty years, and which it is time to break up and fling away. To be a prophet of Art requires almost as high a gift as to be a fulfiller of the prophecy. Mr. Simms has not this gift; he possesses nothing of the magic touch that should cause new intellectual and moral shapes to spring up in the reader's mind, peopling with varied life what had hitherto been a barren waste.[18]

But it may very well be that Hawthorne's feeling that the mould of American historical fiction was outworn influenced his own departure, after *The Scarlet Letter,* from the field of historical fiction.[19]

---

proceeds to a discussion of historical subjects in general, with illustrative suggestions such as "Benedict Arnold as a subject for Fictitious Story" and "Pocahontas: A Subject for the Historical Painter."

[18] Randall Stewart, "Hawthorne's Contributions to the *Salem Advertiser,*" *American Literature,* V, 331-332 (Jan., 1934).

[19] Hawthorne has his share, too, in the negative aspect of the literary nationalism discussion. Passages in the prefaces to both *The Blithedale Romance* and *The Marble Faun* repeat, and rather belatedly, the complaint of many American writers in the first quarter of the century that the American scene, particularly the contemporary scene, did not furnish the proper background and materials for the fiction writer. Hawthorne, in turning from materials in which he had had distinguished success, recurs to the frayed phrases of this complaint as a ready-to-hand explanation for his way of treating a scene in the present. These two prefaces should not be cited (as they have been) exclusively as evidence of a special temperamental quality in Hawthorne or of a special romanticism, for they resemble closely, indeed repeat, what literally scores of his predecessors had said before him. See, for example, a passage in Cooper's *Notions of the Americans* and his preface to *Home as Found* in Robert Spiller, *James Fenimore Cooper* (New York, 1936), pp. 15-16 and 303-304. Bryant in the third of his *Lectures on Poetry* (1825) offers a concise and fair statement of the position of those who find American materials unavailable for literature, a position which he opposes. For a good discussion of the whole problem see William Ellery Sedgwick, "The Materials for an American Literature," *Harvard Studies and Notes in Philology and Literature,* XVII, 141-162 (1935). Henry James seems to have attributed to Hawthorne his own (James's) feeling about the availability of the American scene, in an often quoted passage. See his *Hawthorne* (London, 1887), p. 43.

mated after the bones of the stern Puritan had lain more than a century in the dust."

But there is an emphasis in Choate's theory from which Hawthorne makes a significant departure. He will not use the past only to glorify and idealize it. Choate's motives are worthy enough; he believes that historical fiction would foster a corporate imaginative life and reassemble "the people of America in one vast congregation": "Reminded of our fathers, we should remember that we are brethren." He urges a selection from the varied materials of history to achieve artistic unity; but he urges, too, a selection in which all that is regrettable in Puritan society be suppressed. The writer of historical fiction will neglect that large portion of history which "chills, shames and disgusts us." Choate makes explicit what he thinks unavailable in New England history: "The persecutions of the Quakers, the controversies with Roger Williams and Mrs. Hutchinson, the perpetual synods and ecclesiastical surveillance of the old times; a great deal of this is too tedious to be read, or it offends and alienates you. It is truth, fact; but it is just what you do not want to know, and are none the wiser for knowing." Choate would hardly have wished Hawthorne to include, in "Endicott and the Red Cross," the Wanton Gospeller's question, "Call you this liberty of conscience?" or the suggestion of an answer in the "sad and quiet smile" which "flitted across the mild visage of Roger Williams." Much less would Choate have had Hawthorne write "The Gentle Boy" or "Mrs. Hutchinson"—perhaps not even "The Maypole of Merry Mount," almost certainly not "Young Goodman Brown." While Hawthorne's work has the ethical emphasis in which Choate's theory is representative of the best in New England literary theory, Hawthorne comes, early in his career, to relegate history to background, and to be less interested in the picturesqueness of individual incident than in history as background for the development of a general, not specifically national, moral theme.

Hawthorne himself makes it plain that, in his maturity, his acceptance of the conventional doctrine for the use of American materials was limited. In 1846 Hawthorne reviewed W. G. Simms's *Views and Reviews in American Literature, History and Fiction* (New York, 1845),[17] which has for its main theme a belated repe-

[17] Part I of Simms's book, with which Hawthorne is mostly concerned, begins with a review of an address by Alexander B. Meek on "Americanism in Literature," and then

prime example of the Colonial spirit of liberty, an example to be remembered and taught to succeeding generations.[12]

The literary addresses of Rufus Choate are particularly interesting in reference to Hawthorne because Choate is so eloquently representative of the dominant trend in the critical theory of his time. An address delivered at Salem in 1833, called "The Importance of Illustrating New-England History by a Series of Romances like The Waverley Novels,"[13] sums up impressively the combination of a literary nationalism, natural enough to a new nation, with the influence of Scott. Orians has well called it "the finest expression" of the demand for a Scott-like national literature.[14] It is Choate's contention that the writer of historical fiction vivifies and fills in for the imagination the story of the past, and that every lover of American literature would like, not one, but a thousand American Scotts. Moreover, the American fiction writer ought not only to preserve, but to make intelligible and to universalize history: he must accommodate "the show of things to the desires and needs of the immortal moral nature." Particularly is the Puritan past available for this purpose, and it should be exalted and made to represent an ideal spirit of liberty and nobility.[15] Hawthorne's "The Grey Champion" is as perfect an exemplification of Choate's theory as could be desired; "Endicott and the Red Cross" (1838), is, but for one ironic paragraph, as much so.[16] Hawthorne says the Grey Champion himself is "the type of New England's hereditary spirit," his march "the pledge that New England's sons will vindicate their ancestry"; he makes Endicott's "rending of the Red Cross from New England's banner the first omen of that deliverance which our fathers consum-

[12] *The Works of Rufus Choate*, ed. S. G. Brown (Boston, 1862), I, 356-359.

[13] Ibid., I, 319-346. Something of the representative quality of Choate's address may be seen in a comparison of a passage from it with a stanza from Whittier's "The Garrison of Cape Ann." Choate wishes the American writer to be "like Old Mortality among the graves of the unforgotten faithful, wiping the dust from the urns of our fathers,—gathering up whatever of illustrious achievement ... their history commemorates, and weaving it all into an immortal and noble national literature. . . ." Whittier writes:
   So, with something of the feeling which the Covenanter knew,
   When with pious chisel wandering Scotland's moorland graveyards through,
   From the graves of old traditions I part the blackberry-vines,
   Wipe the moss from off the headstones, and retouch the faded lines.

[14] "The Romance Ferment after *Waverley*," p. 428.

[15] See Choate's "The Colonial Age of New England" and "The Age of the Pilgrims the Heroic Period of Our History," *Works*, I, 347-393.

[16] It is not, of course, contended that Hawthorne had Choate's address consciously in mind in the composition of these tales, though it is likely enough that he heard it. For the resemblance of these tales to the work of Scott, see Woodberry, *op. cit.*, pp. 134-136.

practice so deeply. Tudor says, speaking of the resources of American history for the fiction writer, that "Perilous and romantick adventures, figurative and eloquent harangues, strong contrasts and important interests, are as frequent in this portion of history, as the theatre on which these actions were performed is abundant in grand and impressive scenery." In this single sentence we see something of Hawthorne's early practice in the use of history: the perilous and romantic adventure of "The Grey Champion," the eloquent harangue of "Endicott and the Red Cross," the strong contrast of "The Maypole of Merry Mount," the important interest of "Howe's Masquerade." But it is perhaps more important that two of Tudor's four suggestions of specific historical incidents available for the writer are used by Hawthorne—the career of Ann Hutchinson, in "Mrs. Hutchinson" (1830), and the striking "incident mentioned by President Stiles . . . of Dixwell, one of the regicides, suddenly emerging from his concealment, and by his presence animating an infant settlement . . .," in "The Grey Champion" (1835), though changed to fit Hawthorne's purpose.[9] John Neal, writing in *Blackwood's* in 1825, also suggests the life of Mrs. Hutchinson and the accounts of the regicide judges as story material, as well as "the female Quakers . . . or the witches," the materials of "The Gentle Boy" and "Young Goodman Brown." Neal complains, indeed, of the pre-emption of the story of the regicide judge by Scott in *Peveril of the Peak* (1822).[10] "The Grey Champion" particularly well illustrates the connection between Hawthorne's work and the literary climate about him, for in it Hawthorne is not only fulfilling Tudor's prescription, as three Americans had done before him, and almost certainly deriving (at least his title) from *Peveril of the Peak*,[11] but also changing the traditional story—in which the "infant settlement" was imperiled by Indians—in order to combine it with the history of the resistance in Massachusetts to the government of Sir Edmund Andros. Just the year before the publication of "The Grey Champion," Rufus Choate, in an address called "The Colonial Age of New England," had made the resistance to Andros the

[9] *North American Review*, II, 28-29 (Nov., 1815). Stiles identifies the regicide judge concerned in the incident cited as Goffe, not Dixwell.

[10] John Neal, *American Writers: A Series of Papers Contributed to Blackwood's Magazine (1824-1825)*, ed. F. L. Pattee (Durham, N. C., 1937), pp. 191-192.

[11] G. H. Orians, "The Angel of Hadley in Fiction," *American Literature*, IV, 257-269 (Nov., 1932).

tionalistic fiction patterned after the work of Scott, and to discuss Hawthorne's final attitude toward the critical demand in which his work had its inception.

Hawthorne had been in college but one year when W. H. Gardiner, in some prefatory paragraphs to a review of Cooper's *The Spy*, stated the three great historical resources of the American fiction writer: the Colonial period, the Indian wars, and the Revolution. "What would not the author of Waverley," Gardiner asked, "make of such materials?"[4] Ten years later, when Hawthorne was beginning to write for *The Token*, his first publication outside of *Fanshawe* and a few pieces for the *Salem Gazette*, the young Whittier was calling for the use of the same materials.[5] Hawthorne makes important use of only one of these "three matters of American Romance,"[6] the Puritan material.[7] W. C. Brownell has remarked, rather unaccountably, that Hawthorne's works "are thoroughly original, quite without literary derivation upon which much of our literature leans with such deferential complacence. Even the theme of many of them—the romance of Puritan New England—was Hawthorne's discovery."[8] Actually, parallels in literary theory to Hawthorne's practice in his first period may be found as early as a Phi Beta Kappa address by William Tudor, which was printed in the second volume of the *North American Review* and which helps to mark the beginnings of a distinct New England literary consciousness. Writing almost prophetically at the beginning of Scott's career as a novelist, Tudor stated those characteristics of Scott's work which were to influence American literary theory and

[4] *North American Review*, XV, 255-257 (July, 1822).
[5] *The Literary Remains of John G. C. Brainard*, ed. J. G. Whittier (Hartford, 1832), p. 35.
[6] Carl Van Doren, *The American Novel* (New York, 1933), p. 15.
[7] Hawthorne regrets that he "was shut out from the most peculiar field of American fiction by an inability to see any romance, or poetry, or grandeur, or beauty in the Indian character, at least till such traits were pointed out by others." And he adds, "I do abhor an Indian story" (*Works*, II, 483). He remarks in "Roger Malvin's Burial" that "Lovell's Fight" is "one of the few incidents of Indian warfare naturally susceptible of the moonlight of romance" (II, 381). Even in "The Great Carbuncle," an allegory made from an Indian legend, Hawthorne keeps the tale well away from Indians. Likewise, his use of material from the time of the Revolution is carefully limited, in tales like "Howe's Masquerade" or "Old Esther Dudley," to the use of incidents which have an implicit unity and a symbolic quality. At the end of his career, in *Septimius Felton*, he disclaims interest as an artist in the surrounding action, and seems to feel that there might be danger of its intrusion upon his real theme (XI, 242-243).
[8] *American Prose Masters* (New York, 1923), p. 51.

Hawthorne and Literary Nationalism
Neal F. Doubleday

THE MOST obvious literary influence on Hawthorne is the work of Sir Walter Scott. Scott's influence on Hawthorne, in all its main aspects, has been recognized since G. E. Woodberry's *Nathaniel Hawthorne*.[1] We now realize, too, that Hawthorne's early practice conforms to a critical demand that American materials be treated in the manner of Scott. Scott's work had a great influence on American literary theory in general, because it combined significantly with the patriotic nationalism of American writers and, as G. Harrison Orians has said, "converted the demand for nationalism into a quest for Scott-like ingredients in American life."[2] By 1825 the success of this quest was apparent.[3]

Hawthorne started out in his treatment of historical materials very much as current literary theory prescribed, but he developed away from and modified the theory which had directed his early work. To overlook the influence of current literary theory and fashion upon Hawthorne is to attribute to him an unwarranted isolation; to overlook the individuality of the treatment he gave quite ordinary materials is to miss something of his greatness as an artist. It is the purpose of this note to review the connections between Hawthorne's work and the contemporary desire for na-

---

[1] See G. E. Woodberry, *Nathaniel Hawthorne* (Boston, 1902), pp. 125-126; G. H. Orians, "Scott and Hawthorne's *Fanshawe*," *New England Quarterly*, XI, 388-394 (June, 1938). There is ample evidence of Hawthorne's intimate acquaintance with Scott's work. See Julian Hawthorne, *Hawthorne and His Wife* (Boston, 1885), I, 105, II, 269; G. P. Lathrop, *A Study of Hawthorne* (Boston, 1876), p. 108, Appendix, pp. 341, 343; James T. Fields, *Yesterdays with Authors* (Boston, 1879), pp. 101-102; Hawthorne's *Works*, Riverside ed., VII, *passim*, VIII, 263-274, 504-508, and *passim*.

[2] "The Romance Ferment after *Waverley*," *American Literature*, III, 409 (Jan., 1932).

[3] Jared Sparks, in an 1825 review of ten American novels published within a year, says that he finds "it expedient first to settle . . . the peculiarities" of the *Waverley* pattern, of which most of the ten novels are "acknowledged copies." He makes an excellent statement of the appeal the imitation of Scott had for his time: " . . . the actors in these works have not only a human, but a national, and often a provincial character. . . . The subject of manners and customs is, moreover, one of general interest, and as an adherence to these serves to give individuality to the characters in these narratives, it is so far an improvement on the practice of the older novels, and advantageous to the writer." See *North American Review*, XXI, 78-104 (July, 1825).

to once vibrant but petrifying achievements in the past. For several sound reasons, its volumes prove to be weighted toward the more recent articles, but none of those reasons includes a presumed superiority of insight or of guiding doctrine among the most recent generations. Some of the older articles could benefit now from a minor revision, but the compilers have decided to reprint all of them exactly as they first appeared. In their time they met fully the standards of first-class research and judgment. Today's scholar and critic, their fortunate heir, should hope that rising generations will esteem his or her work so highly.

Many of the articles published in *American Literature* have actually come (and continue to come) from younger, even new members of the profession. Because many of those authors climb on to prominence in the field, the fact is worth emphasizing. Brief notes on the contributors in the volumes of their series may help readers to discover other biographical or cultural patterns.

Edwin H. Cady
Louis J. Budd

But they are worth knowing in their own variety as well as in their instructive differences from us.

On the other hand, the majority of *American Literature*'s authors of the best remain among us, working, teaching, writing. One testimony to the quality of their masterliness is the frequency with which the journal gets requests from the makers of textbooks or collections of commentary to reprint from its pages. Now the opportunity presents itself to select without concern for permissions fees what seems the best about a number of authors and topics from the whole sweep of *American Literature*.

The fundamental reason for this series, in other words, lies in the intrinsic, enduring value of articles that have appeared in *American Literature* since 1929. The compilers, with humility, have accepted the challenge of choosing the best from well over a thousand articles and notes. By "best" is meant original yet sound, interesting, and useful for the study and teaching of an author, intellectual movement, motif, or genre.

The articles chosen for each volume of this series are given simply in the order of their first publication, thus speaking for themselves and entirely making their own points rather than serving the compilers' view of literary or philosophical or historical patterns. Happily, a chronological order has the virtues of displaying both the development of insight into a particular author, text, or motif and the shifts of scholarly and critical emphasis since 1929. But comparisons or trend-watching or a genetic approach should not blur the individual excellence of the articles reprinted. Each has opened a fresh line of inquiry, established a major perspective on a familiar problem, or settled a question that had bedeviled the experts. The compilers aim neither to demonstrate nor undermine any orthodoxy, still less to justify a preference for research over explication, for instance. In the original and still current subtitle, *American Literature* honors literary history and criticism equally—along with bibliography. To the compilers this series does demonstrate that any worthwhile author or text or problem can generate a variety of challenging perspectives. Collectively, the articles in its volumes have helped to raise contemporary standards of scholarship and criticism.

This series is planned to serve as a live resource, not as a homage almost total participation of the profession in the first five numbers of *American Literature.* Cairns, Murdock, Pattee, and Rusk were involved in Vol. 1, no. 1, along with Boynton, Killis Campbell, Foerster, George Philip Krapp, Leisy, Mabbott, Parrington, Bliss Perry, Louise Pound, Quinn, Spiller, Frederick Jackson Turner, and Stanley Williams on the editorial side. Spiller, Tremaine McDowell, Gohdes, and George B. Stewart contributed essays. Canby, George McLean Harper, Gregory Paine, and Howard Mumford Jones appeared as reviewers. Harry Hayden Clark and Allan Gilbert entered in Vol. 1, no. 2. Frederic I. Carpenter, Napier Wilt, Merle Curti, and Grant C. Knight in Vol. 1, no. 3; Clarence Faust, Granville Hicks, and Robert Morss Lovett in Vol. 1, no. 4; Walter Fuller Taylor, Orians, and Paul Shorey in Vol. 2, no. 1.

Who, among the founders of the profession, was missing? On the other hand, if the reader belongs to the profession and does not know those present, she or he probably does not know enough. With very few notable exceptions, the movers and shakers of the profession have since the beginning joined in cooperating to create and sustain the journal.

The foregoing facts lend a special distinction to the best articles in *American Literature.* They represent the many, often tumultuous winds of doctrine which have blown from the beginnings through the years of the decade next to last in this century. Those articles often became the firm footings upon which present structures of understanding rest. Looking backward, one finds that the argonauts were doughty. Though we know a great deal more than they, they are a great deal of what we know. Typically, the old best authors wrote well—better than most of us. Conceptually, even ideologically, we still wrestle with ideas they created. And every now and again one finds of course that certain of the latest work has reinvented the wheel one time more. Every now and again one finds a sunburst idea which present scholarship has forgotten. Then it appears that we have receded into mist or darkness by comparison.

Historical change, not always for the better, also shows itself in methods (and their implied theories) of how to present evidence, structure an argument, craft a scholarly article. The old masters were far from agreed—much to the contrary—about these matters.

Series Introduction

From Vol. 1, no. 1, in March 1929 to the latest issue, the front cover of *American Literature* has proclaimed that it is published "with the Cooperation of the American Literature Section [earlier Group] of the Modern Language Association." Though not easy to explain simply, the facts behind that statement have deeply influenced the conduct and contents of the journal for five decades and more. The journal has never been the "official" or "authorized" organ of any professional organization. Neither, however, has it been an independent expression of the tastes or ideas of Jay B. Hubbell, Clarence Gohdes, or Arlin Turner, for example. Historically, it was first in its field, designedly so. But its character has been unique, too.

Part of the tradition of the journal says that Hubbell in founding it intended a journal that should "hold the mirror up to the profession"—reflecting steadily its current interests and (ideally) at least sampling the best work being done by historians, critics, and bibliographers of American literature during any given year. Such remains the intent of the editors based at Duke University; such also through the decades has been the intent of the Board of Editors elected by the vote of members of the professional association—"Group" or "Section."

The operative point lies in the provisions of the constitutional "Agreements" between the now "Section" and the journal. One of these provides that the journal shall publish no article not approved by two readers from the elected Board. Another provides that the Chairman of the Board or, if one has been appointed and is acting in the editorial capacity at Duke, the Managing Editor need publish no article not judged worthy of the journal. Historically, again, the members of the successive Boards and the Duke editor have seen eye-to-eye. The Board has tended to approve fewer than one out of every ten submissions. The tradition of the journal dictates that it keep a slim back-log. With however much revision, therefore, the journal publishes practically everything the Board approves.

Founder Hubbell set an example from the start by achieving the

Beyond Convention: The Dynamics of Imagery and Response in
Hawthorne's Early Sense of Evil (1980)
David Downing *180*

Nathaniel Hawthorne and His Mother: A Biographical Speculation (1982)
Nina Baym *194*

The Scarlet Letter and Revolutions Abroad (1985)
Larry J. Reynolds *221*

Nature and Frontier in "Roger Malvin's Burial" (1988)
James McIntosh *245*

Nathaniel Hawthorne's Intention in "Chiefly About War Matters" (1989)
James Bense *262*

Index *277*

Contents

Series Introduction *vii*

Hawthorne and Literary Nationalism (1941)
Neal F. Doubleday *1*

Suggestions for Interpreting *The Marble Faun* (1941)
Dorothy Waples *8*

The "Case" of Tobias Pearson: Hawthorne and the Ambiguities (1950)
Louise Dauner *24*

The Double Symbol (1951)
Harold Orel *33*

Hawthorne's Revision of "The Gentle Boy" (1954)
Seymour L. Gross *39*

Hawthorne's *Scarlet Letter*: "The Dark Problem of This Life" (1955)
Hugh N. Maclean *52*

The Character of Flame: The Function of Pearl
in *The Scarlet Letter* (1956)
Anne Marie McNamara *65*

A New Reading of *The Blithedale Romance* (1957)
Frederick C. Crews *82*

Hawthorne's Allegory of Science: "Rappaccini's Daughter" (1960)
Edward H. Rosenberry *106*

Shadows of Doubt: Specter Evidence in Hawthorne's "Young
Goodman Brown" (1962)
David Levin *114*

Hester Prynne's Little Pearl: Sacred and Profane Love (1968)
Robert E. Whelan *123*

Hawthorne and Nineteenth-Century Perfectionism (1973)
Claudia D. Johnson *141*

Hawthorne's Public Decade and the Values of Home (1974)
Terence Martin *152*

Hawthorne's Coverdale: Character and Art
in *The Blithedale Romance* (1975)
James H. Justus *164*

mankind. Out of his need to justify himself he becomes servant and savior of his race and seeks constantly to 'justify the ways of God to man.' Hawthorne, on the contrary, was imprisoned with his feeling of guilt and impelled to state and restate it in tale after tale and romance after romance."[2]

The best part of this passage is its statement that the normal artist conducts a creative justification of mankind. If we test Hawthorne's novel by this demand upon the artist, we may by this very definition find in *The Marble Faun* some bone or muscle, after all, some intellectual or moral content. In the process, we may even discover a connection between the faun and "real psychology" which escaped Henry James. We may find a content acceptable enough to warrant our saying that instead of being merely provincial, out of the stream of contemporary thought, or indicative of abnormality, *The Marble Faun* now shows itself "more definitely modern" than it seemed to James.

It has been asked before this whether "nature caught in the snare of guilt" is indeed the subject of *The Marble Faun*. Is not the subject, rather, nature improved by a share of guilt?[3] This is a theme so daring that though it is reiterated, Hawthorne tempers it to the shorn lambs who may read it; Hilda is allowed to say, perhaps on behalf of the timid reader, that the idea is shocking.

Hawthorne is investigating for himself the nature of good and evil. He puts into Miriam's mouth the question whether the murder had not been a blessing in disguise, a means of education whereby the "simple and imperfect nature" of Donatello had been brought to "a point of feeling and intelligence which it could have reached under no other discipline." Kenyon warns her that she is tending towards "unfathomable abysses." But Miriam professes that "there is a pleasure" in such thoughts.

But these thoughts are on the fall of man: "I delight to brood on the verge of this great mystery.... The story of the fall of man! Is it not repeated in our romance of Monte Beni?" As the romance of Monte Beni repeats Adam's story, so does the life of Donatello repeat the romance of his ancestor of Monte Beni. It is evident,

---

[2] *Expression in America* (New York, 1932), pp. 184, 172-173.

[3] Cf. Lloyd Morris, *The Rebellious Puritan: Portrait of Mr. Hawthorne* (New York, 1927), pp. 79, 142-143, 332; D. H. Lawrence, passages on Hawthorne in *Studies in Classic American Literature* (New York, 1923).

then, that in this novel Hawthorne is attempting to define the Fall; and presently we are obliged to admit that he is also attempting to "justify the ways of God to man," for Miriam proceeds to ask: "Was that very sin into which Adam precipitated himself . . . the destined means by which . . . we are to attain a higher, brighter, and profounder happiness, than our lost birthright gave? Will not this . . . account for the permitted existence of sin, as no other theory can?"[4] When the sculptor cries out that he cannot follow Miriam in these thoughts, it is not because he thinks they are untrue, but because he feels that they are dangerous. "Ask Hilda," advises Miriam. Kenyon, after some solitary thinking, does ask Hilda the same questions. She shrinks from Kenyon and his dangerous probings; but we have already perceived that Hilda's own soul has been made more capacious and her heart has been opened merely by her bystander's knowledge of the crime. Her well-brought-up conscience simply will not let her admit what Hawthorne has told us about her.

Despite Hilda's shrinkings, Hawthorne, tested by Lewisohn's citation of Mann, seems to qualify as a normal artist, so far as his intentions are concerned. The question would be whether his method is interesting and his conclusion acceptable.

I

Now, there is an indication of deeper than superficial insight in the fact that when they consider the educative power of sin, Miriam feels pleasure; Kenyon, attraction and fear; and Hilda, revulsion. Yet this insight is interesting principally if we consider it from a twentieth-century point of view. Compare Hawthorne with Henry James as a writer of psychological novels, and *The Marble Faun* is nonsense; but compare him with an author who has the ideas of this century, such as Thomas Mann, whom Lewisohn cited against him, and *The Marble Faun* shows both profundity and charm.

One reason for this difference is that since *The Marble Faun* was written Sigmund Freud has given statement and currency to some theories of mental behavior which Hawthorne seems to have objectified in the novel. How clearly Hawthorne defined the psychological manifestations in question and how well he embodied them in fiction, will be variously estimated; but even though these matters are disputed, if reading *The Marble Faun* in the light of some

[4] *The Marble Faun* (Boston, 1860), II, 250-251.

contemporary ideas brings out any new values in a novel which has been depreciated, it will not be a valueless activity.

To list some topics which interested both Freud and Hawthorne is distinctly not to attempt psychoanalysis of Hawthorne, in any degree whatever;[5] the purpose here is to use a psychologist's statement of some ideas which are discernible in *The Marble Faun* as ideas, treated by a conscious artist, not as unconscious symptoms.[6]

Five such ideas which are stated by Freud are: timelessness as a characteristic of the unconscious; the connection between myth or symbol and the unconscious; repetition-compulsion; the existence of a death instinct; the contest for the soul between life and death.

Mention of these concepts perhaps will suggest to various readers various contemporaries who have made use of them in fiction. It may be advantageous in this essay not only to demonstrate the similarity of ideas in Hawthorne's novel to these five concepts but also to illustrate his modern use of them by comparison with a contemporary novelist who shares them. Since Thomas Mann has already been mentioned as defining the artist's aim, it is fitting that his work be that chosen for these comparisons.

II

First, then, to be considered, is Hawthorne's use of timelessness. As Thomas Mann's Hans Castorp learned in a sanatorium that months were of different lengths under different circumstances, Hawthorne learned in Rome what comparative antiquity is. After seeing the "Egyptian obelisks . . . put even the Augustan or Republican antiquities to shame," he set down in his notebook that he remembered "reading in a New York newspaper, an account of one of the public buildings of that city—a relic of 'the olden time,' the writer called it; for it was erected in 1825!"[7] And so when Haw-

---
[5] Lewisohn's remarks, professedly Freudian, on the probability of Hawthorne's having had a sense of guilt with an erotic origin, exhibits the kind of errors laymen make in attempts to psychoanalyze; Freud himself says that a sense of guilt is not erotic in origin but arises from aggressiveness turned inward by self-restraint, and that moral anxiety arises from a conflict of the ego with the super-ego, not with the id. See *New Introductory Lectures on Psycho-Analysis* (London, 1933), pp. 103, 104, 141-143.

[6] Régis Michaud, *The American Novel To-day* (Boston, 1928), p. 32, writes that Hawthorne "is, in many respects, very Freudian," but applies this interpretation chiefly to *The Scarlet Letter,* dealing in rather general terms with repressions. L.-E. Chrétien, *La Pensée morale de Nathaniel Hawthorne* (Paris, 1932), appears to have a Freudian interpretation of *The Marble Faun* in mind, but if so, it comes to little more than emphasizing the importance of love as being a recurrent theme in the novel.

[7] *Passages from the French and Italian Note-Books* (Boston, 1892), p. 60.

thorne wished to have his reader in "that state of feeling which is experienced oftenest at Rome," this feeling turns out to be "a vague sense of ponderous remembrances; a perception of such weight and density in a bygone life, of which this spot was the centre, that the present moment is pressed down or crowded out, and our individual affairs and interests are but half as real here as elsewhere." For "Side by side with the massiveness of the Roman Past, all matters that we handle or dream of now-a-days look evanescent and visionary alike."[8] Other passages preserve as the enveloping atmosphere of Rome this dream of confused time and even of place, lest we awake from it.[9]

Now, this sense of timeless dream serves a purpose in the novel. It is not mere texture for its own sake. Timelessness is, we are told, a trait of the unconscious mind.[10] As an element in the atmosphere of this novel, it is of strong effectiveness in bringing out the significance of such a mythological creature as a faun. The connection between the unconscious mind and myth is, of course, now well known.[11] There are interesting indications that Hawthorne saw a connection between certain symbols which appear frequently in myth and the operations of the unconscious mind.

He not only wrote of a spiritualistic séance that it seemed to be "a sort of dreaming awake" because "the whole material is, from the first, in the dreamer's mind," but said this material was "concealed at various depths below the surface." He thought the exploration of these levels of the mind was important, for he said he could not "sufficiently wonder at the pig-headedness both of metaphysicians and physiologists, in not accepting the phenomena so far as to make them the subject of investigation." He makes an ingenious suggestion in interpretation, himself, in the theory by which he accounts for the mischievous spirit, Mary Runnel, who was the only spirit in the séances which did not come "evidently from Dreamland." She, he suspects, "represents that lurking scepticism, that sense of unreality, of which we are often conscious amid the most vivid phantasmagoria of a dream."[12] These statements are

[8] *The Marble Faun*, I, 16-17.
[9] *Ibid.*, I, 131, 137, 149, 152, 190, 192, 197, 201; II, 93, 223.
[10] Freud, *op. cit.*, p. 99.
[11] Compare, for instance, the dream symbol of the bridge with the bridge in mythology. Freud, *op. cit.*, pp. 37-38, writes of the existence of such parallels.
[12] Italian Note-Books, Sept. 1, 1858, MS (Morgan Library). Illustrations from Haw-

indications that Hawthorne had a general interest in the unconscious.

But Hawthorne shows in *The Marble Faun* an interest in specific symbols. The first page of this novel introduces us to a statue which is the "symbol . . . of the Human Soul, with its choice of Innocence or Evil close at hand," and which is equally a personification of the action of the book which is thus opened. The statue is "the pretty figure of a child, clasping a dove to her bosom, but assaulted by a snake," and Hawthorne recognizes that the symbols here used have been apt ones for two thousand years. Echoes of the symbolism of dove and snake are repeated at intervals as if to keep a pattern.[13] A legend is true, he once wrote, "if it is a genuine one that has been adopted into the popular belief, . . . and incrusted over with humanity, by passing from one homely mind to another. Then, such stories get to be true, in a certain sense, and indeed in that sense may be called true throughout, for the very nucleus, the fiction in them, seems to have come out of the heart of man in a way that cannot be imitated by malice aforethought. . . ."[14] Though this was said of the growth of legend, it would serve as a good description of the development of the symbols of mythology, and may be taken as an indication that Hawthorne was aware of the process by which these emerge.

III

The faun concept is the principal element of mythology which connects the timeless Roman atmosphere with the unconscious. The novel is not named for Donatello, but for a marble statue which had set the novelist wondering what the faun's relationship was to man. The novel is his answer to the questions which thus arose. Hawthorne's conclusion was that Praxiteles' sculpture was an expression or symbol of man's delightful escape from his own moral censor: "Perhaps it is the very lack of moral severity, of any high

---

thorne's fiction other than *The Marble Faun* of his knowledge of the unconscious, such as the presence of both invited and uninvited shapes from the past at "A Select Party," would form too long a list here. But Hawthorne's own half-waking dreams and composition in a trancelike state have been mentioned by Arlin Turner ("Autobiographical Elements in Hawthorne's 'The Blithedale Romance,'" University of Texas *Studies in English*, No. 15, pp. 39-62) and E. L. Chandler (Smith College *Studies in Modern Languages*, VII, 31, July, 1926) and perhaps have some bearing.

[13] *The Marble Faun*, I, 75, 120, 218; II, 123, 175, 199.

[14] *Septimius Felton* (Cambridge, 1883), p. 326.

and heroic ingredient in the character of the Faun, that makes it so delightful an object to the human eye and to the frailty of the human heart." Furthermore, the inception of the statue in the sculptor's mind seemed to Hawthorne to be derived, possibly, from a racial memory: "after all, the idea may have been no dream, but rather a poet's reminiscence of a period when man's affinity with nature was more strict, and his fellowship with every living thing more intimate and dear." The faun was "Neither man nor animal, and yet no monster; but a being in whom both races meet on friendly ground! The idea grows coarse as we handle it, and hardens in our grasp. But, if the spectator broods long over the statue, he will be conscious of its spell."

Donatello at first possessed just this charm. Besides this, he had an origin in "the same happy and poetic kindred who dwelt in Arcadia, and . . . enriched the world with dreams, at least, and fables, lovely if unsubstantial, of the Golden Age." He is a personification in fiction as the faun was in marble of one aspect of the mind. Even Kenyon and Hilda seem half aware of a connection between the faun concept and the unconscious. Kenyon is amused and charmed to discover that under Hilda's "little straw hat" "Great Pan is not dead . . . after all!" and "The whole tribe of mythical creatures yet live in the moonlit seclusion of a young girl's fancy. . . ." But on an earlier occasion Hilda has confessed, not without "shrinking a little," that she does not quite like to consider what the source might be of the "nameless charm" which Kenyon felt in a creature "not supernatural, but just on the verge of nature." Hilda, with all her purity, never quite liked to face her own thoughts, and this shrinking may have been shrinking from herself. Hawthorne may have intended Kenyon to be speaking more truly than the sculptor realizes about the habitat of mythical creatures under straw hats.[15]

Since the faun represents only one side of human nature, Hawthorne works out his fable with the help of a second symbolic figure, the spectre of the catacombs. The spectre is not, like the faun, a figure already established in mythology "by passing from one homely mind to another"; but there are indications that he, like the faun, symbolizes in this novel a part of the unconscious mind. The spectre's demon face, which resembles one painted by Guido,

[15] *The Marble Faun*, I, 133-135, 24.

brings up queries about its inception similar to those inspired by the marble faun; had Guido "hit ideally upon just this face" by imagining "the utmost of sin and misery," or was it a portrait of a face that had actually haunted the master "into the gloom" of his last years and after the painter's death had lurked in the ancient sepulchres for centuries until "it was Miriam's ill-hap to encounter him"? Is the spectre's archetype, in other words, a product of an individual's imagination, or a summary of racial experience?[16]

In this double symbolism of faun and spectre, *The Marble Faun* is highly comparable to "Death in Venice," where the figures of life, death, and love seem to be projections from the mind of the moribund artist in the story and yet to have objective life as well. Donatello and the spectre similarly seem to move about Rome like visible characters and mortal men, but to be at the same time eternal symbols of two sides of the human soul. These two sides of the soul engage in a struggle for supremacy; and, as in "Death in Venice," they represent the life instinct and the death instinct at war. For an explanation of this contest between life and death, we must turn to Freud's theory of repetition-compulsion.

IV

Briefly, this theory of repetition-compulsion runs thus: Man feels a compulsion to repeat past events which is a stronger principle in him than is the pleasure principle, since it can drive him to repeat painful experiences by recall. This behavior, and also the tendency to torture others or as a substitute to torture himself, gave rise to the hypothesis that there is in man a positive desire for dissolution, a death instinct. Freud connects this death instinct with the repetition-compulsion by the theory that if "life arose out of inanimate matter," since that moment the repetition-compulsion has sought to "re-establish the inorganic state of things." Thus the instinct for death would be the result of life and inseparable from life, even an indication of life. The impulse to self-destruction may be regarded

[16] There are hints (hardly to be called proofs) that the spectre, like the faun, had his dwelling in the human mind. The chapter title "Subterranean Reminiscences" suggests a mental underworld as well as a physical one. "She has called me forth," says the spectre, as if he might have been kept submerged. The spectre, having been admitted to Miriam's studio, "left his features . . . in many of her sketches." Of certain gloomy paintings repellent to Donatello and evidently done under the spectre's influence, Miriam said: "They are ugly phantoms that stole out of my mind; not things that I created, but things that haunt me" (I, 45-46, 61).

as "the manifestation of a *death instinct,* which can never be absent in any vital process. And now the instincts in which we believe separate themselves into two groups: the erotic instincts, which are always trying to collect living substance into even larger unities, and the death instincts which act against that tendency, and try to bring living matter back into an inorganic condition. The co-operation and opposition of these two forces produce the phenomena of life to which death puts an end." This sounds, Freud says himself, like Schopenhauer, but Freud claims a difference: "We do not assert that death is the only aim of life; we do not overlook the presence of life by the side of death. We recognize two fundamental instincts, and ascribe to each of them its own aim."[17]

The use of repetition in connection with timelessness is well illustrated from Thomas Mann's fiction in those passages in which characters, such as Hans Castorp and Joseph, identify themselves with their ancestors. Frequently Mann connects both repetition and loss of the time sense with myth, as in the repetitions of the essential features of the Adonis myth in various guises over and over in *Joseph and His Brothers,* until the throwing into the pit and the descent into monkeyland seem themselves variations of the myth.

So Donatello is connected with repetition and with myth by more than his resemblance to his Dionysian relatives. He repeats not only the appearance and character of those members of his line who bear the marks of the faun; he repeats also the experience of the knight who wooed and lost the fountain nymph, him who stained the spring with blood. And his story repeats (so Miriam says) Adam's Fall.

Repetition occurs also in the career of the faun's antithesis, the spectre of the catacombs: in the rumors of his agelong existence, during which he is said to have prevailed on "any unwary visitor to take him by the hand" and in the gratification of "his fiendish malignity" by perpetrating some mischief, bringing back some old pestilence or "long-buried evil" or "teaching the modern world some decayed and dusty kind of crime."[18]

[17] Freud, *op. cit.,* pp. 137-140. The idea is more fully developed in *Beyond the Pleasure Principle* (London and Vienna, 1922).
[18] *The Marble Faun,* I, 200, 178, 47.

V

The breath of pestilential death and crime, rising repeatedly from the underground haunts of decay by the willingness of some unwary mortal—this is the spectre's cycle. The animal vitality of Donatello, on the other hand, offers an opposing force. It becomes more and more distinct in the pattern of *The Marble Faun* that the fable of this novel is the struggle between the death instinct represented by the spectre and the life instinct represented by Donatello.

The Borghese Gardens are a world where time works no revenges and where Miriam and Donatello are merged in nymph and faun. Here the venerable ilex trees dream, forgetful that "only a few years ago they were... imperilled by the Gaul's last assault." The tender mingling here of art and wildness is a kind of landscape allegory of the constant tendency of nature to redeem her domain from man's control. Time here is confused, and even age itself may be illusion, for "veritable relics of antiquity" or figures touched by "artful ruin" may close a vista. So the Gardens seem "to have been projected out of the poet's mind." Here is the proper setting for myth: "If the ancient Faun were other than the mere creation of old poetry, and could have appeared anywhere, it must have been in such a scene as this." And here we see the life instinct in Donatello contesting for possession of Miriam against the death instinct in the spectre.

When the faunlike youth entered the Gardens, his spirit took on "new elasticity." For Donatello languished in the "stony-hearted streets." He had disliked the excursion into the underworld of catacombs, though the rest of the party, more normal persons, "went joyously down into that vast tomb, and wandered by torchlight through a sort of dream." He could not bear "all that ghastliness which the Gothic mind loves to associate with the idea of death." His ancestors of Monte Beni had "hated the very thought of death" for generations. They had been a "cheerful race of men in their natural disposition"; so much so that a sinful ancestor had found it needful to order an alabaster copy of his own skull to be handed down to his posterity to correct their indulgence in life's enjoyments. Donatello in time has need of that same skull, but in the Gardens he is purely careless animal vitality.[19]

When Miriam steps into the dreamworld of the Borghese Gar-

[19] *Ibid.*, I, 51, 26, 37, 38; II, 38.

dens, and Donatello drops into the path before her from the tree he has climbed to view the fairyland, she is uncertain whether he comes from the upper or the lower world. More than ever, she is impressed by his likeness to the marble faun, and feels a new affection for him. Fearing the emotion for its very sweetness, she cries out, "Donatello, how long will this happiness last?" Donatello, who knows no more of time than of death and can remember his own boyhood only by his "best effort," answers, "Forever! Forever!"

Yielding to the gaiety of Donatello and the "sweet wilderness," Miriam herself for a while seemed "born to be sportive forever." The scene then was "a glimpse far backward into Arcadian life."

But it was only Donatello's charm that created the timeless Arcadia. The spell presently was broken, and then the Gardens became "only that old tract of pleasure-ground, close by the people's gate of Rome,—a tract where the crimes and calamities of ages, the many battles, blood recklessly poured out, and deaths of myriads, have corrupted all the soil, creating an influence that makes the air deadly to human beings." For Miriam's model, he of the catacombs, has brought, as he always does in the novel, the touch of ruin and of death. No sooner had the "mysterious, dusky, death-scented apparition" thrown his shadow across the Arcadian sunshine of the Gardens, than all joy died there. Miriam exchanged her dream of eternal gaiety for a hope of suicide.[20]

When the spectre first appeared in the novel, his shaggy dress gave him a resemblance to a satyr; but Donatello's instant repugnance disclaims all brotherhood. If he is intended to have any attributes of the satyr, and the shaggy dress is meant to indicate anything beyond mere realism, it must be the violence without the sunny carelessness of the wild part-man. In later appearances, the spectre wears a costume (a monk's habit) more in keeping with his Gothic connection with the catacombs. As Hilda is compared to a dove, so is he to a serpent. When he first emerges to our view in the heart of underground darkness, the actors in the event seem to be surrounded not merely by a place of death but by death itself; the "great darkness spread all round" a little chapel where the party stood shuddering, and seemed "like that immenser mystery which envelopes our little life, and into which friends vanish, one by one." At such a moment one of the friends, Miriam, does vanish from

[20] *Ibid.*, I, 116, 51, 121-122.

their circle, and is discovered with the spectre. The spectre is always obsessed by a sense of guilt, and seems to carry "the time-stains and earthly soil of a thousand years." If, as one tale has it, he ever served as Guido's model, it was for a demon's face.[21]

Perhaps the particular demon face which Hawthorne in his own mind set upon the spectre's shoulders was not drawn by Guido, but by Michelangelo, for in looking through a collection of drawings, much as the artists were doing in the novel when they came upon the sketch of Guido's demon, Hawthorne found that of Michelangelo's drawings in the collection, the "most striking was a very ugly demon." Guido's triumphant Michael, however, had deeply impressed Hawthorne in spite of his not being much attracted to Guido in general. Perhaps when Hawthorne introduced Guido's painting into the novel instead of a drawing by Michelangelo of a single demon, he did so because the theme of the novel, the struggle between two powers, was more adequately echoed by this picture of the "immortal youth" of the angel triumphant over sin and death.[22]

The play of chiaroscuro is so prominent in Hawthorne's work that it has attracted attention everywhere, not merely as a technique of description, but as a pattern of joy and sorrow which Hawthorne saw in life. In "The Maypole of Merry Mount," light and gaiety are associated with classical paganism, gloom with northern Christianity; a connection which resembles *The Marble Faun,* in which the faun derives from Arcadia and the spectre is twice connected with the word "Gothic,"[23] to say nothing of his monastic associations. For normal life, Hawthorne insisted upon the need for both sun and shade, and he went so far as to continue this requirement when sun and shade were life and death themselves.

While Hawthorne was still in Italy and working on *The Marble Faun,* he knew what it was to be attracted to death.[24] This tendency in him has, indeed, been often remarked.[25] *Septimius Felton* decides in favor of the usefulness of death; and the characters in that tale

---

[21] *Ibid.,* I, 75, 120, 40, 186, 197, 51, 178. The order of page references here, as in other footnotes, corresponds to the order in which the respective passages are cited or quoted in the text.

[22] *French and Italian Note-Books,* pp. 398, 163, 310, 505-506; MS, Feb. 21, 1858 (Morgan Library). [23] *The Marble Faun,* I, 38, 197.

[24] See the MS of the Italian Note-Books in the Morgan Library for passages deleted in the published version: Sept. 29, 1858; June 11, 1859; June 12, 1859; May 16, 1860.

[25] Lloyd Morris alone refers to it several times: *op. cit.,* pp. 70, 78, 99, 217.

who appear to have the strongest vitality are the ones who are not seeking to prolong life.

So Hawthorne treats Donatello's extreme fear of death as well as the spectre's constant dwelling in the halls of death as unsuitable for a whole and normal person. Miriam was quite aware that death could be regarded as an "unspeakable boon," that darkness of mood was "just as natural as daylight to us people of ordinary mould." She had a curiosity about death which increased even while Donatello's horror of it, after the murder, was growing. Though it was horror which first called upon Miriam to summon her courage and face death by looking at the monk's corpse, she was able, after this, to see majesty in death, even when it was represented in this man than whom there had been "nothing, in his lifetime, viler." (Compare Hans Castorp's interest in death.) Hawthorne says that Miriam was two women in one. She was able to embrace life and yet to face death as the incomplete faun-man could not. Her wisdom lay in this complete embracing of experience, and in this also lay her power to assist Donatello, to draw him from unthinking animal existence, into thoughtful human life.[26]

For Donatello needed a shadow in his sunshine,[27] but he also needed love. Shut away from Miriam in his tower, with the alabaster skull, Donatello learned to think of death, but the thoughts did not return him to life. At the mere anticipation of meeting Miriam in Perugia, some of his old brightness came back to him. When Kenyon sees him in the Campagna rejoined to Miriam, much of his old charm and vitality glow about him without loss of his new manliness. "It is the surest sign of genuine love, that it brings back our early simplicity to the worldliest of us," Kenyon had once said about this love of Miriam and Donatello. Love brings us out from shadow and unreality into life and eternity, Hawthorne wrote of his own love.[28]

It takes both love and death to form the Garden of Eden. Donatello and Miriam in the Borghese Gardens seemed to be a glimpse into "the Golden Age, before mankind was burdened with sin and sorrow, and before pleasure had been darkened with those shadows

---

[26] *The Marble Faun*, I, 67, 190, 237-242, 107-108.

[27] *Ibid.*, I, 64, 102-103.

[28] *Ibid.*, I, 136. Randall Stewart (ed.), *The American Notebooks by Nathaniel Hawthorne* (New Haven, 1932), p. lxx.

that bring it into high relief, and make it happiness." Death is needed to make Eden of those gardens; and this "final charm is bestowed by the malaria." So Kenyon wanders in the sorrow-haunted vineyards at Monte Beni like an "adventurer who should find his way to the sight of ancient Eden, and behold its loveliness through the transparency of that gloom which has been brooding over those haunts of innocence ever since the fall. Adam saw it in a brighter sunshine, but never knew the shade of pensive beauty which Eden won from his expulsion."

Now, it is a part of Donatello's insufficiency as a man that he felt nothing of the "dreamlike melancholy" of the Gardens. He not only lacked Miriam's premonition that their hour of joy must die, but when the spectre had already killed it, he cried, "Why should this happy hour end so soon?" And yet, in Hawthorne's description, there had been something in the scene all along that had hinted at mortality. The dance in the Gardens resembled "the sculptured scene on the front and sides of a sarcophagus, where . . . a festive procession mocks the ashes and white bones that are treasured up within. You might take it for a marriage-pageant; but after a while" you see some sad break in the gay movement. "Always some tragic incident is shadowed forth or thrust sidelong into the spectacle; and when once it has caught your eye you can look no more at the festal portions of the scene except with reference to this one slightly suggested doom and sorrow."[29]

Thomas Mann's Settembrini, like Hawthorne, was interested in ancient sarcophagi, and for the same reason; the adornment of the tomb with emblems of life revealed, he said, that "These men knew how to pay homage to death. For death is worthy of homage, as the cradle of life. . . . Severed from life, it becomes a spectre. . . ." When death at length comes perilously near to Hans Castorp in the snow, Hans in a dream solves the riddle by recognizing that it is love that overcomes death's attraction; but he discovers, also, that death is close to the shrine of love and life.[30] The debate in *The Magic Mountain* as to whether life is not "only an infection, a sickening of matter," brings up the question whether the creation of life did not constitute the Fall. This idea is developed more fully in the opening of *Joseph and His Brothers,* where Mann weaves together

[29] *The Marble Faun,* I, 114.
[30] *The Magic Mountain* (New York, n.d.), pp. 256, 362, 626.

myths of the origin of life and death. Perhaps the soul was, "like matter, one of the principles laid down from the beginning, and . . . it possessed life but no knowledge." Having no knowledge, it inclined "towards still formless matter, avid to mingle with this and evoke forms upon it." Matter, however, "sluggishly and obstinately preferred to remain in its original formless state." But God, coming to the aid of the soul, created the world, that the soul might engender man; and he also sent "spirit to man in this world," to serve as a reminder to "the human soul imprisoned in matter" that "the creation of the world came about only by reason of its folly in mingling with matter." The spirit's "hoping and striving are directed to the end that the passionate soul . . . will at length . . . strike out of its consciousness the lower world and strive to regain once more that lofty sphere of peace and happiness." Hence, the attraction man feels for death: but "its rôle as . . . grave-digger of the world begins to trouble the spirit in the long run . . . ; while being, in its own mind, sent to dismiss death out of the world, it finds itself regarded . . . as . . . that which brings death into the world." So, Mann says, "It remains controversial which is life and which death."[31]

VI

Now, the transformation of Donatello from the charming but soulless animal into a man by the knowledge of death and love is the fable of *The Marble Faun;* but whereas in the beginning of the book the struggle takes place between the two abstractions of life and of death, the faun and the spectre, with the murder of the spectre this situation undergoes a basic alteration, which is that the struggle between life and death now goes on within Donatello's dawning soul.

This internal struggle of the wretched Donatello is evidently representative of the struggle of the human race. Donatello in his pained retirement at Monte Beni seemed to Kenyon to represent natural man upset by modern civilization.[32] But Hawthorne wrote of the marble faun in terms which would be effective if applied not to one creature but to a certain level of the nature of mankind: the faun had "no principle of virtue" and was "incapable of understanding such"; only his capacity for warm attachment offered a possibil-

[31] *Joseph and His Brothers* (New York, 1934), pp. 38-48.
[32] *The Marble Faun*, II, 17.

ity for his education; through the operation of this capacity, however, "the coarser animal part of his nature might eventually be thrown into the background, though never utterly expelled."[33] If the faun and the early Donatello stand for one level of man's mind, Donatello's struggle to become a man has universal meaning; if they do not stand for this, they would seem to have little meaning whatever. Assuming that they do have this meaning, Hawthorne's education of Donatello into "truer and sadder views of life" by his "glimpses of strange and subtle matters in those dark caverns, into which all men must descend," is a universal experience. When Donatello can strike a balance between his new knowledge of death and his natural vivacity, he will be ready for reconciliation with Miriam and will be a man.

When the transformation is completed and the reconciliation takes place, the action of the story is over. There is added in the book, however, a feeble conclusion which betrays by its very sketchiness how little interest its author took in it. This conclusion, indeed, was so far from a conclusion, left for the literal-minded so many questions unanswered, that Hawthorne was obliged to add (complaining) a further set of explanations. By placing his fable in a realistic setting, Hawthorne brought upon himself the difficulty of having to dispose of his Miriam and Donatello in a practical modern external society. He sent them to a prison and a nunnery to avoid crushing them under lives of hidden guilt. From the calf in the Campagna to the unlikely detail of the bleeding of the corpse, details are drawn from Hawthorne's observations, and the surface of the novel is amazingly realistic. Yet the fable itself is "a fanciful story, evolving a thoughtful moral," and the novel is at its best while the fable is progressing.

It is at its best, that is to say, most acceptable as to its moral content, where it is most modern; where faun and spectre are clear in their symbolic opposition, and where in a mysterious timeless realm the instinct for life and the instinct for death repeat the ancient story of the Fall.

[33] It was to have been expected that Donatello would, if left to his natural development, eventually betray the sensuality and surly selfishness characteristic of his family as the members of it advanced in age. See *The Marble Faun*, II, 12; I, 20-21, 25, 101, 117, 187.

The "Case" of Tobias Pearson: Hawthorne and the Ambiguities

Louise Dauner

IT IS PROBABLY a textbook platitude that Hawthorne presents a constant awareness of, and, one almost suspects, a perverse delight in, the element of paradox. It is for him, as it is for Melville, and Henry James, and Edwin Arlington Robinson, and T. S. Eliot, a "core" realization. Thus, with regard to affirmations or to "taking sides," Hawthorne characteristically refuses to commit himself, often indulging in a perhaps typical New England circumlocution.[1]

At least once, however, in "The Gentle Boy," Hawthorne erects a structure of avowal as unflinching as Melville's basic pronouncement in *Pierre*. It is not as impressive in magnitude, not as eloquently, even melodramatically explored or asserted; but it exists with such clarity of outline that for once we may say of it, and of Hawthorne, "This is the case."

The present juxtaposition of Hawthorne with Melville is not a casual one. Their mutual preoccupations with the great indefinables of human experience—Sin, Free Will, Truth, the very nature of man and his universe—postulate them, uniquely in American literature, as tragic artists. For both, existence objectifies itself as Good-and-Evil, as inevitably hyphenated. Both voice the minor tonalities of disenchantment, although there is an obvious difference in dynamics and instrumentation: the difference between the quiet skepticisms of the observer, remote enough from the anguish of the battlefield to be poised and restrained to the point of ambiguity, and the impassioned avowals of the survivor who needs no other words than his raw wounds to communicate the desperateness of the conflict. Yet one can, and does, illuminate the other.

Ethically speaking, Hawthorne most frequently projects intriguing but finally elusive moral hypotheses. And artistically, with

[1] Miss Esther Bates, the long-time friend of Robinson, who is himself often remarkably Hawthornian, once aptly defined this quality of the noncommittal as "the mind in solution."

regard to symbolic reference, he likes to leave us to the sometimes dubious delight of a "multiple choice."[2] *Did* Donatello have furry ears? *Did* Dimmesdale bear upon his tortured breast a scarlet A? *Did* Young Goodman Brown merely dream the witches' rendezvous in the forest? We may accept with a willing suspension of disbelief; or we may reject with literal rationality—except for the modest but significant fact that in each case the character acts *as though he did,* and that in such instances this "fact" is basic to the structure of the narrative, hence fundamental also to the "statement" of the theme. We are, however, confronted with a slippery blending of fact with fancy, of the symbol with the concrete. Thus a tantalizing uncertainty still persists, rising to affront and check us whenever, in moments of overconfidence, we would presume to formulate for Hawthorne some comfortable "system" of ethical thought. We know not exactly where to have him, for there appears a countering black for every white. In such a quest it is illuminating to turn from Hawthorne's delicate sets of balances to the massive and overburdened scale of *Pierre,* where similar ambiguities find some resolution, sad and sardonic though it may be. (It must of course be interpolated that we need not thus imply either an acceptance of Melville's black iron bed as the only and right psychic bed in which to rest, or an expectation that our literary artists provide us with a menu of neat absolutes.)

Once, however, Hawthorne did, in the figure of Tobias Pearson, venture—or slip—into a dark commitment. True, Pearson is a minor figure and must be made to bear no more than his share of weight. But for whatever it may be worth, the Melvillian ambiguity of his case is firmly drawn and firmly resolved: there is no final lightening of the dark colors, no adjustment for the possibility of alternate choices.

The crucial situation for Tobias develops after the tolerant Puritan has adopted the little Quaker outcast, Ilbrahim, particularly after the brutal attack upon the delicate boy by his contemporaries, and especially by the diabolical boy whom Ilbrahim had befriended after the accident to the former. Tobias has lavished upon Ilbrahim a parental love which had been frustrated by the deaths of his own children. In so doing, he has found his attitude toward the Quakers

[2] F. O. Matthiessen, *American Renaissance* (New York, 1941), p. 276.

imperceptibly changing, though he still retains a contempt for the "tenets and practical extravagances" of the sect. For a time his incipient sympathy for the Quakers struggles with doubt; then the doubt comes to "hold the place of a truth." It is a subtle delineation of the process of a conversion. But it is one step forwards and two steps backwards, for Tobias recognizes in his alloy of feelings and attitudes a contempt for himself which undermines his sense of social security until he imagines a sneer upon every face, a gibe upon every tongue.

In a matter of months, Tobias's internal conflict has realized itself both actually and symbolically in "ignominy and misfortune" for himself and in the "endurance of a thousand sorrows" for his wife, Dorothy. The increasing daily drooping of Ilbrahim and his persecuted mother's far fanatic wanderings and neglect of her maternal obligation are a kind of antiphony to the material and spiritual darkness of the Pearsons.

The final episode, that of Ilbrahim's death, discovers Tobias and an old Quaker sitting in sad company together in the Pearson home. All is gloom—a gloom echoed and intensified by the inclemency of the winter night. The Pearson home itself reveals the present shape of Tobias's world: ". . . the apartment was saddened in its aspect by the absence of much of the homely wealth which had once adorned it; for the exaction of repeated fines, and his own neglect of temporal affairs, had greatly impoverished the owner. And with the furniture of peace, the implements of war had likewise disappeared; the sword was broken, the helm and cuirass were cast away forever; the soldier was done with battles, and might not lift so much as his naked hand to guard his head."[3]

There is more here than the literal acceptance of the Quaker principle of nonaggression. Tobias is a broken man—impoverished, emaciated in body, unhealthy of countenance, diminished in spirit and in will. As the old Quaker seeks to comfort him by reading to him from the Bible, Tobias seems to be in physical pain. Worse, there is for him no comfort in the holy words; the sound of the reader's voice is remote to him, as the words read are cold and lifeless. For Ilbrahim is dying. Now even Tobias's one source of joy is to be taken from him.

[3] Nathaniel Hawthorne, "The Gentle Boy," *The Complete Writings of Nathaniel Hawthorne* (Old Manse ed., Boston and New York, 1900), I, 123.

He has fallen into a sullen resentment. To the Quaker's reproof that his burden is yet light, Tobias returns, impatiently:

"It is heavy! It is heavier than I can bear! ... From my youth upward I have been a man marked out for wrath; and year by year, yea, day after day, I have endured sorrows such as others know not in their lifetime. And now I speak not of the love that has been turned to hatred, the honor to ignominy, the ease and plentifulness of all things to danger, want, and nakedness. All this I could have borne, and counted myself blessed. But when my heart was desolate with many losses, I fixed it upon the child of a stranger, and he became dearer to me than all my buried ones; and now he too must die as if my love were poison. Verily, I am an accursed man, and I will lay me down in the dust and lift up my head no more."[4]

The case, and the irony, are complete. Here then would appear to be an unmitigated presentation of the Melvillian ambiguity—that misfortune, pain, sorrow, and death (his own, or a loved one's) may and indeed often do accrue to the man whose motive and action, so far as he honestly knows, and so far as we can see, have sought only good. It is true that for neither Tobias nor Pierre was the initial act—the championing of Ilbrahim, and Pierre's assumption of responsibility for Isabel—an "expedient" one, calculated to bear fruit of a practically advantageous nature. But the noble or unselfish deed is more often than not at odds with expediency. So, like Pierre, Tobias has become enmeshed in a close-linked chain of causes and effects, until now he is a disillusioned, embittered, and defeated man. It is, partially, at least, the problem of Job, the Good Man, over again. But unlike Job, and again like Pierre, Tobias has not even the martyr's consolation of faith; and certainly there is no joy in him either. So that, in effect, even his conversion becomes ambiguous in quality.

This raises the question as to whether Tobias's misfortunes may not in part be rooted in his own impatient disposition: he does not endure suffering with resignation. Yet the facts remain: he *has* taken in the outcast; he *has* adopted and suffered for his new religious beliefs; he *has,* through overt acts, asserted a "real relationship" between himself and his world; and he has done these things voluntarily, in so far as we do anything voluntarily when we act according to an inner compulsion.

[4] *Ibid.,* pp. 125-126.

There is also the question of the practical possibility of our ever being able to combine and manage equally well both our mortal and immortal "business affairs." In his exploration of "Chronometricals and Horologicals," Melville flatly asserts the contradiction between heavenly wisdom and earthly wisdom: ". . . though the earthly wisdom of man be heavenly folly to God, so also, conversely, is the heavenly wisdom of God an earthly folly to man. Literally speaking, this is so."[5] And again, Melville argues that if the "chronometrical soul" seek "to regulate his own daily conduct" by heavenly time, "he will but array all men's earthly time-keepers against him, and thereby work himself woe and death."[6]

Now Hawthorne, like the good mystery writer that he is (for what deeper mysteries exist than those which he chooses to explore?), usually gives us enough "facts" to assert a kind of practical logic for those who must have it. There are reasons enough then of a purely rational nature to provide acceptable grounds for Tobias's poverty and suffering. But, however we may analyze his fall from prosperity and the mental comfort of an uncomplicated existence, the fact of the fall remains. And the basic fact *in* the fall remains: Had he not encountered, adopted, and loved Ilbrahim, and had he not extended his love to include those who, in effect, produce the Ilbrahims, he would, we must assume, have continued as a happy and successful member of the Puritan community. In their acceptance of the basic irony and ambiguity posed by such instances, Melville and Hawthorne seem to stand agreed.

Since, as suggested, there is for Tobias no joyousness in his brave new world, none of the self-securing overtones of a vivid and vital faith, we must ask: "What does Tobias get out of it?" And we must admit that there seems to be for him little or no compensation on any level. He stands then not as a symbol of the happy martyr, who takes on such weight and momentum of nobility as accrues to his kind, but merely as another example of the vicious irony of life; or as another instance of that flaw, that negative principle in existence which, aesthetically, we know as Tragedy. Like Pierre, Tobias acts according to a simplest Christian ethic, in an impulse of pure generosity and loving-kindness. And like Pierre, the very pil-

[5] Herman Melville, *Pierre or The Ambiguities* (New York, 1929), p. 295.
[6] *Ibid.*, p. 296.

lars of the Christian temple, ironically symbolized here by the persecuting Puritans, shatter about him and crush him in the ruins.

But it may be objected that this interpretation of and bearing down upon the case of Tobias Pearson and the linking of his physical and psychic history with that of Pierre are disproportionate: that it would oppose a highly specific situation, that of the Puritan age and ideology, to a situation which carries no such unique period or cultural implications and which is, therefore, more universal. In this regard, I should like to suggest that Hawthorne's very use of the Puritan scheme is ambivalent: certainly it does erect for us a special world; and certainly Tobias's diminuendo occurs because his "virtue," his tolerance and conversion to Quakerism, obviously opposes the conventional attitudes and behavior which distinguish his time and place. Yet for fallible Mortality, virtue characteristically and timelessly defines itself by its very opposition to the practical conventionalities, which constitute a special "apparatus" for any given period or "world."

Furthermore, it is also true that this very Puritan milieu, this very Puritan strenuosity with regard to the "urgent conscience" are the particular elements and themes which appeal most strongly to Hawthorne as a creative artist. If Puritanism is not for him an individual creed, it *is* an artistic spark which repeatedly fires his creative imagination. His greatest novel, *The Scarlet Letter,* and his perhaps most profoundly searching and intense short story, "Young Goodman Brown," reveal how deeply he "felt" the problems, implicit and explicit, which issue from the rigorous Puritan orthodoxy. Certainly one key to an artist's temperament and psychology lies in the themes and materials to which he recurs and which he thus obviously finds provocative and rewarding. And this, in turn, may suggest the moral depth or value of his characteristic work. With regard to the morality of a work of art and the form in which it appears, we recall that Henry James notes "the perfect dependence of the moral sense of a work of art on the amount of felt life concerned in producing it." James continues: ". . . the question comes back, thus, obviously, to the kind and degree of the artist's prime sensibility, which is the soil out of which his subject springs. The quality and capacity of that soil, its capacity to 'grow' with due freshness and straightness any vision of life, represents, strongly or weakly, the projected morality."[7]

Thus we may further suggest that Hawthorne's appropriation of Puritan material is instinct with his deepest moral intuitions and that quite possibly the very fact that here again the Puritan lines frame a specific circumstance tends to assert that circumstance, symbolically, at least, as a kind of Hawthornian "universal." If this be accepted, we are saying that Hawthorne's truest, most fundamental world, his sharpest intuitions of truth in human experience, are costumed in the trappings and the suits of Puritanism. For Hawthorne, we may even venture, all the world is essentially a Puritan stage. If we need still further evidence of the universality implicit in Tobias's case, it lies in the fact that the crushing climax of his travail of love is the death of Ilbrahim, a "universal" in any time or language.

But Tobias is, again, a minor figure. Both Ilbrahim and his mother Catherine command our major interest. Yet, in addition to Tobias's value as a Puritan symbol, his significance for Hawthorne personally may not be minor. Did Hawthorne, one wonders, deliberately, for once, allow his Puritan skepticism or "realism" an obliquely sharp expression, constraining it merely in that he refers it to a minor character in an obscure position? Did he not here write not only his truest world, but his truest self, more overtly than even he knew?

There is little question about the autobiographical overtones in the moral doubts, the despairs of Pierre; but usually, though Hawthorne's constant striving for "realism" led him to incorporate strangely alien (if often symbolic) items into his fanciful morality-plays—black dogs, perambulating calves, Roman carnivals—Hawthorne himself remains a dimly adumbrated figure behind the scenes. The "real" Hawthorne, like the "real" Shakespeare, cannot yet be comfortably caught and detained. In the case of Tobias Pearson, however, Hawthorne follows to the end of bitter actualities what he usually leaves merely as subtle and tantalizing implications. Characteristically, we feel in Hawthorne a sleight-of-mind adeptness so delicate and swift that the movements of the "trick" are a blur. Often his imaginative and daring speculation, his "cat-like

[7] Henry James, *The Art of the Novel*, ed. R. P. Blackmur (New York, 1947), Introduction, p. xxxi.

faculty of seeing in the dark," as James puts it, lead us to the precarious brink of crucial intuitions and judgments. But then, like Kenyon, he retreats, or hurries down a convenient bypath; or like a kind of literary squid, he conceals himself within the inky cloud of the (deliberately?) vague and fanciful emanations of his genius. Or he simply leaves the resolution to the reader. But in the figure of Pearson, Hawthorne appears, staunchly and for once, to commit himself.

It is perhaps inevitable that, having suggested an analogy between Tobias and Pierre, we should recall the relationship between their creators, so far as to speculate upon a possible cross-fertilization. But then we remember the sad divergence in their artistic and spiritual paths—Melville, it has been suggested,[8] with the realization that Hawthorne was for him a "mistaken identity," and Hawthorne, one suspects, with a temperamental incapacity to absorb or really to understand Melville's violences of rebellion and resentment, and his growing bitter denunciations of the universal scheme. So Melville's skepticism sinks, except for the dawn-struck coda of *Billy Budd,* a step lower than Hawthorne's, until he rejects utterly Hawthorne's too frequent kid-glove shadow-boxing and himself pounds away at the raw stuff of human experience with bare and bloody fists.

There is not much likelihood then of such a cross-fertilization with regard to the ambiguities basic to both *Pierre* and "The Gentle Boy." (In point of fact, there are almost twenty years between them, "The Gentle Boy" dating from 1835.) And we can merely speculate too about the amount of nourishment provided by Hawthorne for Melville's innate and tragic cynicism. Hawthorne was too inherently aloof from the bloody soil out of which grew his beautiful and poisonous purple flowers, except as that dark and sinful earth was sustenance for his creative imagination. Melville, on the other hand, was sinking ever deeper, threshing ever more violently to keep from being buried alive. Yet—and this is the important point—both are conspicuous and subtle anatomizers of our moral nature; hence bound, finally, to reach the quicksand area of the moral ambiguities where each must proceed at his own strength and pace and at his own peril. Melville defined that darksome

[8] Raymond Weaver, Introduction to *The Shorter Novels of Herman Melville* (New York, 1942), p. xxvi.

country as he saw it, and in no uncertain terms. Hawthorne was there and saw it, too, but preferred largely to by-pass the specific verbal and philosophical definition, merely drawing for us a series of intricate shadow-maps. Each writer, however, comprehended the ruggedness of the spiritual terrain; and each detected there many of the same quagmires and volcanic craters. Melville's condor-pen will not do for vignettes; nor will Hawthorne's delicate brushes sweep for us a mural. But Melville brings us high wind and outrageous seas and the ubiquitous and immortal white whale. And Hawthorne points up Chinese prints of unsurpassed subtlety and suggestiveness.

When, rarely, as in the figure of Tobias Pearson, the specific pattern emerges with the clarity of a firm and powerful stroke, for the nonce we are off the tightrope of ambiguity, even though the texture of the rope itself remains ambiguous. The resultant firmness is kinesthetically reassuring. It is also enlightening when we resume the high shadowed vistas of the usual exquisite and airy balance.

The Double Symbol
Harold Orel

CHAPTER XVIII of Hawthorne's *The House of the Seven Gables* deals ostensibly with Judge Pyncheon, a man who sits in a chair. His two relatives, Hepzibah and Clifford, are wildly fleeing from the house, and are indeed at the moment quite a distance away; they have alighted at a solitary way station, and the reader does not know whether they will return at all. Nor, on first reading, can he be sure that the Judge is dead. The author's focus is a motionless figure in a deserted house, and for many readers the chapter has a time-marking inevitability about it. "The melodrama in Judge Pyncheon's demise is like the sensational deaths in the other novels," Stanley Williams has written, "typical of a weaker phase of his art"; and Austin Warren, making an acute stylistic judgment, has pointed out the rhetorical questions are more in keeping with a novel of Dickens than with one of Hawthorne. Nevertheless, it is my contention that this chapter does far more than allow Hepzibah and Clifford sufficient time to return to the House of the Seven Gables; it presents the very essence of an author's method.

The double symbol of the chapter involves light and time. The day changes to night, and the night finally gives way to morning. We consider this light always in relation to Pyncheon, for it casts shadows upon his face, or it illuminates his face, or its absence hides his face. Light or darkness by itself is not enough; it must have relevance to the figure sitting in the old parlor. Also, the Judge clutches in his left hand a watch. The timepiece ticks, the light changes, and finally the watch, neglected by its owner for the first time in five years, runs down. But the clock, symbol of time, has no significance save as it relates to the engagements the Judge is supposed to be keeping at the very moment he is sitting motionless; its significance becomes personal.

The two worlds in which the double symbol has meaning are the outer world and the inner world. The outer world, in which Judge Pyncheon has work to do, places to go, and people to see, is related to the inner world, the room within the house, the body within the room, the soul within the body. The score of drawing-rooms which will welcome the Judge form external appearance. The real estate which the Judge enjoys in town and country, "his railroad, bank, and insurance shares, his United States stock—his wealth, in short, however invested, now in possession, or soon to be acquired; together with the public honors that have fallen upon him, and the weightier ones that are yet to fall," all these are part of the outer world. They measure what seems, not what is. The benevolent actions of the Judge include kindliness to a destitute widow, the renewal of a tombstone, a contribution to the fall campaign, attendance at a charitable society; but the actions exist in a universe of accidents. The universe of essence, as the author makes clear increasingly in veiled insinuations that become finally bald accusations, is something entirely different. The reality of this second world informs us that the Judge will not be kind to the destitute widow unless he receives a bribe; that the tombstone will be renewed only because the person buried beneath it took what the Judge considers to be a seasonable departure; that the Judge has a direct stake in the fall campaign inasmuch as he is a candidate for the gubernatorial candidacy (the chapter itself has the title, "Governor Pyncheon"); that the Judge will not attend the meeting of the charitable society unless he remembers the society's name, and the sheer "multiplicity of his benevolence" renders that unlikely. Two Judge Pyncheons exist, the one people think he is (outer-world Pyncheon), and the one we as readers finally discover him to be (inner-world Pyncheon).

The relationship between the two Pyncheons is ubiquitous. For example, politicians gather to honor the Judge at a banquet. The dinner will include rare treats: turtle, salmon, tautog, woodcock, boiled turkey, Southdown mutton, pig, roast beef, all flavored by a brand of old Madeira. The politicians decide their trip has been in vain when the Judge does not show up, that the Free-Soilers have persuaded the Judge to run on their side; so they eat the dinner. So thoroughly do they devour it that only fragments remain, lukewarm potatoes, and gravies crusted over with cold fat. The cycle of nature (one form of life preys upon another form to exist in its own right) illuminates the Judge who is. The dinner-hour has made him a great beast; he is a person of "large sensual endowments." He would have enjoyed the meal, had he been present.

Far more than food has involvement here, though the emphasis on the Judge's love of peaches, wines, and broiled fowl (mentioned time and again in the chapter) should warn us no accident determines its presence. Animals also form a running motif. The Judge's horse, a big, healthy animal, has stumbled, and "must be at once discarded." A mouse sits on its hind legs, debating whether or not to undertake a journey of exploration over the Judge's body. A cat appears at the window; is it the devil watching for "a human soul?" A common housefly smells out the Judge (at this point ironically named "Governor Pyncheon"), and "alights now on his forehead, now on his chin, and now, Heaven help us! is creeping over the bridge of his nose, towards the would-be chief-magistrate's wide-open eyes!" The imagery of decay, of transition from health to death, brings us to the naked evil of the Judge. The metaphor of the chapter's first paragraph, which claims the story will now betake itself, "like an owl, bewildered in the daylight, and hastening back to his hollow tree," to the House of the Seven Gables, for the first time becomes symbolic.

This technique circles inward, moves from the goodness of day to the sin of night. During the morning the Judge lies abed, "in an agreeable half-drowse," refusing to consider seriously any medical advice his family physician might give on a visit he is destined never to make. But the Judge does not like to look inward. He laughs heartily about the region of the thorax, which is where he ails. Day continues. Lost opportunities and the failure to exploit time lead to a seriousness of diction:

> Up, therefore, Judge Pyncheon, up! You have lost a day. But tomorrow will be here anon. Will you rise, betimes, and make the most of it? To-morrow! To-morrow! To-morrow! We, that are alive, may rise betimes to-morrow. As for him that has died today, his morrow will be the resurrection morn.

The Judge will never rise in this world. Twilight comes into the house, shadows grow deeper on the old furniture, and finally blackness crawls over the Judge's face with its "swarthy whiteness."

Light finally vanishes from the room, and the "infinite, inscrutable blackness has annihilated sight." The universe (outer world) disappears. Everything crumbles away from us, and we, "adrift in chaos, may hearken to the gusts of homeless wind, that go sighing and murmuring about, in quest of what was once a world!"

Light symbolizes the garment of the spirit. When the garment tears to nothingness, when the light goes, we are left without our illusions; chaos is come again. Hawthorne's symbol, unlike Carlyle's, brings us to a terror of night rather than to a greater glory of day. Epiphany follows: a storm begins to howl. The wind veers in from the northwest, takes hold of the aged framework of the Seven Gables, and "gives it a shake, like a wrestler that would try strength with his antagonist." The crescendo rises.

A rumbling kind of a bluster roars behind the fireboard. A door has slammed above stairs. A window, perhaps, has been left open, or else is driven in by an unruly gust. It is not to be conceived, beforehand, what wonderful wind-instruments are these old timber mansions, and how haunted with the strangest noises, which immediately begin to sing, and sigh, and sob, and shriek,—and to smite with sledge-hammers, airy but ponderous, in some distant chamber,—and to tread along the entries as with stately footsteps, and rustle up and down the staircase, as with silks miraculously stiff,—whenever the gale catches the house with a window open, and gets fairly into it.

Outer world crowds upon the inner world. The awful clamor of the wind embodies the relationship itself. We pass from without to within, and we are not again to leave the House of the Seven Gables, even in our fancy, during this chapter. The room in which the Judge is sitting now coffins us. Whatever light we see henceforward comes in from a fabulous beyond, as it must to prisoners in a cell: "a peep of starlight, now here, now there"; moonlight "upon the upper branches of the pear-tree"; the half-illumination indicates the changed nature of things. A fantastic scene recapitulates the history of Maule's curse, but Hawthorne concludes, "we were betrayed into this brief extravagance by the quiver of the moonbeams; they dance hand-in-hand with shadows, and are reflected in the looking-glass, which, you are aware, is always a kind of a window or door-way into the spiritual world."

Spirit or essence lies beneath the light. The grin of benignity with which the Judge has fooled the world is feigned, "insolent in its pretence, and loathsome in its falsehood." At the base of Pyncheon's being rests heavy sin. Subtle, selfish, iron-hearted, hypocritical, the Judge may not tear the sins out of his nature. A higher judge has taken him into custody. "The Avenger" is upon him.

Judge Pyncheon's clock, "undeviatingly accurate chronometer," is of moment only to the living, eventually runs down. But while the faithful timekeeper marks the seconds and the years, eventually to circumscribe the life, it acts as dimension for the two worlds of appearance and reality; within it, accidents and essence co-exist. So long as "the great world-clock of Time still keeps its beat," so long will all things seem possible; so long will it be conceivable that the Judge can rise up from his chair and, through a universal benediction, escape the just penalty for his sins. The ticking of the clock provides an effect of terror, however, which the author does not find in any other accompaniment of the scene, precisely because it suggests the transcendent nature of evil. But when the clock, "this little, quiet, never-ceasing throb of Time's pulse, repeating its small strokes with such busy regularity, in Judge Pyncheon's motionless hand," finally dies into nothingness, the outer world of goodness dissolves; only the inner world of evil remains. No longer must the light have relevance to the Judge's actions; the Judge is incapable of actions; the Judge is dead. Thus, though the morning sunshine glimmers through the foliage, though it be beautiful and holy, light as such will refuse to kindle up the Judge's face.

The double symbol may well provide a clue to Hawthorne's art, in so far as it indicates the general direction pursued by the art. Hawthorne's concern with the return of individuals to their inner beings is really the very thing which so fascinates him with the framework of a crime story, and which finally matures into *The Marble Faun*, with all its strength and weakness. Mistaken identity, where the reader mistakes a person for something or someone he is not, has value as a narrative device only when true identity is established. We may flee from ourselves, as Hepzibah and Clifford do even while the Judge keeps his grotesque vigil in the House of the Seven Gables; eventually we must return, as Hepzibah and Clifford do. We may not flee at all (the Judge sits motionless in a chair), but the true self will emerge. Darkness and light co-exist in the medium of time, measurable by mechanical clocks. We may present to others an aspect of light, but if our souls be dark, eventually we are driven in upon ourselves; if not in this world, then in the next; whatever world it may be, measurable by The Avenger, or God Himself.

Hawthorne's Revision of "The Gentle Boy"
Seymour L. Gross

WHEN HAWTHORNE selected "The Gentle Boy" for inclusion in his 1837 edition of *Twice-Told Tales,* he deemed it necessary to revise that tale from the form in which it had first appeared in Samuel Griswold Goodrich's *Token* of 1832. That this was a consciously artistic revision, rather than a mere "worrying" of material, can be seen in part from the fact that the three other tales[1] which appeared in the same annual were unrevised when subsequently incorporated into his collections. The tale, however, continued to disturb Hawthorne artistically even after his revision. In his preface to a separate reprint of the tale in 1839, he wrote, ". . . there are several among his TWICE TOLD TALES which on re-perusal, affect him less painfully with a sense of imperfect and ill-wrought conception, than THE GENTLE BOY."[2] He took refuge, however, in the cliché of nature-over-art, by concluding "that Nature here led him deeper into the Universal heart than Art has been able to follow."[3]

Some consideration of his changes in the tale should prove profitable, inasmuch as "The Gentle Boy" is the only tale of Hawthorne's in which we have abundant evidence of artistic revision.[4] These revisions are for the most part deletions. And when these deletions are viewed in their totality, they exhibit how Hawthorne has managed to give his piece a firmer point of view through the solidifying of a remarkably perilous balance between Puritan and Quaker. In short, he has clarified the terms of his tragedy.

Hawthorne introduces his tale with an expository sketch of the

[1] "Roger Malvin's Burial" (*Mosses,* 1846); "My Kinsman, Major Molineux" and "The Wives of the Dead" (*Snow Image,* 1852).
[2] Nathaniel Hawthorne, *The Gentle Boy: A Thrice Told Tale* (Boston, 1839), p. 4.
[3] *Ibid.*
[4] Hawthorne's revisions in other short pieces were, for the most part, matters of eradicating tasteless references to contemporaries, or simple word changes. For an analysis of the changes in "The Hall of Fantasy," see Harold P. Miller, "Hawthorne Surveys His Contemporaries," *American Literature,* XII, 228-235 (May, 1940).

historical position of the Quakers in seventeenth-century Massachusetts Bay.[5] With a calm objectivity Hawthorne points up the self-castigating nature of the Quakers, their maniacal courting of "the cross," and their deliberate choice of Massachusetts Bay as a most eligible place to invite martyrdom. As a consequence of these aberrations, an intrinsically holy feeling has been converted into a mad enthusiasm that has driven the Quakers beyond "rational religion." But there is a deliberate counterbalance. The Puritans' vicious reaction in the form of torture, even though terribly provoked, is not absolved of moral culpability. Irony lashes out at them in such a phrase as "The fines, imprisonments, and stripes liberally distributed by our pious forefathers."[6] Further, no matter what theoretical argument Hawthorne could summon up to justify the Puritans (and, indeed, the first deletion is just such a justification), he could not bring himself to accept emotionally the cruelty of torture. Whenever he speaks of the Puritan devices for physical and mental torture, as for example in "Endicott and the Red Cross" and "Main Street," it is with fascinated horror. In fact, one of Hawthorne's most personal remarks is on this subject. In "Main Street," after discussing his own ancestor's guilty responsibility for the whipping of the Quaker Ann Coleman, he prayerfully hopes, with a touch of the inherited guilt he was always to feel, that "as the rain of so many years has wept upon it [the bloody trail of the whip], time after time, and washed it all away, so there may have been a dew of mercy to cleanse this cruel blood-stain out of the record of the persecutor's life!"[7]

The most Hawthorne could concede was that the Quakers' "indecorous exhibitions . . . *abstractly* considered, well deserved the moderate chastisement of the rod."[8] For Hawthorne, then, there was only an *abstract* justification in moderate punishment—no more. But the Puritans' justice was not abstract, and its concrete manifestations were hardly moderate.

[5] For a very thorough discussion of the historical sources of this tale, see G. Harrison Orians, "The Sources and Themes of Hawthorne's 'The Gentle Boy,'" *New England Quarterly*, XIV, 664-678 (Dec., 1941).

[6] George Parsons Lathrop, ed., *The Works of Nathaniel Hawthorne* (Boston, 1883), I 85. (Hereinafter cited as *Works*.)

[7] *Works*, III, 463.

[8] *Ibid.*, I, 86. I am using *abstractly* of *The Token* rather than *abstractedly* of the Riverside edition, since the latter is obviously a misprint.

Once having recognized that Hawthorne has, at the very outset, set up a balance of two evils, abstract guilt and unreasonable retribution, which, as will be seen, is a necessary condition for the subsequent tragedy, the reason for the following deletion becomes evident.

That those who were active in, or consenting to, this measure [the killing of two Quakers in 1659], made themselves responsible for innocent blood, is not to be denied: yet the extenuating circumstances of their conduct are more numerous than can generally be pleaded by persecutors. The inhabitants of New England were a people, whose original bond of union was their peculiar religious principles. For the peaceful exercise of their own mode of worship, an object, the very reverse of universal liberty of conscience, they had hewn themselves a home in the wilderness: they had exposed themselves to the peril of death, and to a life which rendered the accomplishment of that peril almost a blessing. They had found no city of refuge prepared for them, but, with Heaven's assistance, they had created one; and it would be hard to say whether justice did not authorize their determination, to guard its gate against all who were destitute of the prescribed title to admittance. The principle of their foundation was such, that to destroy the unity of religion, might have been to subvert the government, and break up the colony, especially at a period when the state of affairs in England had stopped the tide of emigration, and drawn back many of the pilgrims to their native homes. The magistrates of Massachusetts Bay were, moreover, most imperfectly informed respecting the real tenets and character of the Quaker sect. They had heard of them, from various parts of the earth, as opposers of every known opinion, and enemies of all established governments; they had beheld extravagances which seemed to justify these accusations; and the idea suggested by their own wisdom may be gathered from the fact, that the persons of many individuals were searched, in the expectation of discovering witch-marks. But after all allowances, it is to be feared that the death of the Quakers was principally owing to the polemic fierceness, that distinct passion of human nature, which has so often produced frightful guilt in the most sincere and zealous advocates of virtue and religion.[9]

This is a very curious passage. That this is a rather convincing plea for historical necessity (motivated perhaps by Hawthorne's unconscious need to rationalize his ancestral guilt) seems fairly obvious. But Hawthorne the artist could see in its general tenor a threat to the balanced backdrop of the tale. Even the final sentence,

[9] Nathaniel Hawthorne, "The Gentle Boy," *The Token* (Boston, 1832), pp. 194-195.

in which Hawthorne with characteristic sanity cuts down his seemingly logical argument, was best left unsaid. For after all, the rightness or wrongness of the situation makes little difference here. Caught between forces beyond their control, Ilbrahim and Tobias, like Romeo and Juliet, are tragically destroyed. What ultimately arrests us in both Shakespeare's and Hawthorne's tragedies is not the force itself, the existence of evil, but the tragic waste of decent human beings trapped by life itself.

The next deletion of real importance[10] is somewhat more difficult to explain. After Tobias's good heart has finally conquered his inherited misgivings about the Quaker child whom he has found standing forlornly on his executed father's grave, he takes the boy home to his wife Dorothy, having decided to accept him as their own. After Tobias tells Dorothy to be kind to the child even as she would have been to their own children now dead, the following passage is deleted.

The wife's eyes filled with tears; she inquired neither who little Ilbrahim was, nor whence he came, but kissed his cheek and led the way into the dwelling. The sitting-room, which was also the kitchen, was lighted by a cheerful fire upon the large stone-laid hearth, and a confused variety of objects shone out and disappeared in the unsteady blaze. There were the household articles, the many wooden trenchers, the one large pewter dish, and the copper kettle whose inner surface was glittering like gold. There were the lighter implements of husbandry, the spade, the sickle, and the scythe, all hanging by the door, and the axe before which a thousand trees had bowed themselves. On another part of the wall were the steel cap and iron breast plate, the sword and the matchlock gun. There, in a corner, was a little chair, the memorial of a brood of children whose place by the fire-side was vacant forever. And there, on a table near the window, among all those tokens of labor, war, and mourning, was the Holy Bible, the book of life, an emblem of the blessed comforts which

---

[10] An unimportant but interesting change occurs soon after the story proper begins. As Tobias enters the scene, Hawthorne comments that "a gloomy extent of nearly four miles lay between him and his *home*." In the *Token* edition the final word is *house*. Ordinarily, such a minor change would be attributed to the kind of misprintings one finds in many of Hawthorne's stories, and about which he complained fairly often. But here, where there is ample evidence of close revision, it seems reasonable to attribute the change to artistic scrupulousness. The word *home* has richer, warmer connotations than does *house*, and is therefore substituted. When Tobias asks Ilbrahim where he belongs, the child, pointing to his father's grave, says, "Here is my home." And when Tobias later points to his own "home," "a thrill passed through the child's frame." And finally, Ilbrahim's acceptance of his new parents is complete when he considers "their house as home." Hawthorne's change, then, gives consistency to the distinction.

it offers, to those who can receive them, amidst the toil, the strife, and sorrow of this world. Dorothy hastened to bring the little chair from its corner; she placed it on the hearth, and, seating the poor orphan there, addressed him in words of tenderness, such as only a mother's experience could have taught her. At length, when he had timidly begun to taste his warm bread and milk, she drew her husband apart.[11]

There is nothing in this passage which would contradict Dorothy's character as we come to know her: a warm, considerate, instinctively loving mother. In fact, the inclusion of the passage would have lent something to Hawthorne's portrayal of her as the ideal of "rational piety" and sensitive motherhood. Further, the description of the Puritans' household is effective. The rather casual cataloguing of the items, deftly accentuating the austerity of the entire setting, summons up for the reader the experiental gamut of Puritan life: husbandry, war, domesticity, piety, and death. Perhaps it might be suggested that the over-all effect of the scene with its emphasis on purity and cheerful utility would have run counter to the barbarity that the Puritans are later to exhibit. But the Pearsons are in no way representative of the Puritans in the tale; in fact, they are to be the victims, not the perpetrators, of the "cold sect's" persecutions. The omission of the passage also weakens a later passage in the tale,[12] in which the Pearson home is pictured now destitute of its "homely wealth." Without the previous passage the Pearsons' loss is not dramatically visualized, somewhat vitiating the pathos of their situation. However, Hawthorne must have felt that the warmth of the scene in the home of Puritans, even ones who are later to prove highly unrepresentative, might, unwittingly, upset the precarious balance he felt he needed.

The first foreshadowing of Tobias's ultimate rejection of Puritanism comes when Dorothy asks her husband if the Indians had orphaned the child. "No," he answers, "the heathen savage would have given him to eat of his scanty morsel, and to drink of his birchen cup; but Christian men, alas! had cast him out to die."[13] After Dorothy with an even quicker tenderness than her husband accepts the child as her own, the following description of Ilbrahim is deleted: "She drew near to Ilbrahim, who, having finished his re-

[11] *Token*, pp. 202-203.
[12] *Works*, I, 115.
[13] *Ibid.*, I, 92.

past, sat with the tears hanging upon his long eye-lashes, but with a singular and unchildlike composure on his little face."[14] The key to the deletion is in the words "singular and unchildlike." Although Hawthorne could just as well have kept the rest of the passage, the final words contradict the quiet and lovely childishness of the boy. The two paragraphs which follow the deletion emphasize the pained helplessness of the child: tears that gush forth at the word "mother," the simple and affecting Quaker prayer he insists upon, his pale and spiritual countenance. The "singular and unchildlike composure" would have indicated, not the wretched bewilderment of a child buffeted by circumstances it could but imperfectly understand, but rather an almost premature recognition and acceptance of suffering as a part of the human condition.

The following pages of the tale deal with the Puritans' reaction to the Pearsons' act of Christian charity. They are adamant in their hatred of the child, whose very beauty and winning manners are ascribed to Satanic influences. Their antipathy is increased by their inability to convert the gentle Quaker to the tenets of Calvinism—to them a certain sign of invincible depravity. But more important, Tobias, once a respected member of the community, is now hooted and threatened as a "backslider."

On the second Sabbath after Ilbrahim has become a member of the family, the three Pearsons go to the meetinghouse. Hawthorne's treatment of the scene is stingingly ironic. The signal for commencement is a thundering drum—"a martial call to the place of holy and quiet thoughts."[15] The parishioners on the way to the holy place are full of hate, avoiding the "two parents linked together by the infant of their love."[16] They form a "formidable phalanx," so as to wither the Pearsons with gazes of disapproval. But even in this passage of the scathing contrast between theoretical piety and actual impiety, Hawthorne deleted a passage, which, on the face of it, would have served the vehicle of his critical comment, the military metaphor, very well: ". . . in connexion with which peculiarity [the use of a military drum as the commencement signal], it may be mentioned, that an apartment of the meetinghouse served the purposes of a powder magazine and armory."[17]

[14] *Token*, p. 203.
[16] *Ibid.*
[15] *Works*, I, 96.
[17] *Token*, p. 207.

"The Gentle Boy" Revised 45

Although this deletion would have served Hawthorne's purpose beautifully, he probably could not bring himself to be so unfair as to insinuate, even for artistic purposes, that the whole of the Puritans' religion was one monstrous distortion. He knew that the arsenal was for defense, not aggression, and that the meetinghouse was the most logical place to store arms. Whereas the use of a military drum is explained as being due to the absence of a bell, and carries only a subtle implication, the deleted passage is both too obvious and too baldly unextenuated.

Hawthorne's next deletion is motivated by a desire for unity of effect. Immediately following his description of the rude, unplastered, naked, and drab meetinghouse, there appears in the original version of the tale this obviously inappropriate passage.

> On one side of the house sat the women, generally in sad-colored and most unfanciful apparel, although there were a few high head-dresses, on which the "Cobbler of Agawam" would have lavished his empty wit of words. There was no veil to be seen among them all, and it must be allowed that the November sun, shining brightly through the windows, fell upon many a demure but pretty set of features, which no barbarity of art could spoil. The masculine department of the house presented somewhat more variety than that of the women. Most of the men, it is true, were clad in black or dark-grey broadcloth, and all coincided in the short, ungraceful, and ear-displaying cut of their hair. But those who were in martial authority, having arrayed themselves in their embroidered buff-coats, contrasted strikingly with the remainder of the congregation, and attracted many youthful thoughts which should have been otherwise employed.[18]

This passage individualizes and humanizes the otherwise abstract and faceless force which is ultimately to crush Tobias and Ilbrahim. The figures depicted here seem hardly the same ones who with barbarous self-righteousness had put Ilbrahim's father to death, or shouted after Tobias, "What shall be done to the backslider? Lo! the scourge is knotted for him, even the whip of nine cords, and every cord three knots!"[19] Nor is it possible to imagine these rather attractive people, a moment later, turning their "repulsive and unheavenly countenance[s] upon the gentle boy," and drawing back

[18] *Ibid.*, p. 208.
[19] *Works*, I, 95.

their "earth-soiled garments from his touch," as if to say, "We are holier than thou."[20]

The description of the Puritan minister is also tempered in the final version. Although Hawthorne stresses the minister's having forgotten the lesson of persecution taught by the grim Archbishop Laud, by having the old divine condemn heretics even though but "little children" or "sucking babes," he deletes the aspersions he had originally cast upon the minister's intellectual capabilities. After describing the old man's countenance as "pale and thin,"[21] Hawthorne deletes "yet not intellectual."[22] And following his résumé of the minister's sermon, Hawthorne strikes out the following passage as well:

> Into this discourse was worked much learning, both sacred and profane, which, however, came forth not digested into its original elements, but in short quotations, as if the preacher were unable to amalgamate his own mind with that of the author. His own language was generally plain, even to affectation, but there were frequent specimens of a dull man's efforts to be witty—little ripples fretting the surface of a stagnant pool.[23]

The deletion here is extremely significant. Hawthorne in deleting this satiric passage is underlining the fact that the invidious mantle of evil that is settling down upon the shoulders of the three central characters stems not from a stupid man's pietistic aberrations, but rather is the outgrowth, necessary and indomitable, of the sect's metaphysic, whose self-sufficient righteousness must inevitably doom the tangential believer, be he ever so innocent and intrinsically good. Hawthorne's treatment of the minister's stupidity is amusing; but the Puritans are not a laughing matter. The minister, as a grim symbol of the Puritan force, cannot be, at the same time, an object for Popean satire.

The balance of evils is next affected by the return of Ilbrahim's mother, Catherine, to the meetinghouse. Garbed in the sackcloth and ashes of the conspicuous martyr, she delivers a countersermon. Hawthorne's sharp comment on her impassioned rantings is, "Having thus given vent to the flood of malignity which she mistook for inspiration, the speaker was silent."[24] The only deletion is that of the irrevelant remark, "Having thus usurped a station to which

[20] *Ibid.*, I, 97.
[21] *Ibid.*, I, 98.
[22] *Token*, p. 209.
[23] *Ibid.*, p. 210.
[24] *Works*, I, 101.

her sex can plead no title...."²⁵ This deletion is somewhat allied to the previous one in that the particularity of the criticism detracts from the general evil which Hawthorne felt to be inherent in seventeenth-century Quakerism. For a woman to preach, as Hawthorne could see, was at most a violation of a convention; but for Hawthorne the deepest and most fundamental evil in Quakerism was the "unbridled fanaticism" that destroyed "the duties of the present life" and broke the bonds of natural affection—for Hawthorne the unpardonable sin. Finally, after a tortured struggle, Catherine leaves her son with the Pearsons, and wanders off again to carry out what she believes is her mission. In cataloguing her self-imposed suffering at the hands of other bigots, Hawthorne changes one phrase so as to emphasize the Puritans' cruelty: "For her voice had been already heard in many lands of Christendom; and she had pined in the cells of a Catholic Inquisition before she felt the lash and lay in the dungeons ["ate the bread" in the *Token*] of the Puritans."²⁶

So Ilbrahim becomes a part of the "immovable furniture" of the Pearson household. The child under the consciousness of being loved blossoms into a delighted and delightful boy, although, as Hawthorne observes, "the disordered imaginations of both his father and mother had perhaps propagated a certain unhealthiness in the mind of the boy."²⁷ Ilbrahim is acutely sensitive both to pleasure and pain, and although his is a prevailingly sweet temperament, the slightest rebuke steeps him in an almost unnatural depression. The Puritans are unrelenting. It is with scorn and bitterness that they view the child, whose innocent spirits constantly offend their sense of propriety. But it is the children of the settlement who most hate Ilbrahim—the very children whom he needs for the exercise of his yet "unappropriated love."²⁸ When chance has it that one of these children is injured and has to be confined to the Pearson home for medical reasons, Ilbrahim's tragedy rises to its climax. Ilbrahim woos the injured boy, who is significantly misshapen, with the consideration, patience, and gentleness of an unworthy lover. When the boy is well enough to leave, Ilbrahim imagines that his natural

²⁵ *Token*, p. 211.
²⁶ *Works*, I, 107.
²⁷ *Ibid.*, I, 108.
²⁸ "Unappropriate love" in *Token*.

affection has overcome the inherited malice of the community. One day, completely trusting, Ilbrahim approaches a group of Puritan boys. But with the "devil of their fathers" in their hearts the children attack him mercilessly. The boy whom Ilbrahim had befriended stands apart on crutches. He calls coaxingly to the besieged boy and Ilbrahim drags his bruised body towards the friend to "take his hand." When the Quaker child is close enough, the boy strikes him across the mouth with his crutch. It is all over with the child. Where before he had struggled against the battering of his body, he now, more deeply damaged, turns over to die. The Puritan force in its most elemental state—the children—has done its work. Ilbrahim is saved from actual death by some older people.

Back at the Pearsons' the child, his soul withered, awaits death. But Hawthorne forces us to remember that although the Puritan force has beat its unrelenting hate against the child's fragile being, the soul was crushed against the rock of the Quaker woman's unholy neglect of a mother's duty. Ilbrahim in his agony cries out "Mother, Mother," which "admitted of no substitute in his extreme affliction."[29]

The tragedy of Ilbrahim is complete. Caught between two abstract forces, which the gentle boy could only feel but never understand, he is ironically mangled between a pious love masquerading as hate, and pious hate masquerading as love. His physical death in the arms of his agonized mother later is an anticlimax. When the soul is dead the body will not long endure.

But before Ilbrahim's death Hawthorne had shifted his focus of interest to Tobias. Tobias had always yearned for a more fervid faith than Calvinism, although he had little doubt of its doctrinarian validity. His love for Ilbrahim had softened his attitude towards Quakers, but his contempt for the sect's tenets and outrageous practices remained firm. His struggle for metaphysical values is tortured by the paradox of the head and the heart. Whereas his intellect rejected the spiritual extravagances of the Quakers, his emotional nature was revolted by the Calvinists' torture and castigation, even in the name of a Truth whose theoretical basis he accepted. Even as he becomes assimilated to the "enthusiasts," his contempt for them is not lessened, and he resolves the problem by turning the

[29] *Works*, I, 113.

scorn upon himself. At this point in Tobias's religious predicament Hawthorne deletes this passage.

> At length, when the change in his belief was fully accomplished, the contest grew very terrible between the love of the world, in its thousand shapes, and the power which moved him to sacrifice all for the one pure faith; to quote his own words, subsequently uttered at a meeting of Friends, it was as if "Earth and Hell had garrisoned the fortress of his miserable soul, and Heaven came battering against it to storm the walls."[30]

The reason for this deletion is obvious. First, Hawthorne realized that by projecting Tobias's ultimate spiritual peace into the future he was vitiating, even nullifying, the tragedy which was still to be dramatized. "It is heavy! It is heavier than I can bear!" exclaims the tortured Tobias somewhat later, as he awaits the death of his new-found son.[31] Second, and more important, the passage seems to insinuate that Tobias's choice was the "correct" one: that his conversion enabled him finally to grasp The Truth ("the one pure faith"). But this is not what the form of the tale indicates. The quest for The Truth is not here Hawthorne's concern; on the contrary, it is the ruthless conviction that *the truth* is The Truth which activates the forces of the tragedy. Tobias is not the happy martyr whose anguished pain eventually gains for him the gift of certainty; he "acts according to the simplest Christian ethic, in an impulse of pure generosity and loving-kindness. And ... the very pillars of the Christian temple ... shatter about him and crush him."[32] Ultimately, Tobias's conversion was not toward the dogma of the Quakers, but away from the cruel inhumanity of the Puritans—a desperate and despairing escape, without sweetness or light. It is the tragedy of Ilbrahim that incites the tragedy of Tobias.

The revision of the following passage achieves the same effect as the previous deletion.

> Such was his state of warfare at the period of Ilbrahim's misfortune; and the emotions consequent upon that event enlisted with the beseiging army, and decided the victory. There was a triumphant shout within him, and from that moment all was peace. Dorothy had not been the

---
[30] *Token*, p. 227.
[31] *Works*, I, 117.
[32] Louise Dauner, "The 'Case' of Tobias Pearson: Hawthorne and the Ambiguities," *American Literature*, XXI, 468-469 (Jan., 1950).

subject of a similar process, for her reason was as clear as her heart was tender. (*Token,* pp. 227-228)

Such was his state of mind at the period of Ilbrahim's misfortune; and the emotions consequent upon that event completed the change, of which the child had been the original instrument. (*Works,* I, 114)

The original version indicates a spiritual peace, which is wholly absent from the final one. In revising his original passage, Hawthorne escaped the predicament of the Miracle Plays: the audience's knowledge that the "tragic" happenings of this world would be, at the end, recompensed with Infinite Bliss. The Miracle Plays, therefore, are never tragedies; but Hawthorne's tale is a tragedy.

The final scene of the tale introduces a new character: an old Quaker whose suffering, unlike Tobias's, has gained him the happy acceptance of the convinced martyr. The old man, as Catherine had, deserted a child to follow the compelling inner light. Although the old Quaker is an affecting figure, and his sincere suffering arouses the reader's sympathy, there runs through this section an unmistakable undertone of criticism. For Hawthorne, the inner light which causes an unnatural neglect of duties is, in reality, an inner darkness, and, so as not to mitigate the basic fanaticism which lay beneath the old man's actions, Hawthorne deleted this piece of description: "His features were strong and well connected, and seemed to express firmness of purpose and sober understanding, although his actions had frequently been at variance with this last attribute."[33]

Catherine returns to her final agony: Ilbrahim dies in her arms. And after still more years of even more "unbridled fanaticism," heightened by the absence of any earthly ties, she finally returns to the Pearson household, "her fierce and vindictive nature . . . softened by the same griefs which had once irritated it."[34] In time, her transformation wins over the Puritans, and when she dies many mourners follow her to her grave beside her son's. Both forces have spent themselves.

There remains but one final deletion to consider. Originally Hawthorne had closed his tale with these words: "My heart is glad of this triumph of our better nature; it gives me a kindlier feeling

[33] *Token,* p. 229.
[34] *Works,* I, 125.

for the fathers of my native land; and with it I will close the tale."³⁵ Perhaps Hawthorne omitted this extraneous "story-teller's" comment so as better to preserve the effect of imaginative reality; however, he closed so many another tale in a similar manner that such a conclusion would be extremely tenuous. But it does seem reasonable to assume that he deleted the passage because it would have tended to cast the greatest burden of guilt upon the Puritans; however, as I have attempted to demonstrate, Hawthorne manipulated his material, especially through his revisions, so as to point up the mutuality of guilt. Therefore, it seems to me, the theme of this tale is more than just a dramatized social tract—"a mature study of bigotry and persecution"³⁶—although it is that too. Hawthorne's revisions in this tale so generalize and equalize the terms of the guilt, that, in its final effect, the thematic implication of the story transcends any particular manifestation of evil. For Hawthorne, more than for any of his contemporaries except Melville, the existence of an Evil Principle was a reality;³⁷ and this tale, ultimately, contemplates the tragedy of an innocent child and a Christian adult caught up by this elemental condition of existence, of which the historical act of persecution is but a grim reflection.

[35] *Token*, p. 240.
[36] Mark Van Doren, *Nathaniel Hawthorne* (New York, 1949), p. 77.
[37] "There is evil in every human heart," he wrote in his notebook for 1836 (*Works*, IX, 43).

Hawthorne's *Scarlet Letter:* "The Dark Problem of This Life"

Hugh N. Maclean

I

LIKE all great books, *The Scarlet Letter* continuously stimulates criticism. Hawthorne's genius has not called forth such tremendous surges of critical interest as those which have swept over Blake, James, or Melville; but a steadier and perhaps more progressively constructive stream of studies has added considerably to Hawthorne's stature. An early tendency to consider Hester the "heroine," saved, or at least somehow "improved" by her experiences, has been replaced by a tougher but more accurate interpretation.[1] The placing of Hawthorne in Melville's shadow, as a "conscious allegorist," properly somewhat behind and beneath the "symbolist drawing on the unconscious," has been corrected. Matthiessen's insights, meanwhile, have become critical touchstones, whether they relate to Hawthorne's concern with his own day (as distinct from Brooks's wraith-like aesthete in the ghost town of Salem), his deliberately imposed framework of allegory, or his choice of "romance" for its multilateral nature.[2]

As to the relation of structure and theme in Hawthorne's novel, Professor Gerber has done much.[3] But the text of the novel justifies an extension of his approach. The purpose of the present study is to show that the structure of *The Scarlet Letter* is more deliberately patterned than Gerber suggests, and to show that, by making the fullest use of allegory and of "levels of meaning," its artful balance consciously illuminates the "dark necessity" of Hawthorne's theme.

Critics of the book have often evaded unequivocal statement of

[1] See especially R. H. Fogle, *Hawthorne's Fiction: The Light and the Dark* (Norman, Okla., 1952), pp. 104-107, 117-118; and Darrel Abel, "Hawthorne's Hester," *College English*, XIII, 303-309 (March, 1952).

[2] F. O. Matthiessen, *American Renaissance* (New York, 1949), pp. 192, 250, 267. See also *The Portable Hawthorne*, ed. Malcolm Cowley (New York, 1948), pp. 1-21; Fogle, *op. cit.*, pp. 106-109.

[3] J. C. Gerber, "Form and Content in *The Scarlet Letter*," *New England Quarterly*, XVII, 25-55 (March, 1944).

this theme; this is reasonable, since Hawthorne himself does not absolutely define the fate of Hester and Dimmesdale. Matthiessen finds Hawthorne's "device of multiple choice" peculiarly applicable to *The Scarlet Letter;* Cowley, who recognizes his subject's Calvinist convictions, implies that "a faith in the value of confession and absolution" somewhat mitigates the rigor of Hawthorne's position; Fogle remarks that "The true conclusion of *The Scarlet Letter* is an unresolved contradiction—unresolved not from indecision or lack of thought but from honesty of imagination."[4] Hawthorne, of course, could not give a final answer to "the dark problem of this life." But he resolves the contrast between man's complete weakness (consequent on his sin) and God's complete power (revealed by His grace) in an unmistakably voluntarist manner. That contrast is the theme of *The Scarlet Letter*. There is no evidence that Hawthorne questions the absolute nature of God's predestinate decree. All Hester's strength, intelligence, devotion avail neither her lover nor herself. God alone saves the sinner, and Dimmesdale acknowledges this with his dying breath: "Praised be his name! His Will be done!"[5] He reserves for Hester the accents of fear and doubt. No wonder Sophia, who thought Emerson "the greatest man that ever lived," "took to her bed," when Hawthorne read the last chapters aloud to her, "with one of her old headaches."[6] Her bowdlerizing instincts must have been dumfounded by the stark and uncompromising revelation of her husband's beliefs.

Hawthorne knew very well that he was dealing with a theme "not less but more heroic" than anything which had yet appeared in American fiction. Consciously or not, he clothed his fable in epic machinery. The tale begins *in medias res;* it develops in twenty-four books, of which the first twelve lead outward and "downward"; the concluding twelve home to the heart and to salvation—for Dimmesdale, at least. At the halfway mark Chillingworth seems to be triumphant; Pearl has been described in terms almost exclusively of uncontrolled, chaotic passion. A number of "solutions," political, theological, even necromantic, have been tried (or suggested) and found wanting. Dimmesdale allows himself to be led away by the

[4] Matthiessen, *op. cit.,* pp. 276-277; Cowley, *op. cit.,* p. 13; Fogle, *op. cit.,* pp. 104-105.
[5] *The Best of Hawthorne,* ed. Mark Van Doren (New York, 1951), p. 387. Page references to *The Scarlet Letter* in the text of this article are to this edition.
[6] Matthiessen, *American Renaissance,* p. 230; *The Best of Hawthorne,* p. 19.

leech. But in the concluding twelve chapters all is reversed. Chillingworth steadily declines in power. Pearl's character, though rudderless for a time, is now considered in terms of its potential intelligence and active fiber. The one true solution to "the dark problem" resolves the bewildered despair of the protagonists on a supernatural plane, to which they can be raised only by supernatural aid. This is "epic machinery" without a self-starter. Only God can provide the vital spark.

There are three epic "quests" in the novel. Dimmesdale's search for salvation is a conscious, if largely involuntary quest, which is one long *agon,* pierced (in Chapter XII), by the *pathos* or apparent "death" of his soul, but concluded by the final triumph (really God's triumph) of the struggling "hero." Two other quests turn on the outcome of this central struggle. Chillingworth, the agent of evil, undertakes a conscious and voluntary quest, with the soul of Dimmesdale as object; this mission, appropriately, is perverted in pattern, and ends (after an apparent victory in Chapter XII) in the destruction of the physician. Pearl, who represents man's hopeful future as Chillingworth recalls his bitter and diseased past, has her quest too. It is first announced by Hester: "My child must seek a heavenly Father; she shall never know an earthly one" (p. 241). This quest, which is unconscious and involuntary, appears doomed for a time. As Dimmesdale falls under Chillingworth's spell, Pearl seeks knowledge, not of any "heavenly Father," but of "the Black Man." At length, of course, she finds her "heavenly Father." After the kiss on the scaffold, Pearl, reconciled to the conditions of life, will not "forever do battle with the world, but be a woman in it" (p. 386).

These quests, however, take place on different levels. Although they are closely interdependent, they differ in kind. The quest and career of Dimmesdale (as of Hester) is carried on in society and in nature. Granting all their passion and determination, it remains a fact that both these figures are ineffectual. Dimmesdale accomplishes nothing positive until the eve preceding the "Election Sermon." Hester's frenetic activity is thoroughly futile. To be sure, this is the level of humanity, on which the story of the novel unfolds. But although we call the events on this level "real" and its characters "central," events and characters both are signs and symbols of the eternal battle being waged by forces altogether outside its limits.

Chillingworth, cold and determined, and Pearl, whose heavenly Father waits in the wings, remind us of this struggle. Throughout the action Hester and Dimmesdale, first separately, then together, come under the influence of Chillingworth; and their reactions affect Pearl. Indeed, the actions of Hester and the minister are a kind of "mirror" through which Chillingworth, once he is actively launched on his way of revenge, moves freely into the Pearl-world. Only at the close of the novel does this mirror become opaque, closing Chillingworth out from the New Jerusalem and reflecting merely his own self-destructive image.

The quests of Pearl and the leech, therefore, are in a sense more "real" than those of the two "central" characters. But Hawthorne was careful not to assign a scene to Pearl and Chillingworth alone, as he assigned at least one to every other pair of characters. The child and the physician meet only in the presence of others, and they exchange no word. Hawthorne knew that the past and the future meet only in the present, and that the effect of the one and the hope of the other have meaning for man only in consequence of the thought and action of present time. In *The Scarlet Letter* the level of actuality on which Hester, Dimmesdale, and society move is related both to a threatening symbolic level, acting as it were from below, and also to a hopeful symbolic level, promising more than this world offers. As God knows the necessary outcome, the fate of Chillingworth and Pearl does not literally *depend* on the actions of Hester and Dimmesdale; rather, the manner in which the lives of these four figures turn on each other demonstrates the nature of the divine plan.

The structure of *The Scarlet Letter*, accordingly, is complex; but its complexity is unified by the central theme of God's saving power and man's futility, to which each part of the book directs its readers' attention. The structure is thoroughly balanced and ordered. Professor Gerber finds a four-part progressive division to be the distinguishing principle of the novel's pattern; and it seems to be true that first society at large, then, successively, Chillingworth, Hester, and Dimmesdale take the center of Hawthorne's stage. Yet the parts of the novel *interact* more closely than this interpretation would allow. Chillingworth's quest is the subject of Chapters IV and XIV; Pearl's quest (or "fate") is central first in VI through

VIII, later again in XV and XVI; Dimmesdale's quest (that of all men) is considered especially in IX through XI and again in XVII through XX. The reactions and attitudes of society are discussed, especially as they affect Hester, in Chapters V, XIII, and XXI-XXII. At regular intervals, finally, those "key" chapters centered on the scaffold sum up and comment on the action. In each of them the fearful symbol appears in a different form. The scarlet letter on Hester's breast in Chapter II reminds us of sin in woman; Dimmesdale's revelation in Chapter XXIII confirms the presence of sin in man; the cloudy yet fiery "A" in the heavens, described in Chapter XII, points to the importance of sin in the universal plan. These groupings are enclosed by Chapters I and XXIV, which symbolically anticipate and confirm the theme of the novel.

II

Death and life, darkness and light, ugliness and beauty: these are suggested by the prison-door and the rosebush of Chapter I. But both are *natural* symbols; and although the rosebush is a sign that "the deep heart of Nature could pity and be kind to" the sinner, that is not enough for salvation, as Hawthorne emphasizes in his later account of the forest meeting between Hester and Dimmesdale. There he reminds us that "the sympathy of Nature" stems from "that wild, heathen Nature of the forest, never subjugated by human law, nor illumined by higher truth" (p. 345). Life is not totally dark; but it must always be "a tale of human frailty and sorrow," since the ancient crime at its root effectively prevents the establishment by men of any "Utopia of human virtue and happiness." They are condemned instead to an existence symbolized by "the black flower of civilized society, a prison." The opening chapter of the novel, therefore, promises a description of prisoners and criminals, under sentence of doom, whose hearts may be relieved, but not truly *lifted up,* by moral virtue or natural beauty. The novel ends at a gravestone, confirming the dominance of sin over death as well as life. When the characters have been disposed of in the customary nineteenth-century manner, we are left with the "simple slab of slate . . . relieved only by one ever-glowing point of light gloomier than the shadow." No earthly shadow can be as somber as man's lot; yet within the rigoristic framework of God's plan lies the promise of salvation gained after suffering.

Chapters V, XIII, and XXI-XXII deal with society—and with Hester. Society, which at first condemns Hester, later respects her, and finally takes her for granted, is evidently deluded. Its confidence in the righteousness of social judgments and its assumption that Hester is properly cowed (and presumably "improved") by the punishment are unfounded. "The scarlet letter had not done its office." But Hester also is at fault. Although her suffering is the subject of Chapter V, and her strength of will that of Chapter XIII, both heart and will are pressed into the service of a foolish and fatuous arrogance. That she sets herself, from the first, against man's law is understandable, even part of Hawthorne's theme; but she also challenges the law of God. Hester *"deemed herself* connected with Dimmesdale in a union that, unrecognized on earth, would bring them together before the bar of final judgment, and make that their marriage-altar" (p. 250). This is altogether unwarranted; and Hawthorne confirms our impression by his reference to Hester's "sick and morbid heart," which sheltered "no genuine and steadfast penitence, but something that might be deeply wrong, beneath" (p. 252). Society may be partly accountable for this condition, but that is less important than the fact that Hester presumes to judge her own case. As Hawthorne points out in Chapter XIII, Hester was "little accustomed, in her long seclusion from society, to measure her ideas of right and wrong by any standard external to herself" (p. 311).

Even more significant is Hester's "marble coldness," the result of her turn "in a great measure, from passion and feeling, to thought" (p. 315). Just as Hester's spiritual pain led her, not to true penitence, but to presumption, so she dedicates her strength to a task beyond her, the "saving" of Dimmesdale. Hester is still making her own laws. "She determined to redeem her error, so far as it might yet be possible" (p. 317). Of course, this is not possible. We may sympathize with her courage, and even applaud the moral effect of her conduct upon society; but we cannot miss the futility of her attempt. Chapters XXI and XXII describe Hester as "startled more than she permitted to appear," ". . . in the utmost consternation," and "harassed by . . . terrible perplexity." Her desperate effort on the scaffold to bring off the conjuring trick results only in her lover's admonition to be silent, to recall their mutual error, and to praise the Lord for having saved Dimmesdale. This is cruel; but it is Hawthorne's view of life.

Chillingworth comments openly on his "quest" in only two chapters, IV and XIV. But these chapters reveal a significant development in his nature and his search. The scholar who has "sought truth in books" and "gold in alchemy," and who has "learned many new secrets in the wilderness," is at first confident and then self-reliant. His smile betrays "dark and self-relying intelligence." Chillingworth is quite sure that by his own intellectual powers he can dominate Hester and expose Dimmesdale. He even regards his sojourn among savages as a period of intellectual preparation for his avenging task in the community—almost as a parodied version of Christ's forty days in the wilderness. Pearl is implicitly in his power by force of the mysterious drug; the others he claims more directly. "Thou and thine, Hester Prynne, belong to me." As for the other, "Let him hide himself in outward honor, if he may! Not the less he shall be mine" (p. 247). But his almost casual admission, "Mine was the first wrong," foreshadows his defeat. The reader senses that while Chillingworth means to "ruin" the soul of Dimmesdale, God's purpose has already substituted the soul of the leech. This is made certain by the balancing Chapter XIV, in which Chillingworth, though bound to play out the game, fully recognizes that he is merely a pawn on the board. Hester, with her usual complacency, imagines that she alone can perceive the physician's inner transformation. Chillingworth knows far more than Hester; living with a devil has brought him a special and bitter insight. Man is powerless; the way of the world is governed by a "dark necessity"; and sin itself, which men fondly imagine to be their own, belongs to God too. "Ye that have wronged me are not sinful, save in a kind of typical illusion. . . ." All men are agents, destined to "plant the germ of evil" or of good, not by their own wills, but as instruments in the hand of God. In such an existence, as Chillingworth comes to know, talk of "pardon" between man and man is meaningless and wholly without effect.

In this same Chapter XIV, Hester, glimpsing her own futility, insists passionately that an identical fate awaits all men. "There is no good for him,—no good for me,—no good for thee! There is no good for little Pearl! There is no path to guide us out of this dismal maze!" She is wrong, and especially wrong about Pearl. It is true that in Chapter VI, where Pearl is presented almost entirely through her mother's eyes, the child's chaotic nature receives chiefest emphasis; her wilfulness, her enmity to others, and especially "the warfare of Hester's spirit" which she perpetuates, are at this stage dominant. Further, "the small black mirror of Pearl's eyes" reveals to a horrified Hester the "little, laughing image of a fiend"; Pearl's rejection of her quest ("He did not send me! . . . I have no Heavenly Father") seems to spring from the promptings of an evil spirit. This is only one view of Pearl, and the least reliable; yet the two chapters which follow, and which deal with society's comment on the child, are broadly parallel. Pearl is variously described as one of the "children of the Lord of Misrule," "one of those naughty elfs or fairies," and (by Chillingworth) as a "little baggage" with "witchcraft in her." But even the rigid Puritans conclude their examination of Pearl on an unaccustomed note of humility. At this moment, too, Hester is reminded that "there was love in the child's heart, although it mostly revealed itself in passion"; and Hawthorne ends the chapter on a new note, remarking, as Hester rebuffs Mistress Hibbins, "Even thus early had *the child saved her* from Satan's snare."

Chapters XV and XVI do not positively assert that there *is* "good" for Pearl; that must wait for Dimmesdale's public admission of guilt. Hester, typically, tells the child that although the scarlet letter has meaning, Pearl's green symbol has none. Yet there now begins to emerge from "the little chaos of Pearl's character" courage, "sturdy pride," scorn of falsehood, and a ripening capacity for love. Even Hester is allowed a glimpse of Pearl's destiny.

Hester had often fancied that Providence had a design of justice and retribution, in endowing the child with this marked propensity; but never, until now, had she bethought herself to ask, whether, linked with that design, there might not likewise be a purpose of mercy and benevolence.

Hawthorne, in fact, has in the second group of chapters centered on Pearl prepared his audience for that moment on the scaffold when her kiss announces the breaking of "a spell," and it becomes sure that "she will grow up amid human joy and sorrow, nor forever do battle with the world, but be a woman in it" (p. 386). This does not mean that Pearl will find life completely *happy;* but that Pearl (in the future) can become "the richest heiress of her day, in the New World." She has been freed into a new spiritual life.

III

The quests of Chillingworth and Pearl, and the wanderings of Hester, are *in the novel* properly subsidiary to that of Dimmesdale. Chapters IX, X, and XI describe the gradual decay of his will and spirit under Chillingworth's grinding inexorability. In these chapters the full weight of the physician's malice, knowledge, and ferocious craving for revenge is thrown into the scales against Dimmesdale, who, for his part, understands very well "the perchance mortal agony through which he must struggle towards his triumph" (p. 287). But the very weakening of Dimmesdale's fiber is a subtle part of God's plan, for only in this way can man receive grace. Chillingworth blindly counts on "all the powers of nature," which, he believes, "call so earnestly for the confession of sin" (p. 289). Dimmesdale recognizes his own corruption: ". . . above all things else . . . he loathed his miserable self!" But he knows that "nature" is irrelevant. "There can be, if I forebode aright, no power, short of the Divine mercy, to disclose, whether by uttered words, or by type or emblem, the secrets that may be buried with a human heart." Irresistible grace follows the recognition of total depravity. Penance, however, is not penitence; the bloody scourge in Dimmesdale's closet does not compensate for his secretiveness; his life at this stage is "so false . . . that it steals the pith and substance out of whatever realities there are around him." The minister, overcome by "chill" despondency, is led away by the leech.

The Calvinist knows, of course, that only from such absolute degradation and apparent defeat can regeneration spring. We should not expect a gradual recovery, balancing Dimmesdale's gradual decline; for if man works slowly, God's will is done in an instant. That is why Hawthorne, in Chapters XVII through XX, allows only hints of the approaching climax to appear. Earlier anticipations of the direction and meaning of Dimmesdale's quest are given new emphasis. "As concerns the good which I may appear to do, I have no faith in it. It must needs be a delusion. What can a ruined soul like mine effect towards the redemption of other souls?—or a polluted soul towards their purification?" "Of penance, I have had enough! Of penitence, there has been none!" The mutual forgiveness of the lovers, and the recognition that their sin is not "the worst . . . in the world" (p. 339), appropriately accompany Dimmesdale's bitter self-recrimination. But human power can achieve no more than mutual sympathy and understanding in "things indifferent." Further effort is unavailing. Hester's continual harping on the "happiness" that she can win for both would be almost comic, were it not such a pathetic effort to escape the will of God. Hawthorne points up the irony of Hester's determination by treating her as he had treated Chillingworth, when the physician (in Chapter IV) announced his intention of ruining the soul of her lover. His own soul was in question, although he meant another's. Here too, when Hester whispers dramatically, "Thou shalt not go alone!" it is God who smilingly prepares to "accompany" the minister.

The crucial Chapter XX has two functions. It emphasizes the weakness of the most determined and wily human efforts to gain salvation. But it also shows the immediate results (on Dimmesdale) of irresistible grace. The minister is not buoyed up or strengthened by his interview with Hester; after it, in fact, his mind most completely yields to the insidious persuasions of evil, as his encounters with age, beauty, and innocence show. He is in that "maze" which terrified Hester. But the path out of the maze is at hand: God speaks to Dimmesdale and confirms his election. This is clearly indicated in the closing paragraphs of the chapter. Chillingworth, at the outset of his acquaintance with the minister, had spoken of "saintly men, who walk with God on earth," and of their desire "to walk with him on the golden pavements of the New Jerusalem" (p. 282). The bitter (and apparently Godless) "walk" on earth is over now; Chillingworth, on the threshold of triumph, sardonically compares "a good man's prayers" to "the current gold coin of the New Jerusalem, with the King's own mint-mark on them!" It is God who answers him. Chillingworth, after all, has the unhappy knack of saying precisely the wrong thing (from God's point of view) at such crucial moments as this, and it is artistically right that he should blunder once more. This is how Hawthorne continues speaking of Dimmesdale:

. . . flinging the already written pages of the Election Sermon into the fire, he forthwith began another, which he wrote with such impulsive flow of thought and emotion, that he fancied himself inspired; and only wondered that Heaven should see fit to transmit the grand and solemn music of its oracles through so foul an organ-pipe as he. However, leaving that mystery to solve itself, or go unsolved forever, he drove his task onward, with earnest haste and ecstasy. Thus the night fled away, as if it were a winged steed, and he careering on it; morning came, and peeped, blushing, through the curtains; and at last sunrise threw a golden beam into the study and laid it right across the minister's bedazzled eyes.

An old life is cast into the fire; the foul sinner becomes the recipient of a divine favor totally beyond the grasp of reason. Inspired and ecstatic, the newly elected rises in spirit beyond his dark night of the soul, dazzled but irresistibly drawn into the protective blaze of salvation. There remains only the acknowledgment (on the scaffold) of God's power and the confirmation of God's mercy—which Hester has dimly glimpsed, but which she cannot hope to comprehend.

IV

Most critics have noticed Hawthorne's preoccupation with mirrors. In *The Scarlet Letter,* he uses them as signposts in the structure and to illustrate his theme. There are eight mirrors in the novel, reflecting scenes and images appropriate to the persons who look into each mirror. Hester sees a demon in the mirror of Pearl's eyes (p. 262). Fear, hatred, and self-assertive determination, developed in her by the severity of society, make possible only the view of life which finds "no good for little Pearl." Since the image in this mirror is in a sense of Hester's own making, it is false and unreal. Chillingworth, on the other hand, sees *real* evil—his own doom according to the divine fiat—in the mirror of his imagination. The "frightful shape, which he could not recognize, usurping the place of his own image in a glass" (p. 321), foreshadows the final scenes of the novel, when the physician's carefully developed plans explode and destroy him.

Dimmesdale, the only character to view himself in an actual mirror, sees all—but doubtfully, not with discernment. Devils, angels, dead friends and parents, Hester and Pearl pass over the surface of his mirror, and these shadows bring no certainty either of damnation or salvation. They reflect Dimmesdale's own degeneration of character. "To the untrue man, the whole universe is false, —it is impalpable,—it shrinks to nothing within his grasp. And he himself, in so far as he shows himself in a false light, becomes a shadow, or, indeed, ceases to exist" (p. 301). This mirror signifies that Dimmesdale may yet follow angel or beckoning devil; and it betrays his utter inability to make the right decision for himself, lacking that divine aid which alone can make him a "true" man.

For Pearl there are two mirrors. In Governor Bellingham's armor she sees Hester, and a "gigantic" scarlet letter, symbolizing both her heritage and the fate which may be hers. But in the pool at the water's edge (in Chapter XIV), she sees a "visionary little maid," who beckons her to "a better place." Pearl (in the future) may look on to election as well as to damnation. Her destiny, unlike that of the others, hangs in the balance (for readers of the novel) until the final scene on the scaffold.

The remaining three "mirrors" have to do, not with the characters, but with past, present, and future time, the framework within which their trials develop. In Chapter XVI, "the giant trees and bowlders of granite seemed intent on making a mystery of the course of this small brook; fearing, perhaps, that with its never-ceasing loquacity, it should whisper tales out of the heart of the old forest whence it flowed, or mirror its revelations on the smooth surface of a pool." This suggests that the "wild, heathen Nature of the forest, never subjugated by human law, nor illumined by higher truth," wishes to conceal the past, with its deadly yet dazzling secrets, which deny to Nature the full solace of God's saving promise to the elect. The present, in which God continually works out the consequences of Adam's fault, is made up of hurrying moments; it is man's nature to catch at these. But time is only the stage of the eternal drama; life is short and evanescent. The ephemeral nature of human life and the fleeting opportunities it offers to all men's vision are caught in Hawthorne's second mirror of time: when Hester and Dimmesdale meet in the forest, "The soul beheld its features in the mirror of the passing moment" (p. 335). As for the future, that mirror must be Pearl's; and in fact the final mirror-image in the novel is the brook's reflection of Pearl, "a perfect image of her little figure ... more refined and spiritualized than the reality" (p. 349). This final mirror denies Hester's assumption of Pearl's doom, and confirms the second possibility offered to Pearl by her reflection in the pool. Thus the three mirrors reflect the terrible but inescapable facts of man's past, the challenge of a fleeting but invaluable present, and the divine promise to be realized in the future.

Is not the novel itself, or at least the line of plot which describes the development of Hester and Dimmesdale, a mirror for the reader? As external observer, the reader becomes imaginatively aware of Chillingworth's sidling approach to the mirror's surface, beyond which plays the innocent (yet wise, and even potentially vicious) Pearl. Only with Dimmesdale's revelation does the mirror become opaque, casting Chillingworth's dreadful image destructively back upon himself. But the novel is not by any means merely "a novel," to be read, criticized, "appreciated" by the objective and disinterested reader. We are also internal actors, identifying ourselves with Dimmesdale or Hester, and applying the significance of their actions (and the consequences of those actions) to our lives. In fact, we become the mirror through which evil Chillingworth may strike at us and our posterity. We cannot (Hawthorne would say) alter the course of events; but we may more clearly understand the significance of these events.

F. O. Matthiessen remarks that "what stirred Melville" in *The House of the Seven Gables* "was not any merely abstract speculation about the nature of man," but rather, in Melville's words, "the apprehension of the absolute condition of present things as they strike the eye of the man who fears them not." Matthiessen continues:

Such steady inspection of life, which does not flinch from probing sinister recesses and is determined to make articulate the whole range of what it finds, is indispensable for the great artist. Only thus can he cut through conventional appearances, and come into possession of what Eliot has called "a sense of his own age."[7]

In *The Scarlet Letter* Hawthorne was determined to set forth, not only his "sense of his own age," but his interpretation of the ageless "dark problem of this life." The interlocking structural detail which he chose as suitable vehicle for the epic theme of *The Scarlet Letter* is the most convincing evidence we possess of Hawthorne's artistic genius, as a writer of novels; but it is even more important to see that Hawthorne deliberately chose his complex method as the most effective way in which he could communicate to others his vision of life.

[7] Matthiessen, *American Renaissance*, pp. 192-193.

The Character of Flame: The Function of Pearl in *The Scarlet Letter*
Anne Marie McNamara

IN DISCUSSIONS of Nathaniel Hawthorne's *The Scarlet Letter*, little attention has been given to the significance of Pearl, the illegitimate daughter of Hester Prynne and Arthur Dimmesdale. Indifference to her role in the plot is surprising in view of the general assumption that lack of motivation for the confession of Dimmesdale is a radical weakness in the plot. Since it is obvious that neither Hester nor Chillingworth constitutes an external cause for Dimmesdale's *volte face*, it seems reasonable to consider the possibility that Pearl may be the agent who effects his unexpected public confession of paternity. If Pearl is a part of the "electric chain" formed as she, Dimmesdale, and Hester join hands in the darkness and stand on the pillory as a family for the first time (p. 174),[1] it may not be illogical to assume that she is as dynamic a force in the plot as are the other two members of the chain.

The narrator's extensive treatment of the child, his careful delineation of her physical and spiritual qualities, his presentation of her in juxtaposition to both Hester and Dimmesdale, and his use of her in every decisive scene seem to justify an assumption that she is more than a passive link between her father and mother and more than a static symbol of their sin. Above all, his insistence upon the peculiar preternatural quality of the child and his manipulation of this phenomenon in the crucial scenes (the forest scene and the three pillory scenes) must certainly indicate that she is not merely a fantastically decorative "relief" in the somber story but a functional element in the structural design.[2] It is my purpose to present evidence that Pearl is more than a link, more than a symbol—that she is the efficient cause of the denouement and thus provides the motivation for Dimmesdale's final act.

[1] References by page or chapter of *The Scarlet Letter* are to the Random House edition, New York, 1927.
[2] Pearl is presented in action, mentioned, or discussed in all but four of the twenty-three chapters of the novel proper (i.e., chaps. i, ix, xi, xvii) and in the Conclusion.

Henry James asserted that *The Scarlet Letter* is primarily Dimmesdale's story, not Hester's.

> The story, indeed, is in a secondary degree that of Hester Prynne; she becomes, really, after the first scene, an accessory figure; it is not upon her the denouement depends. It is upon her guilty lover that the author projects most frequently the cold, thin rays of his fitfully-moving lantern. . . .[3]

Agreement with James (and I agree with him) necessitates rejection of Mr. Leland Schubert's statement that the three pillory scenes are "in every sense the high points of the novel."[4] Dimmesdale's story centers in the forest scene. I suggest that the "missing" motivation for Dimmesdale's confession may be found in this great scene. Without it, the first two pillory scenes would be structurally meaningless and the third would never occur.

If *The Scarlet Letter* is Dimmesdale's story, it must trace the change within him from the condition of a sinner, a hypocrite, and a weak capitulator to Hester's plea for flight and resumption of sin, to that of a penitent, sincere and strong enough (and just barely strong enough) to make public confession.[5] But there must be a cause for the change. I suggest that it is Pearl in her "otherworldly" aspect. Since the change in Dimmesdale is in the spiritual order, the cause may be assumed to be in the same order. Pearl is a spirit-child. As such she operates plausibly as an efficient cause within the *ambiance* of ambiguity which pervades the novel. She causes a transformation in the realm of the spirit; the effect is translatable in the terms of the spirit. Above and beyond the literal reality of her action as Hester's and Dimmesdale's child, she moves authoritatively as a regenerative influence on the level of *operative* symbol. On this level, *The Scarlet Letter* is the story of an extraordinary man redeemed by the extraordinary action of an extraordinary child. The progress of such a redemption in such a realm seems to me to take place in four stages: Preparation (Chapters I-XVI); Communication

---

[3] Henry James, *Hawthorne* (English Men of Letters Series, New York, 1887), p. 109.

[4] Leland Schubert, *Hawthorne the Artist* (Chapel Hill, 1944), pp. 137-140.

[5] Hester does not actually change interiorly during the course of the novel. Outwardly she seems to change: she adjusts to her social ostracism and she appears to be repentant. Inwardly, however, she is not repentant, as we see in her bold instigation of Dimmesdale to flee and to undertake a life of deliberate sin with her. She determines to make their "sin of passion" a "sin of principle." Cf. chaps. v (p. 89), xiii (pp. 187-189), and xvii (pp. 126-128).

(Chapters XVII-XIX); Transformation (Chapters XX-XXII); and Revelation (Chapter XXIII).

The first of these stages consists of a meticulous preparation for the cause-effect relationship between Pearl and Dimmesdale, a relationship which depends upon the capability of the one to initiate and of the other to receive the impetus to regenerative action. For such capability in Pearl and for such susceptibility in Dimmesdale the narrator through sixteen chapters most carefully and elaborately provides. By detailing and dissecting the relationship of each of the two with one of the other major characters, he reveals in both certain peculiar spiritual and psychological qualities which he will juxtapose as he brings them face to face in the crucial forest scene for their first major meeting. Before this central scene, he presents Pearl in relation to Hester, Dimmesdale in relation to Chillingworth.[6] Gradually and cumulatively, he draws first one, then the other, carefully keeping them apart except for four brief but pregnant meetings.[7]

In this preparation for their decisive encounter, in which the intercourse between them will be effected on a preternatural plane, he presents each of them on two distinct levels: the ordinary and the extraordinary, or the literal and the figurative, or the natural and the preternatural. Neither the child nor the man, he shows, is merely an ordinary being. Pearl is not merely an ordinary, playful seven-year-old child: she is also precociously intelligent, bewilderingly subtle, frighteningly independent, and penetratingly wise. A double-natured anomaly, torturing her mother with misgivings of her natural origin, she exhibits even in babyhood an uncanny curiosity concerning Hester's scarlet letter. From early childhood, she displays unearthly inquisitiveness about the minister's habit of placing his hand over his heart. Most significantly, by curious questioning and implication and with a prescience that can only be described as preternatural, she insistently associates these two ostensibly disparate phenomena. Similarly, Dimmesdale is not only a well-loved and devoted minister: he is a godlike figure in the community, admired for his delicate understanding and sympathy and superbly

[6] This is not to say that the narrator does nothing else in these chapters. He does much: he delineates Hester's superficial and real natures (v and xiii); he draws Chillingworth's character (ix); he establishes the Hester-Chillingworth relationship (i-iv).

[7] On the pillory (ii); at the Governor's house (vii and viii); from Dimmesdale's window (x); on the pillory at midnight (xii).

endowed with intellectual acumen and spiritual perspicuity. Above all, he is blessed almost beyond human capacity with the gift of communication (p. 160). It is of the utmost importance to observe that in spite of the physical and moral deterioration resulting from his own conscience and from Chillingworth's vindictive ministrations, his profound insight, his acute perception, and his delicate spiritual sensitivity remain unimpaired (pp. 160-162).

With such preparation, the preternaturally endowed child and man are brought together by the narrator in a cause-effect relationship in the great forest scene. I suggest that the second stage in the process of Dimmesdale's redemption takes place in the three chapters which constitute this scene (Chaps. XVII, XVIII, XIX). It is the critical stage of Communication. Everything in the arrangement of details is powerfully suggestive of duality: in the setting, light and darkness, land and water; in the mood, love and disdain, desire and fear, acceptance and rejection, reconciliation and estrangement; in the atmosphere, the real and the preternatural. Against this background, the duality that has already been elaborately established in Pearl and in Dimmesdale begins to operate in a remarkably subtle context of ambiguity.

The double nature of little Pearl functions in this environment on two distinct levels (the natural and the preternatural), in two directions (towards a known and an unknown parent), through two sets of actions (the explicit and the implicit) translatable upon two planes of meaning (the literal and the figurative). She approaches and affects Hester and Dimmesdale in appropriately different ways suited to the capacity of each to receive and understand her meaning. On the natural level she acts on Hester as a real child; on the preternatural level she acts on Dimmesdale as a "more-than-child," an elf-dryad-nymph, a spirit child. In each case, her method of approach is determined by the nature of the desired effect. In Hester the need is for the restoration of the discarded public acknowledgment of adultery, the embroidered scarlet letter. In Dimmesdale the desideratum is the revelation of the private, hidden stigma of the same sin. As a real child, Pearl causes a visible change in Hester by audibly, imperiously, and petulantly demanding that her mother pin the discarded *A* in its customary place on her breast. Hester understands and obeys, and the estrangement between the mother and child is immediately mended: Pearl leaps the brook and embraces her mother.

But the estrangement between Pearl and Dimmesdale is not a temporary condition, induced by one overt act and dissipated by another. The offense of her father against her is the deliberate and guilty concealment of parenthood during her whole lifetime. The healing of this serious breach (divined by the elf-nature but not by the child-nature in Pearl) cannot be effected as was the other, immediately, visibly, audibly, objectively. The spirit child communicates her disapproval in another way, one exquisitely appropriate to Dimmesdale's sensibility—through a silent, indirect, subjective language. In the entire scene at the brookside she does not speak to him with her human voice at all. She addresses him indirectly through her persistent rejection of his advances and through actions ostensibly directed towards her mother. When Hester, restored to Pearl's favor, entreats the child to greet the minister and assures her that he loves her, Pearl phrases in two succinct questions the only terms on which the alienation may be terminated: "Doth he love us? Will he go back with us, hand in hand, we three together, into the town?" (p. 244). Public revelation of the real relationship among the three is to Pearl the only means of reconciliation. She ignores her mother's request that she love the minister. She is not cajoled by the promise of a future home in which the three will be together and in which Dimmesdale will love her dearly. Her only reply is again a question: "And will he always keep his hand over his heart?" (p. 244). She clearly implies that guilt will plague Dimmesdale even if he succeeds in the plans for escape which he and Hester are now formulating. Her mother, not sensing the profound implications of her questions, lightly evades them. Consequently, stubbornly refusing to show any friendliness towards the minister and grimacing with disapproval, Pearl receives his embrace only at her mother's insistence and immediately bathes her forehead in the brook to wash away all vestiges of his "unwelcome kiss" (p. 245).

Pearl's actions at the brookside nettle her mother and produce immediate and tangible results. They work differently on Dimmesdale. For him they have more than their superficial meaning. His fancy that the brook flowing between Pearl and her parents is a boundary between two worlds may suggest his awareness of the double level of Pearl's action. His comment is eloquent: he says that the brook separates Pearl from Hester; he does not say that it separates Pearl from him (p. 240). On the other hand, when Hester is about to call to Pearl to join her and the minister, the child's distance from them is judged differently by the two. To Hester, Pearl is "not far off," but to Dimmesdale she is "a good way off" (p. 234). Does he mean that she seems to be in another world from which she is reaching out to him? Do his observation and insight suggest knowledge of the commencement of the "otherworldly" influence of his child upon his spirit? Does his incipient realization prepare him for an extraordinary meeting of their extraordinary minds? He is nervous and anxious as she mistrustingly delays her approach. He is afraid as the child's penetrating glances apparently at once seek and divine the relationship between Hester and himself: his hand involuntarily steals over his heart—and over the mark of that relationship. He is deeply disturbed as Pearl bursts into passionate cries and gesticulations of protest and demand. Her insistent designation of the cause of her displeasure—the absence of the scarlet letter from her mother's breast—unnerves him. He seems aware that her agitation is more than a childish tantrum, for he uses the word *preternatural* to describe it (p. 242).

Although Pearl's outburst at the brookside is directed towards her mother, it affects Dimmesdale traumatically. This hypersensitive man experiences almost simultaneously the extremes of exaltation and depression—Hester's plan for the resumption of their love affair and Pearl's adamant rejection of his affection. His unacknowledged daughter tells him in her wordless language that his acquiescence to Hester's will to escape is a false answer to his problem and is distasteful to her. She will not enter into arrangements which involve a continuance of his concealment of sin. No wonder that the minister who leaves the elf at the brookside is a minister in a maze.[8]

The narrator's final comment on the forest meeting characterizes it as "fateful" (p. 245). This statement is valid and acceptable on both the natural and the supranatural levels: the interview is fateful as the time of Hester's and Dimmesdale's decision to enter deliberately upon a life of sin; it is fateful as the silent impetus to the agitated minister's subsequent action on the day of the Governor's inauguration.

[8] Cf. the title of chap. xx.

Three passages in a previous chapter entitled "The Interior of a Heart" (Chap. XI) lend credibility to the perspicuity which I have imputed to the minister at this forest meeting. The first prefigures the major action of Pearl at the brookside, her insistent pointing at her mother's breast; the second illustrates Dimmesdale's power of perception—however dim at first—of a subtle influence unperceived by others; the third foreshadows the peculiar ability of Dimmesdale to interpret Pearl's meaning.

The first of these significant foreshadowings occurs in the detailing of Dimmesdale's relationship with Chillingworth after the latter's discovery of the secret stigma. Diabolically playing upon his victim, Chillingworth seeks to overpower him through the agony of fear. In the figure of speech chosen by the narrator to describe the physician's evil plan, the elements of unearthly power and of finger-pointing are adumbrations of the incriminating knowledge and the accusing gesture of Pearl at the brookside. The importance of this association grows as one recalls the triple pattern in which these two elements are found in the forest scene. Three times the narrator repeats the pattern: the child stands on the farther side of the brook, authoritatively pointing her finger at her mother's breast, while beneath, mirrored in the brook, is her image, imperious and beautiful, pointing in the same accusing way. If Dimmesdale had been startled with sudden fear by a "grisly phantom..., a thousand phantoms ... all flocking round [him] and pointing with their fingers at his breast" (p. 159), may he not react similarly to see "the bright-apparelled vision" (p. 234), of Pearl, "now like a child, now like a child's spirit" (p. 234), using the same condemnatory gesture? True, the gesture is not made directly at him by Pearl—since her method of approach to him is indirect—but its repetitive pattern commences immediately after a passage which shows Pearl's uncanny divination of the lovers' relationship and the minister's involuntary, guilty reaction to the suspicious knowledge in her "wild, bright eyes" (p. 240): "his hand ... stole over his heart" (p. 240). May not the thrice-repeated pattern of her direct communication with Hester and her indirect communication with Dimmesdale suggest a real child-Hester relationship but a spirit child-Dimmesdale relationship? The image of the child in the pool, the narrator says, is "more refined and spiritualized than the reality" (p. 239). Moreover, the finger-pointing of Pearl may recall to Dimmesdale his agonizing vigil on the pillory at midnight when, his eyes fixed on the blazing *A* in the night sky, "he was, nevertheless, perfectly aware that little Pearl was pointing her finger towards old Roger Chillingworth, who stood at no great distance from the scaffold. The minister appeared to see him, with the same glance that discerned the miraculous letter" (p. 177). As the real child on the edge of the pool points accusingly at her mother's breast, silently reproaching her for discarding her *A,* Dimmesdale is aware of the image-child in the pool, pointing reproachfully in the same way (pp. 240-241). If the meteor which Dimmesdale saw in the first instance "kindled up the sky . . . with an awfulness that admonished Hester Prynne and the clergyman of the day of judgment," as the narrator points out (p. 177), may not the same fear of doom be generated in Dimmesdale's sensitive mind by his association of the *A* and the finger-pointing of the one instance with the same phenomena in the other?

The second of these foreshadowing references not only offers ground for Dimmesdale's receptivity to subtle influences but also obviates the objection that the lack of *immediate* perceptible evidence of Dimmesdale's understanding of Pearl's meaning at the brookside renders suspect the assumption that she is the cause of his ultimate confession. In the narrator's explanation of Chillingworth's method in his plot to break the resistance of his patient, he says that the evil work "was accomplished with a subtlety so perfect that the minister, though he had constantly a dim perception of some evil influence watching over him, could never gain a knowledge of its actual nature" (p. 159). May not Dimmesdale, then, be said to have at the brookside the first "dim perception" of the redemptive influence of Pearl?

The final foreshadowing concerns the metaphor of the Tongue of Flame. Ascribing Dimmesdale's prestige among the townspeople to his heavenly gift of sympathy for human nature, the narrator uses the Pentecostal Tongues of Flame to symbolize the supernatural penetration and love which distinguished the clergyman in his understanding and expressing the feelings of the human heart (pp. 161-162). The juxtaposition of this passage with that which describes Pearl as the enigmatic symbol of the lovers' secret—the "living hieroglyphic"—shows that the same figure has been used again. "She had been offered to the world . . . as the living hieroglyphic, in which was revealed the secret they so darkly sought to hide,—all written in this symbol,—all plainly manifest,—had there been a prophet or a magician skilled to read the character of flame!" (p. 238). In the Bible narrative, tongues of flame were the symbols of the power of eloquence given by Heaven to men who were chosen to understand and reveal truth in order to effect the salvation of others. In the imaginative narrative with which we are concerned, the narrator interprets them as symbols "not of the power of speech in foreign and unknown languages, but that of addressing the whole human brotherhood in the heart's native language" (p. 161). The scarlet-garbed child—"The character of flame"—addresses an unspoken truth to a man capable in mind and heart of comprehending it. Dimmesdale is the only one of the clergymen of the town marked with "Heaven's last and rarest attestation of their office, the Tongue of Flame." His burden of hidden sorrow gave him sympathetic understanding and the gift of expressing "highest truths through the humblest medium of familiar words and images" (p. 161). The first use of the figure, therefore, is a foreshadowing of and a preparation for the second, and the second recalls the context of the first and lends credibility to the silent communication at the brookside.[9]

In other references in Chapter XI, the narrator emphasizes the "preternatural activity" of Dimmesdale's intellectual and moral perceptions, his power of experiencing and communicating emotion, and his predilection for the autonomy of truth (pp. 160-162). It is obvious that the narrator has taken great care to establish Dimmesdale as a fit recipient for Pearl's cryptic message of truth.

The three chapters which follow the communication in the forest constitute what may be called the phase or stage of Transformation in the process of Dimmesdale's redemption. In the context of ambiguity, the title of the first of these chapters, "The Minister in a Maze," may imply a double effect in the minister as he leaves Hester and Pearl. On a literal level, he is reeling with the physical excitement of plans for escape from Chillingworth and for resumption of his love affair with Hester. On the figurative level, however, he may be stunned and reeling from the spiritual blow dealt him by the elf-child, the meaning of which he as yet only imperfectly realizes. Through her act of rejection she has communicated to him the ne-

[9] Appropriate to the whole artistically ambiguous patterning of the novel, the frame for both uses of this eloquent trope is a conditional clause. By this device of indirection the narrator achieves suggestiveness consonant with the general tone of the novel.

cessity for public declaration of sin as a prerequisite of forgiveness. "So great a vicissitude in his life could not at once be received as real" (p. 246). Now a *vicissitude* is a *change*. The term is capable of double translation: the obvious one, the projected change of his status and environment by escape to Europe; and the subtle one, the incipient interior change of his attitude towards his concealment of guilt. So strange has the experience been that it seems to him to have been a dream. Yet he knows that it was not: he sees Pearl happily dancing along at Hester's side, now that he (the intruder on one level, the hypocritical sinner on the other) has left them. The "indistinctness and duplicity of impression" which the narrator says "vexed him with a strange disquietude" (p. 246) may well be the conflict in his sensitive mind between the two effects of his forest interview: the possibility of freedom (evil seen as good) and the necessity of bondage (good seen as evil). The contention between the two forces for mastery over the soul of the minister is set in motion in this tremendously meaningful chapter, all of which (with the exception of the first three paragraphs) has to do with the element of *change*.

This chapter develops the motivation generated in the forest scene for the minister's confession in the final chapter. It is in perfect harmony with the ambiguous pattern of the whole. Internal change manifested only in the final chapter is suggested here in an account of the minister's strange sense of external change in familiar objects on his homeward walk. In a long passage of eight pages, "this importunately obtrusive sense of change" is developed (pp. 249 ff.). The woods seem wilder; in the town, familiar landmarks seem namelessly but noticeably changed; people are unaccountably but certainly different; his own church seems unreal and dreamlike. The narrator's interpretation of this passage adumbrates the ultimate use to which he will put this provocative material: "This phenomenon in the various shapes which it assumed, *indicated no external change,* but so sudden and important a *change in the spectator* of the familiar scene, that the intervening space of a single day had operated on his consciousness like the lapse of years" (p. 249).[10] The significance of this comment cannot be overestimated. It states and emphasizes the sudden and radical character of the alteration of perspective induced in the minister and strongly looks forward

[10] Italics mine.

to the sudden and radical *volte face* which results in his confession. The narrator's explanation of the transformations as the result of "the minister's own will, and Hester's will, and the fate that grew between them" fits into the ambiguity of the pattern first by suggesting the conflict between Hester's strong will to perpetuate his falsehood and his own weak will to tell the truth, and second, by implying concreteness in the vagueness of its third element, "the fate that grew between them." There is nothing to preclude the conception of this "fate" as Pearl. The explanation may be so construed as to suggest a double meaning in the term *transformation* and to include a double set of agents operative in effecting the change: Dimmesdale's and Hester's plans transforming Dimmesdale into a new and spuriously free man; Pearl's rejection transforming Dimmesdale into a really free man. In this second sense, there is nothing to preclude the operation of Pearl as an efficient cause of the change effected in Dimmesdale between the moment of his meeting Hester and the child in the forest and the moment of his voluntary mounting of the pillory to declare his guilt to the world— "the same minister returned not from the forest" (p. 249). Ostensibly, a morally worse minister returned. Actually, as the final pillory scene shows, a morally better minister returned.

The course which the narrator takes in the development of the important "transformation" or "change" scene in this chapter provides for the objection that if Pearl were the efficient cause of the minister's inner change, the *manifestation* of the effect in him would have come either at the moment of rejection at the brookside or immediately on his arrival in the town among the people whom he had so long deceived. By a series of carefully plotted incidents on his homeward walk, we are made acutely aware that as yet this sensitive and intelligent but weakened and confused man does not know exactly what is happening within him. The evidence for this lies in his behavior during the six chance encounters occurring between the edge of the town and his own abode (pp. 250-253). His actions, described by the narrator as "impulses," carefully identified as "at once involuntary and intentional," and presented as happening "in spite of himself, yet growing out of a profounder self than that which opposed the impulse" (p. 250), indicate a man in whom opposing strengths are striving for mastery as he looks on, bewildered by the fight and uncertain as to the outcome. In the first encounter his impulse to speak blasphemously to a deacon causes him to fear that the strength of the bad impulse will prevail without his consent (p. 251). In the second encounter he is impelled to utter an argument against the immortality of the soul. Later he cannot account for overcoming that evil inclination. In the third his impulse to pervert innocence is thwarted only by mighty effort. In the fourth only his sense of good taste and decorum—not his devotion to principle—prevents his corrupting the young and swearing with the dissolute.

In a passage which concludes the homeward walk, the narrator emphasizes the lack of self-understanding which marks this stage of the transformation in Dimmesdale. In passionate self-address, the tormented man questions himself as to the possibility of his being mad, or leagued with the devil, who now demands evil deeds of his victim (p. 254).

At this point ostensible corroboration of these fears seems to be presented in the unexpected scene between the tortured man and Mistress Hibbins, "the reputed witch lady." The significance of this scene, however, must be evaluated within the context of ambiguity. By twice discounting the authenticity of the meeting,[11] the narrator carefully provides for antithetical interpretations: simultaneous affirmation and denial of the fear that he has succumbed to the bondage of the devil. In the frame of ambiguity his seemingly hypocritical replies to the old woman's malicious insinuations may signify that he is not the lost soul that he seems to be, that he is indeed sincerely interested in salvation.

If these scenes with the deacon, the widow, the maiden, the children, the seaman, and the witch show anything, they show the moral ambivalence of a sensitive, suffering soul startled by the war in his "interior kingdom"—that between attractive evil proposed by Hester and repulsive good proposed by Pearl—and by the exterior manifestations of the conflict in his "profounder self." In every case the evil impulse had been thwarted by an unaccountable power within him. If these scenes look forward to anything, they look forward to the moment after the Election Sermon when, with every human motive urging him on to flight and love, this same man will

[11] "Old Mistress Hibbins . . . *is said* to have been passing by" (p. 254), and "his encounter with old Mistress Hibbins, *if it were a real incident,* did but show his sympathy with wicked mortals and the world of perverted spirits" (p. 255). Italics mine.

yield to the good impulse to turn aside from the procession, to mount the pillory—again "in spite of himself, yet growing out of a profounder self than that which opposed the impulse" (p. 250).

The final section of this chapter which, in overtly tracing the minister's physical journey homeward from the forest, subtly suggests his spiritual journey to peace from a moral wilderness, presents him in his own dwelling, his "refuge" and his "shelter" from the world. Even here there is now the strangeness of change. Yet, it is still the place that it was, the place of his study, his writing, his penance, his prayer, his agony. It is still familiar: he sees his Bible, his unfinished Election Sermon on the table. May not his gazing at his Bible, in its "rich old Hebrew, with Moses and the Prophets speaking to him, and *God's voice through all*" (p. 256),[12] figure the dawning of his full comprehension of the cryptic action-language of Pearl, the preternatural child, at the brookside? She was telling him to abandon sin, to confess, and to repent. May not his "unfinished" Election Sermon, with "a sentence broken in the midst" be a figure of an imminent break with the past? The very word *Election* may operate above its conventional meaning and take on the significance of the Calvinistic connotation of divine predestination.

On the literal, factual, narrative level, this account of manifestations of change in Dimmesdale is pejorative. But on the figurative level, the opposite interpretation is possible and valid in the light of both antecedent and subsequent action. "Another man had returned from the forest. . . ." It may be a man enlightened by subtly communicated knowledge of "hidden mysteries which the simplicity of the former could never have reached" (p. 256). This knowledgeable man may well "stand apart from that former self [i.e., the pious hypocrite] eyeing it with scornful, pitying, but half-envious curiosity" (p. 256).

The final scene in this remarkably suggestive chapter crystallizes the change in Dimmesdale. He confronts Chillingworth with one hand on the Hebrew Scriptures (the voice of God in a cryptic tongue) and the other spread upon his breast (over the hidden sign of his hidden sin) and engages in a conversation which suggests the choice that he will make. To Chillingworth's observation that his paleness indicates that his "journey through the wilderness" had

[12] Italics mine.

been "too sore," he replies that the sight of the Apostle Eliot, whom he had gone to visit, has done him good. He says that he does not now need any more drugs from Chillingworth for "heart and strength" to preach the Election Sermon (pp. 257-258): he does not need the physician's ministrations to maintain him in his deception and to try to keep alive his broken body and his scarred soul. Has he determined upon his own cure, his own way of salvation? Has he determined to be worthy of "election"? Affirmative answers to both these questions may be read in Chillingworth's reply to the minister's offer to requite the physician's "good deeds" with prayers: "A good man's prayers are golden recompense! Yea, they are the current gold coin of the New Jerusalem, with the King's own mint-mark on them!" Intended sarcastically, these words of the evil leech may suggest the minister's real state, unknown to Chillingworth and probably until this moment not completely known to Dimmesdale himself: he is a worthy minister by reason of his strong interior desire to do the deed that will restore him to the favor of the King whom he serves and that will open to him the way to the New Jerusalem, salvation.[13] But to this final remark of the old physician, Dimmesdale makes no verbal reply. Instead, as the old man leaves, he acts with unaccustomed alacrity. Calling for food, he eats "with ravenous appetite," and "flinging the already written pages of the Election Sermon into the fire," he forthwith begins another, which he writes with "such an impulsive flow of thought and emotion" that he fancies himself inspired (pp. 258-259). The complete destruction of the first Election Sermon, conceived and written in deceit and hypocrisy, may be significant of a complete break with the past that produced it. The fluent composition of a new one may figure the tremendous vitality of the soul freed from the shackles of sin and operating under the flow of divine grace. As his physical appetite is satisfied by his ravenous eating, so the appetite of his soul now seems to satiate itself in ecstatic composition that continues unabated throughout the night and ceases only when the morning sun throws a golden beam into the study and lays it "right across the minister's bedazzled eyes" (p. 259). The sun image recalls the forest scene. Is it a figure of the new light that shone

---

[13] Cf. Edward Taylor's *Sacramental Meditation* VI, in Thomas H. Johnson, ed., *The Poetical Works of Edward Taylor* (Princeton, 1939), p. 127, in which the figure of the golden coin as a symbol of a minister's worthiness is similarly used.

upon the darkened soul of the sensitive minister as he saw his little daughter standing in a shaft of sunlight in the gloomy forest—the only ray of light in that wilderness—and recognized in her, however obscurely at first, the prophet of his transformation and redemption?

The answer lies in the final scene at the pillory on Election Sermon Day, the scene for which the narrator has provided through the artistic device of ambiguity in three stages, those of Preparation, Communication, and Transformation. They have led inexorably to the fourth—Revelation. As the minister moves in the procession towards the church, it is evident that he is a changed man. In his gait and air he seems invigorated with physical and spiritual energy. Hester Prynne, standing in the crowd of townspeople, feels depressed as she sees him. She hardly knows him. He seems unsympathetic, unattainable, withdrawn from her world (p. 275). If the visible change in Dimmesdale is the result of capitulation to sin and anticipation of the spurious freedom it will bring, would there not be at least a glance, a meeting of the eyes, between the two lovers? There is none. The minister's thoughts are not on Hester and a new life with her and Pearl in some European city. They are on the Election Sermon which he is about to deliver, the theme of which, as the narrator later reveals, is the Providence of God upon this settlement in the wilderness and the glorious destiny that it will achieve in His hands (p. 286). The application of this theme to the personal problem of the minister is obvious. Through the Providence of God his moral wilderness will be transformed into glory: the change in him is one of spiritual reformation, not one of sinful capitulation. Equally obvious is the narrator's placing of Hester outside the church, separated from the minister. She cannot hear the words that he speaks, but she catches the spiritual sense of the sound of his truly wonderful voice: "the complaint of the human heart... telling its secret... to the great heart of mankind, beseeching its sympathy and forgiveness" (p. 281). The opening paragraphs of the next chapter (Chap. XXIII)—those in which the narrator describes the general effect of the sermon—suggest that the sound conveyed to her the sense of an ending and a beginning: the ending of their plans for escape (indeed, she already knows that Chillingworth has outwitted her, although Dimmesdale does not know it)

(p. 270)[14] and the beginning of a new phase in the minister's life, not that which her will has planned, but another over which she has no control, for it involves his death.

Hester is well aware that she is seeing and hearing a Dimmesdale who is radically different from the Dimmesdale of the forest. She does not know the cause of the change in him. But I suggest that Dimmesdale now knows. It is Pearl. From the moment of her dramatic rejection of him in the forest, he has moved in bewilderment and agony at the conflict within him towards this moment when he will identify her as his daughter to the world. Refusing all human aid except that of the woman who wears the sign of his sin, he stands at the foot of the scaffold and, at the very moment of confession, summons Pearl, his child. This time she does not refuse. Her worried question of the morning, when she had asked Hester why the minister had kissed her in the forest but would not recognize her in the town, is about to be answered. She senses that revelation is at hand. She runs to him. She clasps her arms about his knees. Is it an accident that at this moment of imminent revelation she accepts him with the same gesture which she had used in her reconciliation with her mother in the forest, when Hester had restored the sign of guilt (p. 243)?[15] As the minister mounts the platform of disgrace, supported by Hester and clasping Pearl's hand in his, he thanks God for leading him through "grace" to this moment (p. 291). In that word Pearl is at last identified: she is grace, the instrument of his redemption, a powerful but hidden force urging him to good. When the "dreadful witness" of his sin, his scarlet letter, has been exposed, it is to Pearl that the dying man speaks. He asks her for a kiss, the sign of reconciliation that she had refused him in the forest. Her response is immediate and wholehearted. She kisses his lips (p. 294), as she had kissed the lips of her mother when she had restored the scarlet letter to her bosom in the forest.[16] Moreover, the effect of Pearl's major gesture in the direct communication with her mother and in the simultaneous indirect communication with her father in the forest scene

---

[14] It is interesting to observe that in a Theater Guild adaptation of *The Scarlet Letter* for radio presentation, the text was distorted to give Dimmesdale knowledge of Chillingworth's plan to sail for Europe on the same ship with him. This distortion provided motivation for Dimmesdale's confession. It is significant to observe further that Pearl was omitted entirely from the play.

[15] Cf. *supra*.   [16] Cf. *supra*.

is here fully elucidated in Dimmesdale's passionate disclosure (made almost against his will)[17] that both the angels and the Devil "were forever pointing" at the "brand of sin and infamy" (p. 293)—the hidden wound of the scarlet letter on his breast. Pearl and Chillingworth have probed that wound for seven years, the one for the angelic purpose of redemption, the other for the satanic purpose of damnation. Pearl has won. The subtle power which the minister has called "grace" has moved him to confession and salvation.

From the very beginning the narrator has made clear the nature of Pearl's mission to her mother: she had been sent as a blessing and as a retribution to remind Hester of her fall from grace and to teach her the way to heaven (p. 128). Her mission to her father, however, has been a hidden one. The narrator has chosen to suggest rather than to present it. It has been my purpose to try to elucidate it as another mission of redemption, to show that Pearl, the elf-child, as a figure of grace and through appropriately subtle means, is the cause of Dimmesdale's *volte face*. It is unthinkable that an artist of the stature of Nathaniel Hawthorne should fail to motivate the central action of his most distinguished and most admired work. There must be a cause for Dimmesdale's confession. It is Pearl in her preternatural aspect.

[17] Cf. *supra*.

A New Reading of *The Blithedale Romance*
Frederick C. Crews

MOST CRITICS are agreed that *The Blithedale Romance* is among the least satisfactory of Hawthorne's works. It is felt that the book suffers from a confusion of genres—that, as Yvor Winters put it, the author "began as a novelist, but lost himself toward the close in an unsuccessful effort to achieve allegory."[1] Allegory is indeed a problem in *Blithedale,* and none of the book's admirers—including Howells, James, and Browning[2]—has come to terms with this crucial fact. Recent critics have read the book more carefully. Hyatt Waggoner, Frank Davidson, and W. V. O'Connor have emphasized hitherto unnoticed aspects.[3] Useful as these new insights are, however, I feel that no critic has yet understood the essential movement of the plot. If the present judgment on *Blithedale* differs radically from any previous one, the reason is that my basic reading is different.

If this reading is valid, it would seem remarkable that the novel has been so consistently misunderstood. But a dispassionate look at *Blithedale* will show how this can easily have happened. Several incidental difficulties have been unduly emphasized. Hawthorne's Preface, for example, apologizes for the insubstantiality of the romance, and prepares the reader for an uncomfortable marriage of fabulous and prosaic elements.[4] One is left with the impression that

---
[1] Yvor Winters, *Maule's Curse* (Norfolk, Conn., 1938), p. 17.

[2] See William Dean Howells, *My Literary Passions* (New York, 1895), p. 186; Henry James, *Hawthorne* (New York, 1880), pp. 132-138; and Hawthorne's *English Notebooks,* ed. Randall Stewart (London, 1941), pp. 362-383. In fairness to Browning it should be said that he made no attempt to "explain" *Blithedale,* but simply told Hawthorne that he preferred it to his other works.

[3] Hyatt H. Waggoner, *Hawthorne, a Critical Study* (Cambridge, Mass., 1955); Frank Davidson, "Toward a Re-evaluation of *The Blithedale Romance,*" *New England Quarterly,* XXV, 374-383 (Sept., 1952); W. V. O'Connor, "Conscious Naïveté in 'The Blithedale Romance,'" *Revue des langues vivantes,* XX, 37-45 (Feb., 1954).

[4] *The Complete Novels and Selected Tales of Nathaniel Hawthorne* (New York, 1937), pp. 439 f. Further references to *The Blithedale Romance* are made to this edition, and will be incorporated into the text. In two minor cases of doubtful punctuation I have accepted the more probably correct readings of the first edition (Boston, 1852).

Blithedale will be little more than an improvisation upon the author's recollections of Brook Farm, despite Hawthorne's mild protest to the contrary. Nor does an examination of Hawthorne's notebooks reassure us on this point. The large number of passages lifted directly from journal entries of 1841 and after suggests a rehashing of miscellaneous sketches.[5] Hawthorne is not known to have ever expressed admiration for his book. He seems not to have been annoyed that contemporary readers saw it as a *roman à clef*, and concerned themselves only with trying to identify the prototypes of Hollingsworth and Zenobia.[6] Still another incentive for a prejudicial reading is Julian Hawthorne's statement that his father changed the title when it was "more than half written as 'Hollingsworth.'"[7] This seems to imply an aimlessness of conception. Above all, the tone of the book itself is unsteady. In perceiving that the language of Miles Coverdale, the narrator, vacillates between poetic enthusiasm and scornful bitterness, some critics have inferred that Hawthorne could not make up his mind about the value of his characters or describe them accurately. For this reason F. O. Matthiessen, Mark Van Doren, and Rudolph von Abele are satisfied to dismiss *Blithedale* as an artistic failure.[8]

Although all of these considerations have influenced critical opinion, the influence seems unfair. Hawthorne's Preface is heavily ironical. His apparent silence about *Blithedale* and the fact of his having incorporated many passages from his journals have nothing strictly to do with the book's final merit. Again, assuming that Julian Hawthorne's statement about the title is true, nothing would have prevented Hawthorne from rewriting the first, imperfect half in the light of his new idea. As for the extension of Coverdale's indecisiveness to a hypothetical indecisiveness in his creator, this strikes me as a serious confusion of perspective. Use of the first

---

[5] *The American Notebooks,* ed. Randall Stewart (New Haven, 1932). Most of these correspondences are noted by Arlin Turner, "Autobiographical Elements in Hawthorne's *The Blithedale Romance*," *University of Texas Studies in English*, XV, 39-62 (July, 1935).

[6] This knotty but essentially irrelevant question cannot be entirely solved, because *Blithedale* is not a *roman à clef* at all. Its characters were derived from people Hawthorne knew or had studied, but this is little more than we can say of any novel. We ought not to mistake the author's material for his intent, which is in this case something very different from a representation of his friends.

[7] *The Memoirs of Julian Hawthorne,* ed. Edith G. Hawthorne (New York, 1938), p. 34.

[8] F. O. Matthiessen, *American Renaissance* (New York, 1941), p. 297; Mark Van Doren, *Hawthorne* (New York, 1949), pp. 188-189; Rudolph von Abele, *The Death of the Artist: a Study of Hawthorne's Disintegration* (The Hague, 1955), p. 82.

person singular need not blind us to the fact that a narrator can also be a character. It is possible that Coverdale's shortcomings may be centrally important to the plot, and that Hawthorne stands outside of everything that happens in *Blithedale*. Most critics have briefly entertained this possibility and then rejected it. The real reason they have done so, beyond those listed above, is that *Blithedale* seems to supply no good alternative to the identification of author and narrator. Without a key to the thematic purpose of Coverdale's self-inflicted irony, we must assume that Hawthorne is simply laughing at himself. But I believe that this key can be found. In the interpretation that follows, virtually every sentence in the book can be seen as contributing to a deliberate, clearly definable thematic whole. The point of departure from previous criticism is that whereas Coverdale's limitations as a storyteller have hitherto been ascribed to Hawthorne, I ascribe them only to Coverdale. The "story" that he tells is not in itself the center of attention; it is the act of telling that is important. Once we have grasped Coverdale's function as a character, we can go on to consider the unfolding of *Blithedale's* true plot.

I

Literally and by temperament, Miles Coverdale is a minor poet. In him are joined the vague aspirations of a Transcendentalist, the tastes of an artist, and an acute sense of his own limitations. He yearns to create some permanent and spiritual work of art, divorced from the prosaic aspects of his daily life; but he also has "a decided tendency towards the actual" (p. 522). In one sense these two leanings are complementary, as in this statement of his aim: "to live in other lives, and to endeavor—by generous sympathies, by delicate intuitions, by taking note of things too slight for record, and by bringing my human spirit into manifold accordance with the companions whom God assigned me—to learn the secret which was hidden even from themselves" (p. 533). Here is the artist as novelist, combining "negative capability" with keen observation. But in another sense Coverdale's tendency towards the actual is an impediment to his art. Any work of art is more concise, more vivid, and more purposeful than the mass of experience from which it is derived; an interest in the petty details of life is useful to the artist only insofar as he is willing to select and juxtapose them in a new, more significant order. But this is precisely what Coverdale's tendency towards the actual prevents him from doing. Stated differently, Coverdale has two distinct senses of truth, and he tries to be loyal to both. He is obsessed with the undeniable reality of humdrum life, and equally with the aesthetic conviction that some details in that life are more important than others—more "true" because more universal. The two senses will not let each other alone. When Coverdale tries to think prosaically, his poetic imagination tempts him away. When he thinks poetically, his sense of literal reality calls him back to earth again. Coverdale's dilemma is that he cannot help feeling that "art" and "life" represent incompatible modes of truth. He is swung like a pendulum from one extreme to the other.

This polar view of Coverdale's psychology is more than a metaphor. It is an account of the basic rhythm of his narrative. Torn between poetry and prose, he never achieves a middle style—or rather, he achieves it only once, at the climax of his career. Until then, and afterwards, his language is characterized by alternating passages of rapture and cynicism. Whenever he rejoices in the ambitious spirit of Blithedale, he immediately adds a note of satire. Whenever he begins to praise a friend, he finishes by criticizing him. His own enthusiasm, inspired by a wish for imaginative truth, reminds him of his excess and starts him on the swing back to the other extreme. The two basic concerns of the plot, which give the novel a strict but subtle unity, are subjected to the same rhythm of zeal and disgust, on a larger scale. One of these concerns is the question of social and moral reform, epitomized in the Blithedale colony. The other has never been noticed, and must be introduced more carefully.

In order to interpret the "romance" that Coverdale recounts between Hollingsworth, Zenobia, and Priscilla as the subject of *Blithedale,* or even as an accurate version of the facts, the reader must overlook a great deal of evidence to the contrary. In the first place, Coverdale never supplies answers to some of the principal questions of fact involved in the romance: "Zenobia's whole character and history; the true nature of her mysterious connection with Westervelt; her later purposes towards Hollingsworth, and, reciprocally, his in reference to her; and, finally, the degree in which Zenobia had been cognizant of the plot against Priscilla, and what . . . had been the real object of that scheme" (p. 566). Without this information, which Hawthorne hints at but deliberately withholds, we are not equipped to use Coverdale's impressions as a basis for judging the other characters. More importantly, Coverdale's unreliability as a philosopher extends to his storytelling; and Coverdale is our only source of information about the romance. Most of the important scenes he recounts are observed from an inconvenient distance, or are not observed at all. Two of his most significant chapters are imaginative reconstructions of someone else's words,[9] and for the most crucial meeting of Hollingsworth, Zenobia, and Priscilla he arrives "half an hour too late" (p. 564). These considerations in themselves prove nothing, but they become significant when connected with the language with which Coverdale surrounds many of his "facts." In order to describe the first day at Blithedale he must "rake away the ashes from the embers in my memory, and blow them up with a sigh, for lack of more inspiring breath" (p. 443). After describing Hollingsworth's self-centeredness he adds, "Of course I am perfectly aware that the above statement is exaggerated, in the attempt to make it adequate. . . . The paragraph may remain, however, both for its truth and its exaggeration . . . and as exemplifying the kind of error into which my mode of observation was calculated to lead me" (p. 480). He recalls an image of Hollingsworth and Priscilla "with the evening twilight a little deepened by the dusk of memory" (p. 484). His first view of Westervelt "had almost the effect of an apparition" (p. 493). He admires Priscilla not for herself but "for the fancy-work with which I have idly decked her out" (p. 498). She has "always seemed like a figure in a dream" (p. 538). He concludes an important dialogue between Westervelt and Zenobia with this reflection: "Other mysterious words, besides what are above written, they spoke together; but I understood no more, and even question whether I fairly understood so much as this. By long brooding over our recollections, we subtilize them into something akin to imaginary stuff, and hardly capable of being distinguished from it" (p. 501). And his summary of Moodie's confession is characterized by "a trifle of romantic and legendary license, worthier of a small poet than of a grave biographer" (p. 546). Such language makes it difficult to see how Richard Fogle arrived at the conclusion that "Coverdale's interpretation is final," and that he is possessed of "infallibility."[10] On the contrary, Hawthorne has taken

---

[9] These are Zenobia's Legend of the Veiled Lady and Moodie's autobiography.

[10] Richard H. Fogle, *Hawthorne's Fiction: The Light and the Dark* (Norman, Okla., 1952), p. 157.

considerable pains to suggest that Coverdale's story is not to be trusted.

Another series of unusual statements raises this unreliability to paramount importance. Not only does Coverdale take liberties with the facts in relating them; he has had a suspiciously accurate foreknowledge of the whole course of events. He tells us that a record of his dreams during the first night at Blithedale "would have anticipated several of the chief incidents of this narrative, including a dim shadow of its catastrophe" (p. 460). A little later he has what Zenobia calls "an idea worthy of a feverish poet": that she is actually the Veiled Lady's sister. Speaking of the Blithedale colony, the narrator says, "I shall never feel as if this were a real, practical, as well as poetical system of human life, until somebody has sanctified it by death" (pp. 515-516). When he rediscovers Zenobia and Priscilla in town, "it was with no positive surprise, but as if I had all along expected the incident" (p. 530). On his way back to Blithedale, "the thought stared me in the face that some evil thing had befallen us, or was ready to befall" (p. 561). And just after Zenobia —not having told Coverdale of her intention—has gone off to drown herself, he "must have fallen asleep, and had a dream, all the circumstances of which utterly vanished at the moment when they converged to some tragical catastrophe" (p. 574). Clearly, there is a direct relationship between the workings of Coverdale's imagination and the tale that he asks us to believe.

If this relationship is not already apparent, another look at Coverdale's language will make it so. His interest in Hollingsworth, Zenobia, and Priscilla is specifically literary.

My own part in these transactions was singularly subordinate. It resembled that of the Chorus in a classic play, which seems to be set aloof from the possibility of personal concernment, and bestows the whole measure of its hope or fear, its exultation or sorrow, on the fortunes of others, between whom and itself this sympathy is the only bond. Destiny, it may be,—the most skilful of stage-managers,—seldom chooses to arrange its scenes, and carry forward its drama, without securing the presence of at least one calm observer. It is his office to give applause when due, and sometimes an inevitable tear, to detect the final fitness of incident to character, and distil in his long-brooding thought the whole morality of the performance. (p. 496)

This self-image is recalled again and again. "After all was finished, I would come, as if to gather up the white ashes of those who had perished at the stake, and to tell the world . . . how much had perished there which it had never yet known how to praise" (p. 534). He refers to his three friends as "these three characters . . . on my private theatre" (p. 480), and speaks of their habits in terms of suitability for "a sufficiently tragic catastrophe" (p. 486). "These three had absorbed my life into themselves" (p. 553). In brief, Coverdale is trying to make Hollingsworth, Zenobia, and Priscilla into a work of art. The narrative we read is not a description of his friends, but a tale which attempts to idealize them dramatically—a Blithedale romance.

This statement should be quickly amended. The romance that Coverdale is imagining, like his enthusiasm for the moral ideals of the colony, does not occupy the whole of his narrative. Together they are subject to what I called the rhythm of his mind—his tendency to swing between the real and the ideal. The Blithedale colony and Coverdale's Blithedale romance are both representative of the ideal. One embodies a vision of moral perfection; the other, aesthetic perfection. Both demand a transcendence of the actual. Blithedale is an effort to ignore and supersede all existing institutions, and the Blithedale romance is an effort to create an aesthetically meaningful world, above physical reality. For as Coverdale sadly observes, "real life never arranges itself exactly like a romance" (p. 500). Since Coverdale's respect for real life—both as an artist and as a friend of reform—is no weaker than his desire to transcend it, the action of the book consists largely in a running debate within Coverdale's mind over the suitability of his two ambitions. Every other "action" in *Blithedale* is subordinate and contributory to this debate.

The best evidence for this reading of the book will appear later—namely, its usefulness in making sense out of the many chapters which must otherwise be dismissed as incongruous. The awkward contrast between the ethereal romance and its prosaic setting; the sudden shifts of tone and scenery; the thickly suggestive language with no apparent referents; the seemingly frivolous episodes involving the Veiled Lady, and especially Zenobia's tale on this subject; the interlude with the Blithedale masqueraders; the shockingly vivid description of Zenobia's drowned body; and above all, Coverdale's obsessive interest in his friends—all of these become pieces in a complete and ingenious mosaic. Nor is this view of *Blithedale's* plot so thorough a contradiction of previous criticism as it may seem. In one form or another, Davidson, Waggoner, Matthiessen, and von Abele all recognized that Coverdale is distinct from Hawthorne. Von Abele deals specifically with the fact that Coverdale's attitude toward his friends is artistic; and although his analysis of the book is impaired by a random Freudianism, there is no real contradiction between saying that Coverdale has an artistic viewpoint and that he puts this viewpoint to practical use. Furthermore, there is no reason for thinking that this sophisticated relationship between the author, the narrator, and the narrator's experience is beyond Hawthorne's powers of refinement. The majority of the heroes in his fiction are isolated, like Coverdale, by some intellectual passion, and two of his tales are directly concerned with the clash between human and aesthetic values: "The Artist of the Beautiful" and "The Prophetic Pictures." *The Marble Faun* deals with the same question. And Hawthorne's notebooks indicate a persistent awareness of such problems. Indeed, it is possible that the genesis of *Blithedale* can be traced to this journal entry of October 25, 1835: "A person to be writing a tale, and to find that it shapes itself against his intentions; that the characters act otherwise than he thought; that unforeseen events occur; and a catastrophe comes which he strives in vain to avert.... he having made himself one of the personages."[11] This is slightly different from *Blithedale's* plot as it actually developed, but the same basic concern is present.

This plot will be traced in a moment, but first we must become better acquainted with the questions upon which it is built. The matter of social reform is relatively simple. On the one hand is the appeal of an ideal society; on the other, a distrust of novelty, an awareness of practical obstacles, and a skepticism about the wisdom of devoting oneself single-mindedly to any kind of project. It is true that the issue is complicated by Hollingsworth's minority plan for the reformation of criminals, for Hollingsworth's scheme lacks the poetic attractions of Blithedale; but Coverdale brings the same values to bear upon both of them. The artistic question is of greater complexity, and is debated on a level farther beneath the surface of the narrative—the level of symbolic language. For convenience we

[11] *The Heart of Hawthorne's Journals,* ed. Newton Arvin (Boston, 1929), p. 8.

may separate it into two components, which might be phrased as "Should art be made to resemble life?" and "Should life be made to resemble art?" The first of these is introduced covertly on the first page of the book, where the narrator is recalling a demonstration of clairvoyance by the Veiled Lady.

> Nowadays, in the management of his "subject," "clairvoyant," or "medium," the exhibitor affects the simplicity and openness of scientific experiment; and even if he profess to tread a step or two across the boundaries of the spiritual world, yet carries with him the laws of our actual life, and extends them over his preternatural conquests. Twelve or fifteen years ago, on the contrary, all the arts of mysterious arrangement, of picturesque disposition, and artistically contrasted light and shade, were made available, in order to set the apparent miracle in the strongest attitude of opposition to ordinary facts. (p. 441)

Readers who are familiar with Hawthorne's Prefaces—including the Preface to *Blithedale*—will not fail to recognize that this passage states a fundamental artistic problem, the opposition of realism and romance as techniques of fiction. Should a writer strive to give the illusion of real life, however prosaic? Or should he rather admit that fiction must always be different from life, and strive to cultivate this difference through frankly artificial devices? These two extremes correspond to the two poles of Coverdale's temperament, his tendency towards the actual and his love for the spiritual and ideal. Neither extreme can therefore be expected to satisfy him. Coverdale's true conception of a proper art is presented later on, when he is examining some paintings in a saloon. He expresses distaste for a picture of a drunken man asleep on a bench: "The death-in-life was too well portrayed" (p. 542). However, he is charmed by certain still-lifes, equally realistic in detail, but with an important difference. "All these things were so perfectly imitated, that you seemed to have the genuine article before you, and yet with an indescribable ideal charm; it took away the grossness from what was fleshiest and fattest, and thus helped the life of man, even in its earthliest relations, to appear rich and noble, as well as warm, cheerful, and substantial" (p. 542). In short, Coverdale's artistic ideal is a marriage of actual life with an ennobled taste. Real people must be the subject of his romance, but they must give forth "an indescribable ideal charm."

Where, then, is the cause for debate? It lies in the fact that Coverdale, for all his belief in this desired ideal, cannot put it into practice. He can concentrate alternately on corporeal life and on pure spirit, but he is emotionally incapable of fusing them. If he were satisfied either to record only the meanest details of his experience or to create a wholly fictitious romance, he might well succeed. But his integrity betrays him. He is committed to base his art on the real transactions among Hollingsworth, Zenobia, and Priscilla, and at the same time to make these relationships "artistic." But the subjects of his attention resent his efforts to see them in an unreal light. Hollingsworth and Zenobia, especially, deliberately ridicule his conception of the affair, and thus they force Coverdale into a moral corner. He cannot easily deceive himself into thinking that his friends are involved in a ready-made romance, and yet he wants very badly to compose his romance according to the observed truth. Here is where the second part of the question comes in: "Should life be made to resemble art?" Since life refuses to be artistic *in se,* to what degree should an artist alter his notion of reality to suit his purpose as artist? It is only a small exaggeration to say that *Blithedale* is a symbolic treatise on this subject.

II

Coverdale begins with the best intentions. Through the first four chapters he shows no sign of contemplating a romance. These chapters are principally concerned with developing the contrast between Blithedale and the neighboring city, presumably Boston, and with introducing the main characters of the book. But Priscilla, the last of these to appear, stimulates Coverdale's fancy. When he expresses his interest to Zenobia, she says: "Since you see the young woman in so poetical a light . . . you had better turn the affair into a ballad" (p. 457). Here is the germ of Coverdale's trouble. On the same evening he is stricken with a fever, the significance of which is made fairly plain. "During the greater part of it [the night], I was in that vilest of states when a fixed idea remains in the mind, like the nail in Sisera's brain, while innumerable other ideas go and come, and flutter to and fro, combining constant transition with intolerable sameness" (p. 460). The sentence which immediately follows has already been quoted. "Had I made a record of that night's half-waking dreams, it is my belief that it would have anticipated several of the chief incidents of this narrative, including a dim shadow of its catastrophe." Coverdale has begun to entertain his romance, and his fever is that of an artist in the first stage of expanding an inspirational idea.

This fever lasts for two more chapters, during which time Coverdale is content to lie in bed and observe his three attendants, and to formulate his poetic conception of them. For in sickness, "Vapors then rise up to the brain, and take shapes that often image falsehood, but sometimes truth. The spheres of our companions have, at such periods, a vastly greater influence upon our own than when robust health gives us a repellent and self-defensive energy" (p. 466). On May Day he gets up and emerges into the "genial sunshine" of Blithedale. He tells us that his illness has purged him of everything pertaining to his old self. "In literal and physical truth, I was quite another man. I had a lively sense of the exultation with which the spirit will enter on the next stage of its eternal progress . . ." (p. 474). Here Coverdale is expressing the poetic, unrealistic side of his nature, nursed by his recent isolation from daily toil. But as soon as he accepts his new duties as a farmer, this poetic attitude is challenged. "The clods of earth, which we so constantly belabored and turned over and over, were never etherealized into thought. Our thoughts, on the contrary, were fast becoming cloddish" (p. 477). Thus begins one of the most prominent metaphorical tensions in the book, between the real, prosaic earth and the clouds, vapors, or breezes of poetic truth. Every reference to earth occurs in defiance of one or both of Coverdale's ambitions, and every escape from earth is an escape to the ideal.

Chapter IX is entitled "Hollingsworth, Zenobia, Priscilla," and this is its opening paragraph:

> It is not, I apprehend, a healthy kind of mental occupation, to devote ourselves too exclusively to the study of individual men and women. If the person under examination be one's self, the result is pretty certain to be diseased action of the heart, almost before we can snatch a second glance. Or, if we take the freedom to put a friend under our microscope, we thereby insulate him from many of his true relations, magnify his peculiarities, inevitably tear him into parts, and, of course, patch him very clumsily together again. What wonder, then, should we be frightened by the aspect of a monster, which, after all,—though we can point to every feature of his deformity in the real personage,—may be said to have been created mainly by ourselves. (p. 479)

At this stage in his thinking, having just tested his preliminary ideas about Blithedale and its colonists against the intractable reality of the soil, Coverdale is taken aback. Perhaps he has been at fault in thinking of his comrades only in terms of his private scheme. He is by no means convinced, but from this point onward he is plagued by doubts. The rest of the chapter contains numerous expressions of uncertainty, but Coverdale persists in his conjectures. It is at this point, also, that he first confesses his awareness of a growing alienation from the others. "While these three characters figured so largely on my private theatre, I . . . was at best but a secondary or tertiary personage with either of them" (p. 480). A human problem thus complicates the artistic one. In order to see his friends in a sufficiently artistic light, Coverdale recognizes that he must detach himself from a personal concern for them, and this detachment inspires scorn in return.

The next two chapters, which bring the mysterious figures of Moodie and Westervelt briefly into the foreground, are devoted to the further development of Coverdale's ideas; but the second also hints at an impending change in his attitude. The spot where Westervelt is seen in the Blithedale woods is lent a peculiar significance. ". . . I abated my pace, and looked about me for some side-aisle, that should admit me into the innermost sanctuary of this green cathedral, just as, in human acquaintanceship, a casual opening sometimes lets us, all of a sudden, into the long-sought intimacy of a mysterious heart" (pp. 491-492). Coverdale is seeking to crystallize his romance. Westervelt's arrival momentarily breaks his reverie, for the mesmerist's attitude towards Hollingsworth, Zenobia, and Priscilla is exactly opposite to that which Coverdale is trying to maintain. He speaks of them in the most cynical manner, without poetic flavor. His very appearance "had an indecorum in it, a kind of rudeness, a hard, coarse, forth-putting freedom of expression, which no degree of external polish could have abated one single jot" (p. 493). Although Westervelt displays a close familiarity with Coverdale's three "characters," the poet's instinctive rudeness to him soon puts an end to their conversation, and Westervelt disappears "among the windings of the wood-path." The full import of this encounter will be seen later, but for the moment this much can be said: Coverdale is not yet so dedicated to a deliberate *manipulation* of his characters that he will recognize a kinship between himself and a charlatan like Westervelt. However, the evil seed has been sown. "But after a little reflection, I could not help regretting that I had so peremptorily broken off the interview while the stranger seemed inclined to continue it. His evident knowledge of matters affecting my three friends might have led to disclosures or inferences that would perhaps have been serviceable" (p. 496). It should be added that Westervelt, in this chapter and in every subsequent appearance, is conspicuously linked with references to the Devil. In the romance, he tempts Zenobia into marriage and later tempts Hollingsworth, through Zenobia, to betray Priscilla into his power. But outside the romance he is a symbolic tempter of a deeper sort. He represents Coverdale's impulse to complete his romance at the expense of literal truth, and when Coverdale has been tempted, Westervelt reminds us of his fall.

Every backdrop in *Blithedale* is significantly associated with the type of action occurring there. The city from which Coverdale first departs comes to stand for the restrictions and also the comforts of conventional life, in contrast with the more adventurous but more uneasy country.[12] At Blithedale itself, as Coverdale becomes increasingly aware of his isolation from the others, he connects certain localities with certain aspects of his experience. It is obvious that the farmhouse is the scene of community life, and that the farmland itself is the scene of physical labor, the enemy of intellect and art. But Coverdale's romance also has a special locality—the woods. Not only do many of the significant developments in his tale occur on wood-paths, but he himself has a private retreat for artistic contemplation. This, as the title to Chapter XII informs us, is "Coverdale's Hermitage," "an admirable place to make verses" (p. 497). This little nook, shielded from the sun of literal truth, is formed by the intertwining of a wild grape vine "of unusual size and luxuriance" with three or four trees—that is, by the intertwining of poetic fancy with the material of romance. The richness of symbolic suggestion in these paragraphs can scarcely be overstated. These two sentences, for example, prefigure both the maturing of the romance and its grim climax: "I counted the innumerable clusters of my vine, and fore-reckoned the abundance of my vintage. It gladdened me to anticipate the surprise of the Community, when, like an allegorical figure of rich

---

[12] See, for example, Coverdale's first voyage from city to farm (pp. 444-445) and his partial readjustment to the city (pp. 525-526).

October, I should make my appearance, with shoulders bent beneath the burden of ripe grapes, and some of the crushed ones crimsoning my brow as with a blood-stain" (p. 497). Henceforth, every mention of overhanging trees heralds a new complication in the romance, and every mention of grapes or wine implies the joy of artistic creation.

Perched in his tree-hermitage, Coverdale now surveys the farm. Hollingsworth at toil appears ludicrous, and so does his philanthropy. Priscilla evokes sympathy, but only for the "fancy-work" with which Coverdale has adorned her. Under the influence of "the pleasant scent of the wood," Coverdale confesses to "a mood of disbelief in moral beauty or heroism" (p. 498). He laughs aloud, and his laughter is echoed—by Westervelt's.[13] Westervelt has already affected his thinking. "I recognized as chiefly due to this man's influence the sceptical and sneering view which, just now, had filled my mental vision, in regard to all life's better purposes.... I detested this kind of man; and all the more because a part of my own nature showed itself responsive to him" (p. 499). This renewed connection with the materialistic show-master, coming as it does when Coverdale is reappraising his friends from a purely artistic point of view, can only signify that his conception of the romance is being cheapened. The episode that now ensues between Westervelt and Zenobia contributes appreciably to the progress and "atmosphere" of the romance; but it is also bombarded on all sides by images of falsehood, error, and fancy.

Appropriately enough, the next scene is one of fancy almost wholly divorced from fact. "Zenobia's Legend," as retold by Coverdale, is completely out of character in its motivation. There is no conceivable reason why Zenobia should want at this point to suggest to the assembled colonists that Priscilla is the Veiled Lady; and equally strangely, no one seems to draw this unmistakable inference. Nor does Zenobia's apparent maliciousness here seem to effect the slightest change in the relations among the three characters. It is not even mentioned again. These facts, plus the poetic license that Coverdale stresses, can only mean that the legend is not a literal part of the romance, but is partly or entirely a fabrication of Coverdale's.

[13] In their earlier meeting it was Westervelt who laughed first, and was joined involuntarily by Coverdale. The reversal of this order here is suggestive of Coverdale's increasing "possession" by Westervelt.

Its theme of the skeptic who refuses to have faith in the beauty beneath the veil is intended as a symbolic gloss to his romance. But it is also a condemnation of that romance—Coverdale being now exclusively concerned with "veils"—and in addition a judgment on all of the real characters in *Blithedale,* as we shall see in retrospect. The legend marks the end of a progression of chapters that are increasingly "romantic," beginning with Zenobia's first mocking suggestion that Coverdale "turn the affair into a ballad." The next chapter brings us back to earth. Its locale, "Eliot's Pulpit," is a place of moral judgment, and as such it belongs to the self-righteous Hollingsworth (as his name implies) rather than to Coverdale. The issue debated is the status of women, and the question as Coverdale phrases it—"Will it be possible ever to redeem them?"—bears on the real fortunes of Zenobia and Priscilla as well as on Coverdale's rather different plan for immortalizing them. The influence of Eliot's Pulpit is a sobering one. When a brief "wood-path" episode near the end of the chapter brings Coverdale's favorite subject back into focus, these are some of the questions he asks himself: "But was it a vision that I had witnessed in the wood? Was Westervelt a goblin? Were those words of passion and agony, which Zenobia had uttered in my hearing, a mere stage declamation? Were they formed of a material lighter than common air?" (p. 514). These questions are disingenuous. Hawthorne is informing us, through Coverdale's imagery, that his narrator is engaged in distorting the truth. And Coverdale himself is displaying a vague consciousness of this fact.

Chapter XV, "A Crisis," comes at the literal and thematic midpoint of *Blithedale*.[14] Hollingsworth, in his growing distrust of the colony's usefulness, is prepared to break off on a private tangent. His ideas of reform divorce practical utility from the Utopian affectations of Blithedale. When Coverdale is asked to join him, the contrast is sharpened between Hollingsworth's fanatical but down-to-earth philanthropy and Coverdale's loyalty to the Utopian affectations. As Hollingsworth justly observes, the real reason for Coverdale's interest in Blithedale is that "It has given you a theme for poetry" (p. 516). The two men part in anger, and in the next

[14] That is to say, every previous chapter has drawn Coverdale farther away from the truth, although an undercurrent of misgivings has been accumulating. Hereafter, the misgivings will be of superior weight; Coverdale will be drawn closer and closer to a despair of completing the romance on false terms, until he must finally submit to the factual truth.

chapter Coverdale has decided to leave the farm, "and take an exterior view of what we had all been about" (p. 522). Hollingsworth's accusations have shaken his faith in Blithedale's reality—and also, of course, in the reality of his Blithedale romance. "I was beginning to lose the sense of what kind of a world it was, among innumerable schemes of what it might or ought to be." His purpose in returning to town is at once philosophical and artistic: "to correct himself by a new observation from that old stand-point." The side of Coverdale's nature that responds to corporeal reality—as symbolized in this chapter by his leave-taking of the pigs—will now be temporarily served.

Situated comfortably in a hotel, Coverdale now savors the contrast between Blithedale and the town. The contrast is essentially between artistic techniques, as a close reading of the chapter will show. Coverdale's detailed and random observations of his neighbors—between whom and himself a symbolic grapevine grows—are apparently collected to furnish a more solid basis for the romance. But here again, Coverdale senses his inability to connect the mundane with the romantic. The last paragraph of the chapter is a metaphorical statement of this fact.

> There was nothing else worth noticing about the house, unless it be that on the peak of one of the dormer-windows which opened out of the roof sat a dove, looking very dreary and forlorn; insomuch that I wondered why she chose to sit there, in the chilly rain, while her kindred were doubtless nestling in a warm and comfortable dove-cote. All at once, this dove spread her wings, and, launching herself in the air, came flying so straight across the intervening space that I fully expected her to alight directly on my window-sill. In the latter part of her course, however, she swerved aside, flew upward, and vanished, as did, likewise, the slight, fantastic pathos with which I had invested her. (p. 529)

This dove reappears in the next chapter, but now in her proper context: Zenobia, Priscilla, and Westervelt are seen in this same house. Their reappearance is a sign of Coverdale's slavery to his romance as it has been previously established. "After the effort which it cost me to fling them off,—after consummating my escape, as I thought, from these goblins of flesh and blood, and pausing to revive myself with a breath or two of an atmosphere in which they should have no share,—it was a positive despair, to find the same figures arraying themselves before me, and presenting their old problem in a shape that made it more insoluble than ever" (pp. 531-532). From this point onwards Coverdale makes no pretense of human sympathy for his friends, but devotes himself only to working out their tragedy. "I began to long for a catastrophe. If the noble temper of Hollingsworth's soul were doomed to be utterly corrupted by the too powerful purpose which had grown out of what was noblest in him; if the rich and generous qualities of Zenobia's womanhood might not save her; if Priscilla must perish by her tenderness and faith, so simple and so devout,—then be it so! Let it all come!" (p. 532). Coverdale is positively looking forward to these events. Although Zenobia sees him from across the street and angrily lets down a curtain, "like the drop-curtain of a theatre, in the interval between the acts" (p. 533), Coverdale pays a call, trying to extort "some nature, some passion, no matter whether right or wrong, provided it were real" (p. 536). His heartless interest in drama has obliterated his sense of moral values; and remembering his moralistic ideal of art, we may say that it is destroying his art as well. When Zenobia refuses to answer all his questions, Coverdale goes to a less reliable source—Old Moodie. Moodie, like Westervelt, is central to the romance but only incidentally a subject of Coverdale's attention. His story, related at second-hand by the narrator, comes close to answering the questions I listed earlier as withheld by Hawthorne. But it does not answer them, for Moodie's biography is not only sketchy, it is lent the same legendary quality as Zenobia's tale of the Veiled Lady. As Coverdale's readers, we shall never know what Moodie really said; but we can be sure that Coverdale has adapted his words to the purpose of his romance.

III

Now we are ready for two of the richest chapters in *Blithedale*. In "A Village Hall" we have a literal scene, an episode in Coverdale's romance, a symbolic judgment on that romance and on Blithedale itself, and a hint of their ultimate failure, all embodied in a single concrete event. Coverdale is by now fully aware that his obsession is unhealthy. "Hollingsworth, Zenobia, Priscilla! These three had absorbed my life into themselves. Together with an inexpressible longing to know their fortunes, there was likewise a morbid resentment of my own pain, and a stubborn reluctance to come again within their sphere" (p. 553). Now they reappear in a setting such as to suggest an utterly fraudulent and prostituted art— a country lyceum-hall, fit for ventriloquism, thaumaturgy, pantomimes, wax museums, and the like. Before a vulgar and superstitious audience, Westervelt is to present the hypnotized Veiled Lady. The analogies between Westervelt's debased art and Coverdale's, which have been accumulating throughout *Blithedale,* are pointed devastatingly. "Human character was but soft wax in his hands; and guilt, or virtue, only the forms into which he should see fit to mould it" (p. 556). Coverdale denounces this blasphemy, but to no avail; Westervelt's introductory remarks are a parody both of Coverdale's art and of the Blithedale experiment. "He spoke of a new era that was dawning upon the world; an era that would link soul to soul, and the present life to what we call futurity, with a closeness that should finally convert both worlds into one great, mutually conscious brotherhood" (p. 557). The supreme blow is dealt to Coverdale's art-worship when Westervelt borrows some of his most reverent vocabulary and twists it into this: "Slight and ethereal as it [the veil] seems, the limitations of time and space have no existence within its folds. This hall—these hundreds of faces, encompassing her within so narrow an amphitheatre—are of thinner substance, in her view, than the airiest vapor that the clouds are made of. She beholds the Absolute!" (p. 558). When this final analogy between Westervelt's Priscilla and Coverdale's has been drawn, the ensuing action is a symbolic defeat for Coverdale as well as a tangible defeat for the mesmerist. Hollingsworth, the anti-poet, climbs onto the stage, breaks Westervelt's spell over Priscilla, and bears her off to safety. Reality has conquered fiction.

Chapter XXIV, "The Masqueraders," has been ignored or condemned as irrelevant in previous interpretations of *Blithedale.* Although its symbolism is a trifle more strained than that of the preceding chapter, it is a masterpiece of relevancy. Surrounded on all sides by impediments to his romance, Coverdale makes the only choice that may possibly extricate him. He decides to return to Blithedale and check his version against the truth. The closer he gets to the colony, the more certain he becomes that the truth will mock him. He even doubts the very existence of the place as he has remembered it, and when the thick earth of the farm partly reassures him, he gratefully renounces all of his spiritual aspirations. "The red clay of which my frame was moulded seemed nearer akin to those crumbling furrows than to any other portion of the world's dust. There was my home, and there might be my grave" (p. 560). But it is too late to get off so easily. Fearful of "some evil thing," he turns off into the woods and seeks out his hermitage. Although he passes the very spot where Zenobia is to die, he refuses to dwell on his vague presentiment; his summer grapes are completely ripened, and ready to be pressed into the wine of art. "And I longed to quaff a great goblet of it that moment!" (p. 562). Thus committed to pursue his work, but afraid to base it on the truth, he plunges into the woods again—in search of a method. First he sees some cows, who make him "foolishly angry" by their indifference to him; thus the method of prosaic realism is quickly rejected. Next, he meets a band of masqueraders who represent allegorical figures. Some of these are dancing to the music of a Devil. Coverdale knows they are only Blithedale residents on a picnic, and the absurdity of their disguises makes him laugh; allegory is shallow. Recognizing his laughter, the dancers threaten him with tortures appropriate to their various roles. " 'The voice was Miles Coverdale's,' said the fiendish fiddler . . . 'My music has brought him hither. He is always ready to dance to the Devil's tune!' " "The whole fantastic rabble. . . . streamed off in pursuit of me, so that I was like a mad poet hunted by chimeras" (p. 563). Glad to escape from such a specious and unmanageable technique, Coverdale entertains one final possibility. He finds a pile of cut logs, moss-covered with age—or symbolically, a historical situation that is real but "dated." "I found something strangely affecting in this simple circumstance. I imagined the long-dead woodman, and his long-dead wife and children, coming out of their chill graves, and essaying to make a fire with this heap of mossy fuel!" (p. 564). Thus Coverdale has rejected the use of indiscriminate realism, of allegory, and of historical romance. He has exhausted his alternatives to the real adventures of his friends. It is thus with full symbolic import that he next hears the voices of these very people, calling to him from the seat of moral judgment, Eliot's Pulpit. "But you come half an hour too late," says Zenobia, "and have missed a scene which you would have enjoyed!" (p. 564). While Coverdale has been searching for a less honest technique, the central action of his romance has transpired unobserved.

In the next two chapters any lingering hope of resuming his fiction is erased. Finally in the presence of a real crisis between real people, he feels ashamed. "The intenseness of their feelings gave them the exclusive property of the soil and atmosphere, and left me no right to be or breathe there" (p. 565). The human tragedy whose next-to-final scene he is witnessing is more dramatic than anything he might fabricate, and it has been quietly developing all the while that he was busy trying to romanticize it. Now a sudden flood of genuine sympathy nullifies his artistic detachment. When Hollingsworth departs with Priscilla, the center of controversy, at his side, Coverdale's grief is scarcely less than Zenobia's. For as he confesses in the last line of the book, he has loved Priscilla all along. That is to say, he has loved her as a romantic heroine. When Coverdale is left alone with Zenobia, "the analogy that I saw, or imagined, between Zenobia's situation and mine" (p. 570) becomes clear; they have each been deprived of an ill-founded and consuming hope. At first Zenobia refuses to recognize the change in Coverdale's attitude. "Ah, I perceive what you are about! You are turning this whole affair into a ballad. Pray let me hear as many stanzas as you happen to have ready" (pp. 570-571). But she sees her mistake, and eventually takes him into her confidence. Ironically enough, Zenobia speaks like a tragic heroine only when she is sure that she is no longer in the presence of a writer of tragedies.

Coverdale's romance has been partly truth, partly fiction, but its catastrophe is entirely true—so true that it invalidates the rest. This is the meaning of his dream, "all the circumstances of which utterly vanished at the moment when they converged to some tragical catastrophe, and thus grew too powerful for the thin sphere of slumber that enveloped them." During this dream Zenobia has drowned herself. When Coverdale, at the start of Chapter XXVII, throws "a tuft of grass with earth at the roots" into Hollingsworth's room, we are symbolically informed that brute reality is to be confronted at last. In the middle of the night Hollingsworth, Coverdale, and a prosaically minded farmer named Silas Foster dredge the river for Zenobia's body. This scene has justly been acclaimed as the most vivid in *Blithedale*. It is the most vivid because it is the only one that Coverdale makes no attempt to touch up. And yet it is also the symbolic climax of the whole book. The most prominent metaphor throughout *Blithedale* has been one of disguise, and particularly of white or silvery veils.[15] Now every veil has been lifted except one, the black veil of the river. Underneath it is pure, stark reality.

> Her wet garments swathed limbs of terrible inflexibility. She was the marble image of a death-agony. Her arms had grown rigid in the act of struggling, and were bent before her with clenched hands . . . it seemed as if her body must keep the same position in the coffin, and that her skeleton would keep it in the grave. . . . (p. 578)

This rigidity denies every vain delusion in *Blithedale*. It even challenges the spirit of tragedy: "could Zenobia have foreseen all these ugly circumstances of death . . . she would no more have committed the dreadful act than have exhibited herself to a public assembly in a badly fitting garment!" (p. 579). Zenobia's funeral in the next chapter is devoid of affectation, despite the very different plans that the Blithedale residents had projected earlier. "She was buried very much as other people have been for hundreds of years gone by" (p. 580). And when Coverdale meets the cynical Westervelt by her grave, he is justified in denouncing Westervelt's expressions of regret that Zenobia did not live to achieve worldly success. He can secretly agree that her suicide was unnecessary, but he has been made aware that worldly success—be it in the form of personal influence, useful philanthropy, or literary fame—is less real than death, and less important than something else—love. Zenobia learned this at the cost of her life. Coverdale did so at the cost of his romance. And Hollingsworth, as we presently learn, did so at the cost of his self-respect.

Blithedale's theme is the most common one in Hawthorne's work. It is what he called the Unpardonable Sin: "the separation of the intellect from the heart."[16] Each of the book's characters is guilty of denying the heart—except Priscilla, who is not a character at all but an abstract symbol of the heart. Zenobia pursued an image of herself as grandly independent. Hollingsworth embodied his ego in a project of reform. Westervelt scorned the very existence of the heart, and Moodie betrayed it for the sake of external display. And

---

[15] Waggoner's treatment of this symbol is adequate, although his conclusions about structure seem to me over-simple (*Hawthorne*, pp. 179-181).

[16] *American Notebooks*, p. 106.

Coverdale drained himself of human sympathy to make room for his romance.

However, it must not be thought that *Blithedale* is a condemnation of all art. Insofar as it deals with Coverdale, it is a condemnation of divorcing the moral consciousness from the aesthetic. A better artist than Coverdale could base his work on a proper relationship to his material—a relationship involving a respect for truth and at the same time a respect for the human beings under scrutiny. Coverdale's romance was justified in aspiring to present an exalted view of humanity. But the "indescribable ideal charm" should have arisen from a perception of ideal virtues within the subject itself, not in the detached fancy of the artist.[17] And an exactly parallel judgment is passed on the Blithedale colony. The desire for an ideal society was good, but it became worthless when detached from a concern for *actual* society. In each case the fundamental error was the same: a lack of faith that spiritual qualities are inherent in real life. Hollingsworth, Zenobia, Coverdale, Westervelt, and Moodie each failed to see that the symbolic Priscilla was neither real nor ideal, but *both*. Hollingsworth made partial amends, but everyone suffered for his mistake.[18] The unifying moral of this complicated book is simply that the highest truth is intrinsic in the lowest. If Miles Coverdale can see only one of them at a time, the fault is not in nature; it is in a consciousness that unjustly divorces intellect from heart. In this sense—remembering the evident pun in "Westervelt" —it is not unfair to read *Blithedale* on its highest level as a parable of the modern mind.

IV

However, the ambition of this paper is only to show that *Blithedale* has been misread on the very lowest level, that of plot. If my reading is correct, it is only fair to Hawthorne that we discount as irrelevant all previous value-judgments about this book. For in

[17] In warning his fiancée against the dangers of mesmerism, Hawthorne wrote: "And thou wilt know that the view which I take of this matter is caused by no want of faith in mysteries, but from a deep reverence of the soul. . . . Keep thy imagination sane—that is one of the truest conditions of communion with Heaven" (*Love Letters of Nathaniel Hawthorne*, 2 vols. Chicago, 1907, II, 64-65)

[18] Strictly speaking, however, it is wrong to say that Westervelt suffered. Like Priscilla, he is only a symbol—the symbol of everything that Priscilla is not. He tempts the others into a cheap materialism and personifies it, but, like Priscilla, he remains morally unaffected by the events around him.

order to speak of a book's faults and virtues, we must at least have some idea about what is transpiring in its plot. The surface difficulties of *Blithedale* have goaded its various critics into generalizations which bear little or no reference to Hawthorne's achievement. And those who have admired *Blithedale* have on the whole been less acute than its detractors, for if this book is not principally concerned with Coverdale's mind, surely it is one of the most absurd and self-defeating romances ever written. But if we take the trouble to read it in the terms that Hawthorne established—not in the title or the Preface, which are ironical, but in the language of Coverdale's narrative—we may emerge with a very different estimate of its value.

The Blithedale Romance is a symbolic commentary on several types of activity. It is not a romance, nor is it a novel in any usual sense of the term. To judge it on the traditional grounds of character and action is to miss the point—despite the fact that Miles Coverdale is one of the most subtly conceived characters in American fiction. The real achievement of *Blithedale* lies in the complexity and consistency of its structure. Hawthorne is attempting what few writers have dared: a surface plot, an imaginative reconstruction of that plot by a narrator, and a symbolic commentary on both. Indeed, *Blithedale* has claims to uniqueness, for in no other book that I know does the narrator's changing attitude toward his narrative constitute a rival plot which overtakes and is eventually matched against the other. The nearest approach is Henry James's *The Sacred Fount,* and James's failure is the measure of Hawthorne's success. James was forced to eliminate everything from his book except the tedious, falsifying mind of his narrator, but Hawthorne can give us glimpses of the truth *within* the false narrative—and a symbolic means of distinguishing between them—so that we can see the two plots separating and then converging.[19] Some parts of the book are less successful than others in maintaining this complex purpose, but there is not a single chapter that can be called unfunctional or inconsistent. *Blithedale* belongs to a tradition that includes *Gulliver's Travels* and *Ulysses*—books whose greatness lies in the author's ability to express his deepest judgments through a narrator who is himself a subject of judgment. Historically, as a precursor of the modern

---

[19] James's *The Turn of the Screw* may provide a more exact parallel, if Edmund Wilson's well-known interpretation is correct.

novel, and biographically, as the most complex expression of Hawthorne's mind, *Blithedale* deserves considerable respect; but for its own sake it demands attention as an extraordinary work of art. If it lacks the warmth and surface drama of *The Scarlet Letter,* it eliminates the half-visible puppet-master who asks us to suspend disbelief. Or rather, it sublimates him into Miles Coverdale. Hawthorne's discomfort with the too obvious devices of romance led him into something far deeper and more challenging to his powers of expression. His success must be judged in terms of his purpose.

Hawthorne's Allegory of Science: "Rappaccini's Daughter"
Edward H. Rosenberry

"R APPACCINI'S DAUGHTER" is one of the major unsolved enigmas in Hawthorne's work. The problem, difficult as it has been to solve, is easy to define. The knowledgeable reader looks for a clear pattern of second meanings in a Hawthorne story. In this one, as if to ensure the expectation, Hawthorne made prefatory remarks about his "inveterate love of allegory" and the fact that if his tales are not taken "in precisely the proper point of view . . . they can hardly fail to look excessively like nonsense." Few readers would reject "Rappaccini's Daughter" as nonsense; on the other hand, none has seemed to find "precisely the proper point of view" to unravel its mysteries. Many of the best analyses of the tale hang fire on uncertainties or discrepancies in likely allegorical patterns, and as a result critics have disagreed whether it is "below its author's highest art" or "one of Hawthorne's greatest tales."[1] The purpose of this essay is to contribute to a clearer reading and more settled estimate of the story by proposing a consistent allegory underlying its admittedly complex narrative.

The interpretation to be developed here is grounded on two assumptions about Hawthorne's *donnée*. First, the title establishes the center of meaning in Beatrice Rappaccini, and specifically in her capacity as her father's child. Second, the opening sentence establishes the narrative point of view in Giovanni Guasconti, and specifically in his capacity as a student.[2] The focal point and the frame

[1] The judgments belong respectively to Austin Warren, ed., *Nathaniel Hawthorne: Representative Selections* (New York, 1934), p. 367, and Mark Van Doren, *Nathaniel Hawthorne* (New York, 1957), p. 131. Some of the frustrations in good recent studies may be seen in Richard Harter Fogle, *Hawthorne's Fiction: the Light and the Dark* (Norman, Okla., 1952), p. 92; Hyatt H. Waggoner, *Hawthorne, a Critical Study* (Cambridge, Mass., 1955), pp. 115-116; Roy R. Male, *Hawthorne's Tragic Vision* (Austin, Texas, 1957), p. 55.

[2] Critical differences about the story are generally reducible to divergence on these fundamental points. Traditional interpretation has placed central emphasis on Rappaccini (e.g., Warren, *loc. cit.*). More recent critics favor Beatrice (e.g., Fogle, Waggoner, and Male), or sometimes Giovanni (F. L. Gwynn, "Hawthorne's 'Rappaccini's Daughter,'"

of the picture thus defined, the vital elements of the setting and their figurative suggestions take shape with reasonable clarity of outline.

The opening tableau of Giovanni at his window, gazing with kindled interest upon the exotic garden of Dr. Rappaccini, is plainly enough the picture of an impressionable young student discovering in his traditional and somewhat boring educational world an exciting laboratory of experimental science. The waters that nourish this garden and the ruined fountain from which they flow are identified for us as "immortal spirit" and "perishable garniture" respectively; or, in terms of a strictly academic symbolism, intellectual energy, the spirit of learning, as opposed to its transitory uses, forms, and disciplines. The meaning of the great central shrub with gem-like purple blossoms follows from context. In its position with respect to the garden as a whole and the symbolic fountain, this plant represents the crowning product of a potent but lawless force of mind. In its physical character, it suggests a marvelous new source of energy, expressed to the visual observer in terms of light: "a show so resplendent that it seemed enough to illuminate the garden even had there been no sunshine." In the midst of the symbolic laboratory appears Rappaccini, the standard Hawthorne man of science, conveying, as he moves among his flowers, a sinister impression of not loving his plants but fearing them, as "one walking among malignant influences . . . which, should he allow them one moment of license, would wreak upon him some terrible fatality." He works with gloves and a mask and a wary "perception of harm in what his own hands caused to grow." This is Hawthorne's "Adam" in his "Eden of the present world." It is an ironical but not otherwise distorted picture of science seen from the gloomiest point of view—a picture which has been rushing rapidly enough toward reality in the intervening century to justify the author's irony and gloom.

When Rappaccini finds his work at last too perilous and calls his daughter to help, the action of the allegory may properly be said to begin. Three things are at once stressed about the new and all-important figure of Beatrice: she is young, she is attractive, and she is almost horribly at ease with plants her father is in mortal fear of. As he gives the great purple shrub into her care, she welcomes the

---

Nineteenth Century Fiction, VII, 217-219, Dec., 1952; Bernard McCabe, "Narrative Technique in 'Rappaccini's Daughter,'" *Modern Language Notes*, LXXIV, 213-217, March, 1959), but do not define and relate their roles in the way that is suggested here.

charge with a mystical fervor in striking contrast to her father's dread. What is the meaning of this crucial symbolic act? Evidently the old scientist is passing the torch to the next generation. Both narrative and allegorical contexts seem to say this. But they say it in different ways; Hawthorne here requires the native ambivalence of symbolism, which no one has seen fit to grant him on this point. Beatrice is an old man's child so long as he remains an old man. But in his allegorical incarnation as Scientist, Rappaccini has no physical offspring, only spiritual or intellectual. To the man of learning, "the next generation" can only be those he teaches, the children of his intellect, the inheritors and habitual possessors of objects and ideas which he has, often fearfully, brought into being. It is an old but vital story that Hawthorne is telling here: how the adventure of one age is the custom of the next, and how long familiarity can make a safe and stable haven of the very brink of disaster.

In addition to being young and unafraid, Beatrice is extremely attractive. Hawthorne has given this fact all the emphasis in his power by making her the first of a famous gallery of his heroines remarkable for a darkly voluptuous sexual magnetism. So successful is he that the reader brings himself with some difficulty to translate her literal charms into the necessary symbolic causes of Giovanni's intellectual infatuation. The young man is about to be captivated by the glamor of Science. Of course, he will be entranced, too, by a ravishing young woman, because this is a story and that is what happens in it; but to read Beatrice as woman on the allegorical level of the tale is to deny her essential duality as a symbol. Having established, then, the figurative sex appeal which Science exerts on Giovanni, Hawthorne provides a hedge against quick disillusionment by having the student check his dreamy twilight experience "in the light of morning," which "brought everything within the limits of ordinary experience, so that he was inclined to take a most rational view of the whole matter." Both head and heart are now enthralled, and our freshman is ripe for his fateful academic heresy.

At this point Hawthorne introduces the fourth and last major element into his human equation, the professor to whom Giovanni's father (orthodox intellectual tradition?) has sent the young man. Professor Baglioni has given readers of the tale more trouble, if possible, than Beatrice has. In the excitement of measuring him for some strictly ethical equivalence, it is easy to forget that Baglioni is a professor, as Giovanni is a student, and that his entire role in the story is devoted to representing an academic philosophy diametrically opposed to that of his rival, Rappaccini. If he does so ineffectually, at times pettily, the manner will of course qualify the role, but it will in no sense define or alter it. What are the facts as Hawthorne gives them?

Baglioni is, first, "of genial nature." Unlike Rappaccini, he is a sociable man, a drinker, and a talker. His opinion of his dehumanized colleague is colored by enough prejudice and professional jealousy to make his character humorously human; but it fairly reflects the basic irreconcilability of their positions. To an uninfected mind Baglioni's indictment of the pure scientist, for all its asperity, must be decisive. But Giovanni, like the rest of us, wonders whether "so spiritual a love of science" may not be rather a "noble" thing. Here speaks the Romance of the Laboratory, an epidemic and durable mode of hero-worship. What is the humanitarian to say to this? Indignant, and frustrated by his loss of ground in this "warfare of long continuance," Baglioni grows sarcastic. With a conservative's disdain, he dismisses the radical methods of his rival, deprecates his professional successes, and hints waspishly at dark designs to place his learned daughter in Baglioni's own chair. These are not heroic sentiments. They are most appropriately human ones. And they are significantly in tune with the views of his creator. One of the plainest attitudes in Hawthorne's writings is a contemptuous distrust of science, which he personified in villain after villain of Rappaccini's stamp: Cacaphodel, Aylmer, Brand, Chillingworth—even the mild and sagacious Dr. Heidegger, whose fiancée "had swallowed one of her lover's prescriptions, and died on the bridal evening." If Baglioni seems at times contemptible himself, perhaps it is because he, too, was a Hawthorne physician. In any event, his antagonism toward two scientists of another camp, and his somewhat officious unwillingness to surrender Giovanni into their hands, are hardly symptomatic of any real or symbolic depravity. The professor's tribute of jealousy and resentment is, after all, only another form of the student's tribute of adoration.

The plot now thickens. Giovanni, observing Beatrice a second time in her garden, is struck with a new aspect of her beauty, most important to the total tale in view. This is an "expression of simplicity and sweetness,—qualities that had not entered into his idea of her character, and which made him ask anew what manner of mortal she might be." Her moral innocence becomes at once a part of her fatal attraction for Giovanni; but neither he nor the reader for him can anticipate at this point that it will become in time the principal irony of the drama and a key to Beatrice's meaning in the allegory. To add to his perplexity, Giovanni notices (or fancies) that the girl and the flower she so mysteriously resembles have a lethal effect on small, normal plants and animals. But here Hawthorne takes immediate pains to ensure that the reader will not share Giovanni's mystification. "Beatrice," he tells us, "observed this remarkable phenomenon, and crossed herself, sadly, but without surprise; nor did she therefore hesitate to arrange the fatal flower in her bosom." The episode may, characteristically, speak too softly of Hawthorne's symbolic thinking in the story; but its imagery surely does all that imagery can do to portray both the awful power of modern science and the moral insulation of the youthful manipulator of its deadly marvels, to whom attendant death and desolation are sincerely regrettable but for whom there is no other way of life than that which assumes for its own high purposes the tragic risks of technological progress. Perhaps no fact about the allegorical Beatrice is more significant than that "her experience of life had been confined within the limits of that garden." How could she know what her father had not taught her? How should she, the "sister" of his dreadful inventions, see them with the eye of an *homme moyen sensuel?* To the innocent Beatrice, her wizard parent is a benevolent Prospero, as her admirer is a Ferdinand, and she herself a Miranda, deriving "a pure delight from her communion with the youth not unlike what the maiden of a lonely island might have felt conversing with a voyager from the civilized world." She is, of course, a tragic Miranda, for, as she must discover to her destruction, her father lacks humanity and her lover lacks purpose and understanding.

While the story must be told from Giovanni's point of view, he plays a part at least as villainous as Dr. Rappaccini's. His demerits are less spectacular but far more devastating to the simple soul whose knowledge of the world is so fantastically circumscribed. From first to last, his manner to Beatrice is selfish and disingenuous. Attracted by curiosity and vanity rather than by any valid interest in science, he bribes his way into her world through a back door, flatly disregarding an all but certain apprehension of its diabolical character, and sweeps poor Beatrice off her feet with his Grecian beauty and his Latin charm. His ultimate disillusionment and rejection of her are inevitable. His love is mere fascination; and his intelligence, apt enough to see the satanic meaning of Rappaccini's botanical creations, is blind to the kindred nature of the daughter. It is the paradox of their relationship that Beatrice, the unwitting agent of death, is a "heavenly angel" in her capacity for love, while Giovanni, though grounded in humane tradition, proves a vain and shallow adventurer. No wonder she asks with her final breath, "Was there not, from the first, more poison in thy nature than in mine?" As the only true murderer in the story, Giovanni changes, in effect, from a moth at a flame to a bull in a china shop. Difficult as the change must have been for Hawthorne to manage, it was the one structural device that enabled him finally to establish Beatrice as the tragic center between the opposing emotional forces of Giovanni and her father without sacrificing the initial advantage of Giovanni's suspension between the contending intellectual forces of the Rappaccinis and Baglioni.

If Baglioni has fared badly at the hands of the story's interpreters, it is probably because his jarringly Chaucerian personality has overshadowed the moral importance of two acts which his author gave him to perform. First, he tells Giovanni the old legend out of Sir Thomas Browne on which the tale is based and which effectively defines the danger of an intimacy with Beatrice Rappaccini. Second, he provides Giovanni with the antidote intended to counteract the poison in Beatrice's system and thus bring her back, in Hawthorne's oft-repeated phrase, "within the limits of ordinary nature." It is true that Baglioni lacks the fine conscience of a Hawthorne or a Henry James hero. But Hawthorne could hardly have intended him for either hero or villain, and it would seem a distortion of the author's aim to assess Baglioni's irascibility and sentimentality as "ignoble motives" which his creator held in significant contempt.[3] In the same way, the point of the tale is shifted or obscured if we

[3] Chester E. Eisinger, "Hawthorne as Champion of the Middle Way," *New England Quarterly*, XXVII, 48-49 (March, 1954).

suppose that Baglioni's antidote was placed in a Cellini vase in order to suggest that to him Giovanni's affair is "on the same level as Cellini's amorous adventures"; or if we read Baglioni's concluding taunt to his stunned rival as "the revenge of the mediocre over the exceptional."[4] Such interpretations cannot fail to drive one to Arvin's conclusion that "Rappaccini's Daughter" represents a "disparagement of the intellect."[5]

Both Baglioni and his mental superior, Rappaccini, demonstrate a tragic intellectual fallibility as they stand aghast before a catastrophe which they could neither anticipate nor avert; and surely this common failure of mind, whether pragmatic or empirical, speaks critically enough of two major camps of modern intellectualism. Yet the point of the story does not lie wholly in this weakness, nor in the equal and opposite emotional weakness of Giovanni, nor in the conflict of the two.[6] It does not even lie in the destructive impact of these forces on Beatrice, though this is clearly a part of what Hawthorne has to say—is, indeed, precisely what he means in referring to her, finally, as "the poor victim of man's ingenuity and of thwarted nature, and of the fatality that attends all such efforts of perverted wisdom." Had Hawthorne ended the story there he would have had a point, but no further point than the one he had already made more cogently in "The Birthmark."

In the earlier tale, as in this one, innocent humanity in the guise of a beautiful girl is beguiled by the scientist-who-would-be-God into a state of unquestioning and finally self-destructive discipleship. In "The Birthmark" the idea behind this pattern was to dramatize the tragedy of cabalistic hubris and public hero-worship in a civilization in which science has become a religion.[7] Georgiana was Aylmer's wife, bound to him by romantic love and contractual fealty, and her conscious sacrifice to his fanaticism takes its meaning from analogy with martyrdom. Beatrice, on the other hand, is conceived as the daughter of the god-scientist because only the filial relationship could dramatize the split personality of science itself: the scientist as villain and as victim, at once the sorcerer and the sorcerer's

---

[4] Male, p. 66; Fogle, p. 100.
[5] Newton Arvin, *Hawthorne* (Boston, 1929), p. 139.
[6] S. R. Price, "The Head, the Heart, and 'Rappaccini's Daughter,'" *New England Quarterly*, XXVII, 399-403 (Sept., 1954).
[7] Robert B. Heilman, "Hawthorne's 'The Birthmark': Science as Religion," *South Atlantic Quarterly*, XLVIII, 575-583 (Oct., 1949).

apprentice. In "The Birthmark" these figures in the pattern were totally discrete and somehow oversimplified—the arrogant Aylmer, the ethereal Georgiana, the gross Aminadab. There, too, the tale is wholly concerned with the scientist's operations upon the girl to change her nature, and when the change is complete the tale is done. In this sense, "Rappaccini's Daughter" takes up where "The Birthmark" leaves off. The crucial change in the girl's nature is quite complete before the story begins. For this reason, the ultimate fatality of that change can hardly be considered the sole, or even the chief, point of the story.

Hyatt Waggoner, in pointing out the subordinate role of Rappaccini, concludes that it is not the original poisoning, but "present evil, a woman poisoned, that is the chief subject of the story."[8] My extension of his view might be defined, if not quite defended, by a more literal translation of the French title Hawthorne gave the story in his whimsical preface—"Beatrice; ou la Belle Empoisonneuse." To the extent to which Beatrice is merely a woman *poisoned* her story has nothing to say, since she lives in her deadly garden, like Housman's Mithridates, "easy, smiling, seasoned sound." It is only when she becomes "the fair *poisoner*"—when her father's experiment, that is, becomes political rather than simply botanical—that there can be tragic meaning in her death and in the final cry of Baglioni with which the tale concludes: "Rappaccini! Rappaccini! And is *this* the upshot of your experiment!"

Beatrice is more than the innocent victim of Rappaccini's experiments; she is, without the least loss of personal innocence, the transmitter of them to a foolish and unwary society to which her training has made her effectively a stranger. Randall Stewart has correctly placed this tale in the first rank of those embodying Hawthorne's obsessive theme of social estrangement.[9] By virtue of its unique symbolic multiplication of the personality, it also stands high among his studies of the scientist as an ethical being and of the ambiguous warfare of guilt and innocence in the human soul. Perhaps in no other tale did Hawthorne attempt so ambitious a program, and its extraordinary complexity has made for interpretive difficulty proportional to its richness of texture and variety of esthetic rewards.

[8] *Hawthorne*, p. 107.
[9] *The American Notebooks of Nathaniel Hawthorne* (New Haven, 1932), p. lxxi.

Shadows of Doubt: Specter Evidence in Hawthorne's "Young Goodman Brown"
David Levin

I CHOOSE FOR MY TEXT two statements written in the autumn of 1692, after twenty Massachusetts men and women accused of witchcraft had been executed. The first is by Increase Mather, the second by Thomas Brattle.

. . . the Father of Lies [Mather declared] is never to be believed: He will utter twenty great truths to make way for one lie: He will accuse twenty Witches, if he can thereby bring one honest Person into trouble: He mixeth Truths with Lies, that so those truths giving credit unto lies, Men may believe both, and so be deceived.[1]

Brattle was astonished by the ease with which witnesses avoided a crucial distinction:

And here I think it observable [he wrote], that often, when the afflicted [witnesses] do mean and intend only the appearance and shape of such an one, (say G[oodman]. Proctor) yet they positively swear that G. Proctor did afflict them; and they have been allowed so to do; as tho' there was no real difference between G. Proctor and the shape of G. Proctor.[2]

Nathaniel Hawthorne's protagonist Goodman Brown commits the very mistakes that Brattle and Mather belatedly deplored in 1692. He lets the Devil's true statements about the mistreatment of Indians and Quakers prepare him to accept counterfeit evidence, and he fails to insist on the difference between a person and the person's "shape," or specter. Most modern critics who have discussed the story have repeated both these errors, even though Hawthorne clearly identifies the chief witness as the Devil and the setting as the Salem Village of witchcraft days. In the last decade,

---

[1] Increase Mather, *Cases of Conscience Concerning Evil Spirits Personating Men* (Boston, 1693), reprinted in *What Happened in Salem?*, David Levin, ed. (New York, 1960), p. 122.

[2] Letter of Thomas Brattle, dated October 8, 1692, and reprinted in *ibid.*, p. 130. The letter was probably circulated in manuscript; the name of the addressee is unknown.

several articles have rightly contended that Hawthorne meant to reveal the faultiness of Goodman Brown's judgment;[3] but the first and most cogent of these did not prevent so distinguished a critic as Harry Levin from alluding to "the pharisaical elders" whom Goodman Brown sees "doing the devil's work while professing righteousness."[4] And the cogent article itself insists that "it is not necessary to choose between interpreting the story literally and taking it as a dream"; that Brown neither goes into a forest nor dreams that he goes into a forest. What Brown does, says D. M. McKeithan, is "to indulge in sin (represented by the journey ...)."[5]

I believe that one must first of all interpret the story literally. The forest cannot effectively represent sin, or the unconscious mind of Goodman Brown, or the heart of the dark moral wilderness, until one has understood the literal statements about the forest in regard to the literal actions that occur therein. Instead of agreeing with one recent critic that "the only solution to the problem" of what happens in the forest "lies in the tale's complex symbolic pattern,"[6] let us try to accept Hawthorne's explicit statements of fact. Instead of inventing a new definition of the word "witch," as another critic has done,[7] let us try to read the story in the terms that were available to Hawthorne. A proper reading of the literal action removes some of the ambiguity that it is now so fashionable to admire, but it should leave open a sufficient variety of interpretations to satisfy those who insist on multiple meanings, and it will clarify the fine skill with which Hawthorne made the historical materials dramatize his psychological insights and his allegory.

Hawthorne knew the facts and lore of the Salem witchcraft "delusion," and he used them liberally in this story as well as others. He set the story specifically, as the opening line reveals, not in his native Salem, but in Salem Village, the cantankerous hamlet (now Danvers) in which the afflictions, the accusations, and the diabolical

[3] D. M. McKeithan, "Hawthorne's 'Young Goodman Brown': An Interpretation," *Modern Language Notes*, LXVII, 93-96 (Feb., 1952); Thomas F. Walsh, Jr., "The Bedeviling of Young Goodman Brown," *Modern Language Quarterly*, XIX, 331-336 (Dec 1958); Paul W. Miller, "Hawthorne's 'Young Goodman Brown': Cynicism or Meliorism? *Nineteenth-Century Fiction*, XIV, 255-264 (Dec., 1959).

[4] Harry T. Levin, *The Power of Blackness: Hawthorne, Poe, Melville* (New Yor 1958), p. 54.

[5] McKeithan, p. 96.

[6] Walsh, p. 336.

[7] Miller, p. 259 n. 10.

sabbaths centered in 1692. Among the supposedly guilty are the minister of Salem Village and two women who were actually hanged in that terrible summer. Hawthorne not only cites testimony that Martha Carrier "had received the Devil's promise to be queen of hell"; he also quotes Cotton Mather's description of her as a "rampant hag," and he even violates Goodman Brown's point of view in order to introduce another actual rumor of 1692: "Some affirm that the lady of the governor was there [at the witches' sabbath]." He takes great care to emphasize the seeming presence at the witches' sabbath of the best and the worst of the community—noting with superbly appropriate vagueness, just before the climax, that the "figure"[8] who prepares to baptize Goodman Brown "bore no slight similitude, both in garb and manner, to some grave divine of the New England churches."

There can be no doubt that Hawthorne understood clearly the importance of what was called "specter evidence" in the actual trials. This was evidence that a specter, or shape, or apparition, representing Goodman Proctor, for instance, had tormented the witness or had been present at a witches' meeting. Hawthorne knew that there had been a debate about whether the Devil could, as the saying went, "take the shape of an angel of light," and in both "Alice Doane's Appeal" and "Main Street" he explicitly mentioned the Devil's ability to impersonate innocent people.[9] He was well aware that Cotton Mather had warned against putting too much confidence in this sort of evidence; he also knew that after the Mathers and Thomas Brattle had opposed even the admission of

---

[8] The first published versions of the story used the word "apparition" here. See *The New-England Magazine*, VIII, 257 (April, 1835); and *Mosses from an Old Manse* (New York, 1846), p. 80. The word was changed to "figure" in Hawthorne's last revision of *Mosses from an Old Manse* (Boston, 1857).

The text of this story has often been erroneously printed. One important change seems to have been made by George P. Lathrop in the edition he published nineteen years after Hawthorne's death. Every earlier version that I have seen, including Hawthorne's last revision, says that "the chorus of the desert" at the spectral meeting in the forest seemed to include "the roaring wind, the rushing streams, the howling beasts, and every other voice of the unconverted wilderness. . . ." Lathrop and almost every editor after him changed the word "unconverted" to "unconcerted." I have been following Hawthorne's last revision.

[9] Hawthorne even joked casually about this kind of imposture. Of his participation in the experiment at Brook Farm he wrote: "The real me was never an associate of the community; there has been a spectral Appearance there, sounding the horn at day-break, and milking the cows . . . and doing me the honor to assume my name." Quoted in Randall Stewart, *Nathaniel Hawthorne, A Biography* (New Haven, 1949), p. 60.

specter evidence (the Mathers on the ground that it was the Devil's testimony), the court had convicted almost no one and not a single convict had been executed. It seems certain, moreover, that Hawthorne had read Cotton Mather's biography of Sir William Phips, in which Mather the historian not only echoes his father's language about truths and lies, but clearly suggests that one of the Devil's purposes had been the traducing of Faith.

> On the other Part [Mather wrote in 1697], there were many persons of great Judgment, Piety and Experience, who from the beginning were very much dissatisfied at these Proceedings; they feared lest the *Devil* would get so far into the *Faith* of the People, that for the sake of many *Truths,* which they might find him telling of them, they would come at length to believe all his *Lies,* whereupon what a Desolation of *Names,* yea, and of *Lives* also, would ensue, a Man might without much *Witchcraft* be able to Prognosticate; and they feared, lest in such an extraordinary Descent of *Wicked Spirits* from their *High Places* upon us, there might such *Principles* be taken up, as, when put into *Practice,* would unavoidably cause the *Righteous to perish with the Wicked,* and procure the Blood-shed of Persons like the *Gibeonites,* whom some learned Men suppose to be under a false Pretence of *Witchcraft,* by *Saul* exterminated.[10]

If we set aside the alternative possibilities for a while and examine the story from the seventeenth-century point of view—the perception of Goodman Brown through which Hawthorne asks us to see almost all the action—we will find a perfectly clear, consistent portrayal of a spectral adventure into evil. Goodman Brown goes into the forest on an "evil" errand, promising himself that after this night he will "cling" to the skirts of his wife, Faith, "and follow her to heaven." Once in the wilderness, he himself conjures the Devil by exclaiming, "What if the Devil himself should be at my very elbow!" Immediately, he beholds "the figure of a man," and this figure quite unambiguously tells him that it has made the trip from Boston to the woods near Salem Village—at least fifteen or twenty miles—in fifteen minutes. Brown refuses the Devil's staff and announces that he is going back to Faith, but the Devil, "smiling apart," suggests that they "walk on, nevertheless, reasoning as we go."

[10] Cotton Mather, *Magnalia Christi Americana: or, The Ecclesiastical History of New-England* (London, 1702), Book II, p. 62.

The reasoning proceeds from this point, as the Devil tries to convince Brown that the best men are wholly evil. Most of the argument that follows corresponds to the traditional sophistry of the Devil—the kind of accusation with which Satan nearly discourages Edward Taylor's saint from joining the church in *God's Determinations Touching His Elect*. It is here that the Devil mentions true sins (the mistreatment of Indians and Quakers) in order to induce despair: men are so wicked that nothing can save them.[11] Against this first argument Goodman Brown resists longer than some modern critics have resisted, for he sees that the alleged hypocrisy of elders and statesmen is "no rule for a simple husbandman like me." Foolishly, however, he believes the Devil's testimony (as his neighbors did in 1692), and he frankly tells him that "my wife, Faith," is the foundation of his reluctance to become a witch.

This admission invites the Devil to proceed, and it determines the organization of the rest of his argument. With typical subtlety he pretends to give up at once, because

". . . I would not for *twenty* old women like the one hobbling before us that Faith should come to any harm."

As he spoke he *pointed his staff at a female figure* on the path, *in whom Goodman Brown recognized* a very pious and exemplary old dame. . . .[12]

The Devil has of course conjured this "figure," which moves "with singular speed for so aged a woman," and he appears to it in "the very image"—soon afterward, "the shape"—"of old Goodman Brown, the grandfather of the silly fellow that now is." When the woman's figure has served his purpose, the Devil throws his staff "down at her feet," and she immediately disappears. Brown accepts this evidence without question, for by this time the Devil is "discoursing so aptly that his arguments [seem] rather to spring up in the bosom of his auditor than to be suggested by himself."

[11] Here again we should notice that Cotton Mather had used language very close to Hawthorne's. In a sermon called "The Door of Hope," Mather cautioned against "A sinful and woful Despair." Some men, he said, "rashly conclude" that "because they see no *help* to their Souls in themselves, . . . there is no *hope* for their Souls any where else." And among several *"Reasons* of Despair" to which he offered answers at the end of the sermon, the fifth reads: "I doubt I have committed the *unpardonable Sin;* and then, all my hope is lost forevermore." *Batteries Upon the Kingdom of the Devil* (London, 1695), pp. 100 ff.

[12] The italics are mine.

But Goodman Brown holds back once again, and the Devil, assuring him that "You will think better of this by and by," vanishes. Just as Brown is "applauding himself greatly," he is assaulted by another kind of airy evidence: disembodied voices. The "mingled sounds" *appear* to pass "within a few yards," and although the "figures" of the minister and deacon "brushed the small boughs by the wayside, it could not be seen that they intercepted, even for a moment, the faint gleam from the strip of bright sky athwart which they must have passed." Brown cannot see "so much as a shadow," but "he could have sworn"—as witnesses in 1692 did indeed swear—that he recognized the deacon and the minister in "the voices, talking so strangely in the empty air."

Now, as Brown doubts that "there really [is] a heaven above him," the Devil has only to produce evidence that Faith, too, is guilty. Hearing the voice of Faith from a "black mass" of cloud that "hurried" across the sky although no wind is stirring, Brown calls out to her in agony, and the "echoes of the forest"—always under the Devil's control—mock him. Then the Devil sends his final argument, Faith's pink ribbon, as her voice fades into the far-off laughter of fiends. At the end of the story we learn that this evidence, too, was spectral, for Faith wears her ribbons when her husband returns home in the morning; but now, in the forest, Brown is convinced that his "Faith is gone," that the world belongs to the Devil. He takes up the Devil's staff and "seems to fly along the forest path rather than to walk or run, . . . rushing onward with the instinct that guides mortal man to evil."

With beautiful care Hawthorne makes his descriptive language reinforce these meanings through the rest of the horrible experience. "Flying" among the black pines, Brown finally sees the "lurid blaze" of the witch-meeting and pauses "in a lull of the tempest that had driven him onward." The verse that he hears is sung "by a chorus, not of human voices, but of all the sounds of the benighted wilderness, pealing in awful harmony together," and his own cry sounds in "unison with the cry of the desert." At the sabbath itself he sees, "quivering between gloom and splendor," *faces* belonging to the best people of the colony. A congregation shines forth, then disappears in shadow, and again grows, "as it were, *out of the darkness, peopling the heart of the solitary woods at once*."[13] Brown believes that he recognizes "a score" of Salem Village church members before he is "well nigh ready to swear" that he sees "the figure" of the minister, "the shape of his own dead father," "the dim features" of his mother, and "the slender form" of his wife. When he stands with the form of Faith, they are "the only [human] pair, *as it seemed*," who hesitate "on the verge of wickedness in this dark world." It is "the shape of evil" that prepares to baptize them, and the figure that stands beside Brown is that of his "pale" wife.[14] When he implores her to "look up to heaven and resist the wicked one," the whole communion disappears, and he cannot learn "whether Faith obeyed."

The clarification that this reading achieves for the story should remove some of the objections that have been raised against it even by its admirers. When we recognize that the Devil is consistently presenting evidence to a prospective convert who is only too willing to be convinced, we do not need to complain with F. O. Matthiessen against Hawthorne's "literal insistence on that damaging pink ribbon"; nor need we try, with R. H. Fogle, to explain the ribbon away.[15] One might insist that even here Hawthorne restricts his language admirably to Brown's perception, for he says that *something* fluttered lightly down through the air and that Brown, after seizing it, *beheld* a pink ribbon. Brown's sensory perception of the ribbon is no more literal or material than his perception of the Devil, his clutching of the staff, or his hearing of the Devil's statement about the fifteen-minute trip from Boston to the woods near Salem Village. But such an argument is really unnecessary. The seventeenth-century Devil could produce specters, with or without the consent of the people they resembled, and he could make cats, birds,

---

[13] The italics are mine.

[14] Here it might be argued that Hawthorne says Faith was actually present, for he writes that "the wretched man beheld his Faith, and the wife her husband," and just before Brown cries out Hawthorne writes, "The husband cast one look at his pale wife, and Faith at him. What polluted wretches would the next glance show them to each other...!" It is more consistent with Hawthorne's practice throughout the story to read these references to Faith's observation as Goodman Brown's view of her reaction. All the action has been seen from Brown's point of view, and Hawthorne has never entered Faith's mind. Surely the exclamation is in Brown's mind only, for it prompts him to act, and his plea that she look up to heaven leaves him standing alone. Her specter vanishes with the others.

[15] F. O. Matthiessen, *American Renaissance: Art and Expression in the Age of Emerson and Whitman* (New York, 1941), p. 284; and R. H. Fogle, "Ambiguity and Clarity in Hawthorne's 'Young Goodman Brown,'" *New England Quarterly*, XVIII, 451 (Dec., 1945).

and other familiars seem to materialize before terrified witnesses.[16] For such a being, and with a witness overcome by "grief, rage, and terror," a ribbon posed no great difficulty.

Hawthorne's technique thus gives a clear view of his meaning. When we stop looking for what we may wish to believe about Puritans who whipped Quakers and burned Indian villages, we can recognize just what it is that Goodman Brown sees. Hawthorne does not tell us that none of the people whom Brown comes to suspect is indeed a diabolical agent, but he makes it clear that Brown has no justification for condemning any of them—and no justification for suspecting them, except for the shadowy vista that this experience has opened into his own capacity for evil. Asking whether these people were "really" evil is impertinent, for it leads us beyond the limits of fiction. The story is not about the evil of other people but about Brown's doubt, his discovery of the *possibility* of universal evil. Before reading the Devil's statements here in the light of ideas that Hawthorne suggested elsewhere, we must read them in their immediate context. At the witch-meeting, the "shape of evil" invites Goodman Brown to "the communion" of the human "race," the communion of evil, but we have no more right than Brown himself to believe the Father of Lies. Indeed, Hawthorne's brilliant success depends on this distinction. He gives us an irresistible picture of a "crisis of faith and an agony of doubt";[17] we must notice that Brown finally does exorcise the spectral meeting, but that he can never forget his view of the specters or the abandon in which he himself became "the chief horror" in the dark wilderness. He lives the rest of his life in doubt, and the literal doubt depends on his uncertainty about whether his wife and others are really evil. If he were certain that they had been present in the forest, he would not treat them even so civilly as he does during the rest of his life. It is the spectral quality of the experience—both its uncertainty and its unforgettable impression—that makes the doubt permanent.

[16] Cf. Cotton Mather, *Magnalia Christi Americana*, Book II, p. 60; and Cotton Mather, in *Memorable Providences, Relating to Witchcraft and Possessions* (Boston, 1689), reprinted in Levin, *What Happened in Salem?*, pp. 96-97: "Other *strange* things are done by them in a way of *Crafty Illusion*. They do craftily make of the *Air*, the *Figures* and *Colors* of things that never can be truly created by them. All men might *see*, but, I believe, no man could *feel* some of the Things which the *Magicians of Egypt*, exhibited of old."

[17] The phrase is Harry Levin's. See *The Power of Blackness*, p. 54.

The question, then, is not whether Faith and the others were really there, in their own persons, at the witch meeting. When Hawthorne asks whether Goodman Brown had "fallen asleep in the forest and only dreamed a wild dream of a witch meeting," and replies, "Be it so if you will," he offers an alternative possibility to the nineteenth-century reader who refuses to take devils seriously even in historical fiction. The choice lies between dream and a reality that is unquestionably spectral. Neither Hawthorne nor (at the end) even Goodman Brown suggests that the church members were present in their own persons. Brown's question is whether the Devil, when he took on their shapes, had their permission to represent them. That is why Hawthorne can say, "Be it so if you will." For the meaning remains the same even if Brown, having for some odd reason fallen asleep in the woods before the story begins, has dreamed the entire experience.

By recognizing that Hawthorne built "Young Goodman Brown" firmly on his historical knowledge, we perceive that the tale has a social as well as an allegorical and a psychological dimension. Hawthorne condemns that graceless perversion of true Calvinism which, in universal suspicion, actually led a community to the unjust destruction of twenty men and women. But we ought also to be reminded of some general truths about proper ways to read this wonderfully shrewd writer. We must not underestimate his use of historical materials, even when he is writing allegory; nor should we let an interest in patterns of image and symbol or an awareness that he repeatedly uses the same types of character obscure the clear literal significance of individual stories. Working over an amazingly—some critics have said, an obsessively—narrow range of types and subjects, he nevertheless achieves a remarkable variety of insights into human experience.

Hester Prynne's Little Pearl: Sacred and Profane Love
Robert E. Whelan

IN HIS INTRODUCTION TO *"Rappaccini's Daughter,"* Hawthorne confesses to "an inveterate love of allegory," telling us that "he generally contents himself with a very slight embroidery of outward manners,—the faintest possible counterfeit of real life,—and endeavors to create an interest by some less obvious peculiarity of the subject." He at the same time warns us that his works "can hardly fail to look excessively like nonsense" unless "the reader chance to take them in precisely the proper point of view" (II, 107-108).[1] In *The Scarlet Letter* Hawthorne seems to further warn us that we shall with difficulty make sense of the history of Arthur Dimmesdale and Hester Prynne unless we take Pearl in precisely the proper point of view:

In [Pearl] was visible the tie that united them. She had been offered to the world, these seven years past, as the living hieroglyphic, in which was revealed the secret they so darkly sought to hide,—all written in this symbol,—all plainly manifest,—had there been a prophet or magician skilled to read the character of flame! (V, 247-248)

Certainly Hawthorne's reference to Pearl as a hieroglyphic suggests that this character of flame will be somewhat difficult to decipher unless the reader, like Champollion, also becomes possessed of the Rosetta Stone. That the Rosetta Stone has not been found accounts, I should say, for the uncertain answers still given by so many critics to the poignant question Hester addresses to Dimmesdale in his dying moments: "Shall we not spend our immortal life together? Surely, surely, we have ransomed one another, with all this woe!" (V, 303).[2]

[1] Volume and page references to Hawthorne's works are to *The Complete Works of Nathaniel Hawthorne*, ed. George Parsons Lathrop (Riverside ed.; Boston, 1882-1883).
[2] Both Marius Bewley, *The Eccentric Design: Form in the Classic American Novel* (New York, 1959), pp. 173-174, and Richard Harter Fogle, *Hawthorne's Fiction: The Light and the Dark* (Revised ed.; Norman, Okla., 1964), pp. 132-135, feel that Hawthorne has left the ultimate destiny of Hester and Dimmesdale darkly ambiguous. Hyatt H. Waggoner,

Both Hester and Dimmesdale can, however, be placed irrevocably in heaven once the reader recognizes that Pearl's sole reality is that of an allegorical mirror which multitudinously reflects the intricate tangle of love and passion uniting Hester and Dimmesdale.[3] Sick as they both are "with the plague of sin" (II, 287), neither Hester nor Dimmesdale can be released from "that saddest of all prisons, his own heart" (I, 67), except by what Hawthorne considers the sole remedy for sin—Love, "the flower that grew in heaven and was sovereign for all the miseries of earth" (II, 287-288). Pearl is sovereign for all Hester's and Dimmesdale's miseries because she is just such a flower: she is the "sweet moral blossom" (V, 68) which Hester plucks off "the bush of wild roses that grew by the prison-door" (V, 138), and which Hawthorne presents to the reader in order to "relieve the darkening close of a tale of human frailty and sorrow" (V, 68). In short, it is because the love between Hester and Dimmesdale is the oneness of their being that Hawthorne can prophesy their salvation through his comments on Pearl, the allegorical embodiment of that love: "And Pearl was the oneness of their being. Be the foregone evil what it might, how could they doubt that their earthly lives and future destinies were conjoined, when they beheld at once the material union, and the spiritual idea, in whom they met, and were to dwell immortally together?" (V, 248).

Since Pearl is "the scarlet letter in another form; the scarlet letter

---

Hawthorne: A Critical Study (Revised ed.; Cambridge, Mass., 1963), also thinks it possible to doubt that either Hester or Dimmesdale truly repented; and he further asserts that "the redemptive love and knowledge that worked the cure of Roderick Elliston in 'Egotism' do not enter the picture here" (p. 154).

[3] We should agree, then, with Marius Bewley both when he tells us that "Hawthorne explicitly presents Pearl as a symbol of [Hester's and Dimmesdale's] love in its full play of complex contradictions"; and when he suggests, though very tentatively, that "the emotional transformation of little Pearl as she kneels by her dying father on the scaffold may be read to symbolize a kind of spiritual resurrection for both her parents" (*The Eccentric Design*, p. 173). Mr. Bewley speaks far more truthfully here than he realizes since he himself does not perceive how accurately Pearl dramatizes the vicissitudes of Hester's and Dimmesdale's misbegotten love. In other words, he recognizes, along with other critics, that Pearl is an allegorical figure; but the language of allegory—Pearl's antics and words, and the comments which the other characters and Hawthorne himself make about her—this he leaves for the most part untranslated.

Anne Marie McNamara, "The Character of Flame: The Function of Pearl in *The Scarlet Letter*," *American Literature*, XXVII, 537-553 (Jan., 1956), limits the value of her interpretation by identifying Pearl merely with divine grace (pp. 552-553). Roy R. Male, *Hawthorne's Tragic Vision* (Austin, Texas, 1957), also wrongly restricts Pearl's symbolic function when he identifies her merely with truth and grace (p. 95).

endowed with life" (V, 127), she is an obvious heart-symbol—a diamond "that sparkles and flashes with the varied throbbings of the breast on which it is displayed" (V, 272). It is Pearl, the gem on her mother's unquiet bosom, who throughout the tale betrays to the reader, "by the very dance of her spirits, the emotions which none could detect in the marble passiveness of Hester's brow" (V, 272)—especially the passionate love for the minister which Hester, of fearful necessity, takes such great care to hide. Indeed, the most important question Hawthorne asks in this tale is whether there is "anything in Hester's face for Love to dwell upon"—anything in her "bosom, to make it ever again the pillow of Affection" (V, 198). That that something is there we are certain, for in all seasons of calamity "Hester's nature showed itself warm and rich; a wellspring of human tenderness, unfailing to every real demand, and inexhaustible by the largest. Her breast, with its badge of shame, was but the softer pillow for the head that needed one" (V, 195). Both this badge of shame and Pearl, its living counterpart—allegorical emblems as they are of Hester's heart—are intended by Hawthorne to travel through the same range of meanings: "Adultery," "Able," "Affection," and "Angel." Once, therefore, that Pearl and the scarlet letter can legitimately mean holy Affection, they can also mean Angel; for both Hester and Dimmesdale will have become angelic in the sense that a profane love has become sacred and, in so doing, has led them to Heaven.

The history of little Pearl is, however, predominantly the allegorical history of Hester's love for the minister. Providence, as we know, "had assigned to Hester's charge the germ and blossom of womanhood, to be cherished and developed amid a host of difficulties" (V, 200). Indeed Hester's very salvation is made dependent upon her guiding her child to Heaven—a point that is emphasized by Dimmesdale in his defense of Hester's right to little Pearl:

"This boon was meant, above all things else, to keep the mother's soul alive, and to preserve her from blacker depths of sin into which Satan might else have sought to plunge her! Therefore it is good for this poor, sinful woman that she hath an infant immortality, a being capable of eternal joy or sorrow, confided to her care,—to be trained up by her to righteousness,—to remind her, at every moment of her fall,—but yet to teach her, as it were by the Creator's sacred pledge, that, if she bring the child to heaven, the child will also bring its parent thither!" (V, 141-142)

Since Hawthorne intends the relationship between Hester and her misbegotten child to be the allegorical embodiment of Hester's misbegotten love for Dimmesdale, Hester's loving her child "with the intensity of a sole affection" (V, 216) aptly mirrors her all-absorbing love for the minister; and consequently the beneficent influence that Pearl has on her mother's heart properly mirrors the beneficent influence that Hester's love for Dimmesdale has on her soul. Loyalty to the logic of Hawthorne's allegory also reveals to the reader that Hester must bring her love for the minister into accord with God's will if she is to be saved. Moreover, since, according to the literal story, Pearl is intended by God "to connect her parent forever with the race and descent of mortals, and to be finally a blessed soul in heaven" (V, 113), the child serves the most important function of keeping her mother within the magnetic chain of humanity; and, of course, on the allegorical level this very same function is served by Hester's attachment to Dimmesdale. At this point, however, we must not forget that Pearl is also Dimmesdale's child. As his child, she can—and occasionally does—mirror his love for Hester. Indeed, Hawthorne intends any return of affection that Pearl shows either Dimmesdale or Hester to be emblematic of love beneficently at work within their hearts.

Of course, the love that exists between Hester and Dimmesdale cannot lead them to Heaven until they and their love escape the cowardice that is the deepest cause of their impenitence—that cowardice which induces Dimmesdale to lead a life of hypocrisy; and which also persuades Hester to consent, out of concern for the minister's life and reputation, to that life of destructive secrecy. In other words, *The Scarlet Letter* essentially presents a battle of the virtues and the vices within the hearts of Hester and Dimmesdale: it is a war that Love and Truth under the guise of little Pearl wage with Cowardice and Falsehood under the guise of old Roger Chillingworth. Indeed the illegitimate child and the vengeful husband, inasmuch as they are the not unnatural consequences of adultery, are ideally situated to assume unobtrusively their roles as the allegorical reflectors of the inner lives of Hester and Dimmesdale.

Because love in some way or other dominates Hester's heart

throughout the story, the allegory demands that little Pearl be almost always at her side. In truth, Pearl's birth, her troubled childhood, her deep grief at Dimmesdale's death, her attainment of womanhood, her marriage, and her subsequent motherhood—all mark allegorically the different stages of Hester's love for Dimmesdale. Since love, "whether newly born, or aroused from a death-like slumber, must always create a sunshine, filling the heart so full of radiance, that it overflows upon the outward world" (V, 243), it is not at all surprising that Hawthorne chooses the birth of Pearl, the child who has "an absolute circle of radiance around her" (V, 114) and is "all glorified with a ray of sunshine" (V, 249), to allegorize the birth of love within Hester's heart. It is to this birth that Hawthorne refers when he tells us that "it was as if a new birth, with stronger assimilations than the first, had converted the forest-land, still so uncongenial to every other pilgrim and wanderer, into Hester Prynne's wild and dreary, but life-long home" (V, 103); for it is Hester's passionate love that keeps her "within the pathway that had been so fatal": "There dwelt, there trode the feet of one with whom she deemed herself connected in a union, that, unrecognized on earth, would bring them together before the bar of final judgment, and make that their marriage-altar, for a joint futurity of endless retribution" (V, 103). Under the guise of little Pearl, therefore, a lawless and passionate love has been born into the world—a love that is able to face hardships and suffering, but that has no home and apparently no way to build one. Indeed the only marriage and home that the moral pattern of *The Scarlet Letter* can allow our erring lovers is the Eternal Home of Heaven and the spiritual union that this implies for all who enter there.

As Hester's love for the minister develops both in courage and in truth, so there can be seen emerging in the little chaos of Pearl's character "the steadfast principles of an unflinching courage,—an uncontrollable will,—a sturdy pride, which might be disciplined into self-respect,—and a bitter scorn of many things, which, when examined, might be found to have the taint of falsehood in them" (V, 216). But until Hester's love for the minister has been disciplined to recognize and obey the will of God—until "the taint of deepest sin" is removed from "the most sacred quality of human life" (V, 77)—Pearl's affections must remain "acrid and disagreeable, as are the richest flavors of unripe fruit" (V, 216). It is only after Hester's repentance that little Pearl's love for her mother, which up to then had "mostly revealed itself in passion, and hardly twice in her lifetime . . . been softened by" tenderness (V, 143), becomes "a continual remembrance" (V, 310) flowing from a fond heart. It is then that the alert reader of Hawthorne's allegory knows that Hester's love for the minister has been redeemed. In other words, Pearl, "an imp of evil, emblem and product of sin, . . . [has] no right among christened infants" (V, 118) until Hester's and Dimmesdale's love for one another—the love that Pearl symbolizes— is christened. It is when Pearl grows to noble womanhood, marries, and bears a child that we learn through allegory that Hester's love for Dimmesdale has borne the fruit of salvation. Then it is that Hester's words to Dimmesdale in the forest—"But the child hath strong affections! She loves me, and will love thee!" (V, 248)— are fulfilled in their deepest sense; for it can then be truly said that little Pearl—the personification of the love that Hester and Dimmesdale have for one another—has loved each of them so wisely that she has led both of them to heaven.

What we are saying, then, is that Pearl, although her aspect has "nothing of the calm, white, unimpassioned lustre that would be indicated by" her name (V, 113), will actually become for Hester the Pearl of Great Price once the impure love within Hester's heart has been converted into the love of God and man. This is why Hawthorne has the Reverend Mr. Wilson say, "Pearl, . . . thou must take heed to instruction, that so, in due season, thou mayest wear in thy bosom the pearl of great price" (V, 138). We must not assume, however, that this love of Hester's is mere earthly passion; and we must remember that Hawthorne distinguishes sharply between pure and immortal love in which "there is no falsehood or forgetfulness" and "an earthly passion" that is "mingled with little that is spiritual, and must therefore perish with the perishing clay" (XII, 73). Although Hawthorne's description of the conception and birth of little Pearl makes clear that Hester's adulterous relationship found its beginnings in merely guilty and lustful passion, it is also this same description that allegorically marks the sudden and unexpected flowering within Hester's heart of something really resembling true love for Dimmesdale; for Hawthorne refers to Pearl both as "the unpremeditated offshoot of a passionate moment" (V, 127) and as "that little creature, whose innocent life had sprung, by the inscrutable decree of Providence, a lovely and immortal flower, out of the rank luxuriance of a guilty passion" (V, 113).[4] Since Hester's intense love of her child is the living emblem of her love for the minister, Hawthorne can emphasize once again, through the distinction Dimmesdale draws between Hester's former sin of lust and her present devotion to her child, the difference between Hester's once mere unhallowed lust and her present passionate and self-sacrificing love for the minister. Dimmesdale, in his defense of Hester's right to little Pearl, attempts to persuade the other magistrates that there is "a quality of awful sacredness in the relation between this mother and this child" (V, 141); and in so doing he urges that if they were to judge the relation otherwise, they would have to conclude that "the Heavenly Father, the Creator of all flesh, hath lightly recognized a deed of sin, and made of no account the distinction between unhallowed lust and holy love" (V, 141). Those aspects of Hester's love that might properly be termed "holy" are spelled out allegorically for the reader by the reasons Hester gives in defense of her continued custody of her child: " 'She is my happiness!—she is my torture, none the less! Pearl keeps me here in life! Pearl punishes me too! See ye not, she is the scarlet letter, only capable of being loved, and so endowed with a million-fold the power of retribution for my sin?'" (V, 139). To be sure, Hester's love for the minister is her only happiness. In fact, it keeps her in life, for without it she would long before this have committed suicide. Moreover, Hester's love for Dimmesdale is endowed with a million-fold the power of retribution for her sin of unhallowed lust because it is only this love that gives her the courage to stay within the limits of the Puritan settlement and bear the public ignominy which has become her daily lot. Indeed, as Hawthorne suggests later through allegory, one of Providence's merciful and beneficent purposes in sending Hester this love is ultimately "to help her to overcome the passion, once so wild, and even yet neither dead nor asleep, but only imprisoned within the same tomb-like heart" (V, 217). Since, however, such problems as Hester's vanish only if the woman's "heart chance to come uppermost" (V, 201), it is important to recall again

[4] Some light can be thrown on the redemptive role that Pearl is to play as the incarnation of the love that exists between Hester and Dimmesdale if we compare this quotation with what Hawthorne says of the young couple in "The Ambitious Guest": "Perhaps a germ of love was springing in their hearts, so pure that it might blossom in Paradise, since it could not be matured on earth" (I, 371).

that Hester's love for Dimmesdale—her little Pearl—is the "sole treasure" that keeps "her heart alive" (V, 139); for it prevents her complete isolation from mankind and thereby interferes with her intellect gaining—as it almost succeeds in doing—an absolute ascendancy within her soul (V, 198-200). Beyond question, then, Hester's love for Dimmesdale, despite its guilty origin and despite the impurities imbuing it, is the best and most beautiful part of her being. It can therefore be truly said that this love which is Hester's better self can no more remain in being without God's concurring power than Hester herself can. This is a truth that Hester herself insists on by way of allegory just after little Pearl denies that God is her Heavenly Father: "Hush, Pearl, hush! Thou must not talk so! .... He sent us all into this world. He sent even me, thy mother. Then, much more, thee! Or, if not, thou strange and elfish child, whence didst thou come?" (V, 124). It is in this fashion that Hawthorne has chosen, here and elsewhere, to dramatize the interplay of light and shadow within the love that was born amiss within Hester's heart.

Since Hester, by falling in love with Dimmesdale, "has evoked a spirit [Pearl], but, by some irregularity in the process of conjuration, has failed to win the master-word that should control this new and incomprehensible intelligence" (V, 117-118); and since she therefore wanders "without a clew in the dark labyrinth of mind" (V, 201), she and the love within her heart will ultimately have to turn to Dimmesdale for wiser and better guardianship than she herself can provide. Indeed, one of the arguments given by the leading inhabitants of Boston for depriving Hester of her child underlines allegorically the need Hester's misbegotten love has for just such spiritual direction; for these good people felt that "if the child ... were really capable of moral and religious growth, and possessed the elements of ultimate salvation, then, surely, it would enjoy all the fairer prospect of these advantages by being transferred to wiser and better guardianship than Hester Prynne's" (V, 125). That this is the kind of control Dimmesdale will exercise over the love he has begotten in Hester's heart, we cannot doubt; for Hawthorne has Governor Bellingham say to Mr. Wilson, "Care must be had ... to put the child to due and stated examination in the catechism, at thy hands or Master Dimmesdale's" (V, 142). Hester herself, with unconscious irony, indicates Dimmesdale's future role as a catechist to the unruly love within her heart when, during her forest meeting with the minister, she says of Pearl, "She is a strange child! I hardly comprehend her! But thou wilt love her dearly, as I do, and wilt advise me how to deal with her" (V, 244). In this way, then, does little Pearl, the allegorical child, enable Hawthorne to prophesy that Hester will find salvation for her soul if she allows her love for Dimmesdale to be instructed by the lessons he will teach through his heroic confession on the scaffold.

A good and golden year can therefore "pass over the poor old world" of Hester's heart only when Dimmesdale, having cast off the "old man," begins, as a "new man," to rule over Hester's heart, and thereby fulfils his pastoral responsibility to her soul; all of which Hawthorne predicts allegorically when Hester, on the day of Dimmesdale's return to God, explains to Pearl the reason for the holiday (or holy day) in language that is reminiscent of the parable of the prodigal son: " 'The children have come from their schools, and the grown people from their workshops and their fields, on purpose to be happy. For, to-day, a new man is beginning to rule over them; and so . . . they make merry and rejoice; as if a good and golden year were at length to pass over the poor old world!' " (V, 274). Dimmesdale does truly become for Hester the "mouth-piece of Heaven's messages of wisdom, and rebuke, and love" (V, 174): obedience to God's will, hatred of sin, and trust in God's mercy are the truths he bequeaths her with his dying breath. His last words are without doubt the prayers of a truly penitent man; and since a good man's prayers, as Chillingworth tells us, are "golden recompense" or "the current gold coin of the New Jerusalem, with the King's own mint-mark on them" (V, 268), it is most probable that these words of the minister's will enrich the heart of the grief-stricken woman who listens so attentively to them. Moreover, since the minister's dying words are indeed his Election Sermon in that he elects as the inmate of his heart the God of truth, love, and courage rather than the demon of cowardice and hypocrisy,[5] we can say that his last words affect Hester just as his Election Sermon af-

---

[5] Anne Marie McNamara interprets the Election Sermon in almost the same way: "The complete destruction of the first Election Sermon, conceived and written in deceit and hypocrisy, may be significant of a complete break with the past that produced it. The fluent composition of a new one may figure the tremendous vitality of the soul freed from the shackles of sin and operating under the flow of divine grace" ("The Character of Flame," p. 550).

fects the people of Boston: "It was as if an angel, in his passage to the skies, had shaken his bright wings over the people for an instant,—at once a shadow and a splendor,—and had shed down a shower of golden truths upon them" (V, 295). Indeed, another flight to heaven—that of Governor Winthrop at the time of the midnight scaffold scene—looks forward to the kind of inheritance Dimmesdale is to leave Hester. For when the Reverend Mr. Wilson returns home by lantern light from the death chamber of the Governor, Dimmesdale observes him and imagines that he is "surrounded, like the saint-like personages of olden times, with a radiant halo, that glorified him amid this gloomy night of sin,—as if the departed Governor had left him an inheritance of his glory, or as if he had caught upon himself the distant shine of the celestial city, while looking thitherward to see the triumphal pilgrim pass within its gates" (V, 182-183).

Triumphal pilgrim Dimmesdale certainly becomes, for through his heroic confession the weed of falsehood—the black weed that typifies the hideous secret buried within his heart (V, 160)—is uprooted, to wilt and die beneath the meridian sunshine of truth; all of which Hawthorne tells us allegorically when he informs us that very soon after Dimmesdale's death all Chillingworth's "strength and energy—all his vital and intellectual force—seemed at once to desert him; insomuch that he positively withered up, shrivelled away, and almost vanished from mortal sight, like an uprooted weed that lies wilting in the sun" (V, 307). Thus, after the death of old Roger Chillingworth—after, in other words, the death of Dimmesdale's falsehood and cowardice—Roger's last will and testament aptly allegorizes those dying words of the minister that are for Hester "a shower of golden truths"; for old Roger bequeaths "a very considerable amount of property, both here and in England, to little Pearl, the daughter of Hester Prynne" (V, 308). And since to know and do the will of God is to come into one's richest spiritual inheritance, then how appropriate it is that Pearl, the living mirror of her mother's inner life, should become "the richest heiress of her day, in the New World" (V, 308). In having Chillingworth thus bequeath his wealth to Pearl—in having Dimmesdale, in other words, teach Hester practically a Golden Rule—Hawthorne is merely reworking an idea that appears in one of his notebooks: "An old man to promise a youth a treasure of gold;—and to keep his promise by teaching him practically a Golden Rule."[6] Furthermore, "in the spiritual world, the old physician and the minister—mutual victims as they have been—may, unawares, have found their earthly stock of hatred and antipathy transmuted into golden love" (V, 308); for the detestation that the minister feels for his cowardly and hypocritical self in the guise of old Roger Chillingworth disappears of necessity when he kisses little Pearl and allows holy and golden love to reign in his heart.

It is also at the moment of this kiss that Hester's love for Dimmesdale—her little Pearl—experiences the grief it so much needs: "a grief that should deeply touch her, and thus humanize and make her capable of sympathy" (V, 221). In other words, it is at this moment that Hester, from whom "some attribute had departed . . . , the permanence of which had been necessary to keep her a woman" (V, 198), receives that magic touch to which Hawthorne refers when he says of her: "She who has once been a woman, and ceased to be so, might at any moment become a woman again if there were only the magic touch to effect the transfiguration" (V, 198). And although formerly there had seemed "to be no longer anything in Hester's face for Love to dwell upon; . . . nothing in Hester's bosom, to make it ever again the pillow of Affection" (V, 198), that very bosom now becomes "the pillow of Affection"; for after Dimmesdale collapsed on the scaffold, "Hester partly raised him, and supported his head against her bosom" (V, 303). Thus, through the instrumentality of Dimmesdale's heroic confession and his ensuing death, is broken the "bewildering and baffling spell, that so often came between [Hester] and her sole treasure" (V, 117)—that is, between Hester and her love for the minister: "Towards her mother . . . Pearl's errand as a messenger of anguish was all fulfilled" (V, 303). Like one of her literary ancestors, the diamond with the evil spirit in "The Antique Ring," Pearl is purified only "by becoming the medium of some good and holy act, and again the pledge of faithful love" (XII, 55). In truth, Hester, as a consequence of the

[6] *The American Notebooks by Nathaniel Hawthorne*, ed. Randall Stewart (New Haven, 1932), p. 102. My interpretation of Chillingworth's last will and testament is not altogether original. It is partly anticipated by Roy R. Male, *Hawthorne's Tragic Vision*, p. 97; and Leslie A. Fiedler, *Love and Death in the American Novel* (New York, 1960), pp. 512-513. Both Male and Fiedler, however, wrongly claim that Pearl's allegorical role ceases after she becomes a wealthy heiress; Male can be permitted to speak for both Fiedler and himself when he asserts that, "as Dimmesdale ascends, [Pearl] moves down from her allegorical function and into fully temporal existence" (p. 97).

last scaffold scene, could have legitimately addressed to Dimmesdale those words that Hawthorne wrote to Sophia Peabody on October 4, 1840:

Thou only hast taught me that I have a heart—thou only hast thrown a light deep downward, and upward, into my soul.... Indeed, we are but shadows—we are not endowed with real life, and all that seems most real about us is but the thinnest substance of a dream—till the heart is touched. That touch creates us—then we begin to be—thereby we are beings of reality, and inheritors of eternity.[7]

It is well to note here that Dimmesdale's Election Sermon, allegorical embodiment as it is of Dimmesdale's dying words, is an expression of love as well as a catechetical lesson; for it breathes "passion and pathos, and emotions high or tender, in a tongue native to the human heart, wherever educated" (V, 289). Through his response both to repentance and to Hester's love the minister converts the "atmosphere ... into words of flame" (V, 294): the fire not only of truth but also of love—God's as well as man's. He thereby gains in its fullest measure the power "of addressing the whole human brotherhood [and Hester Prynne in particular] in the heart's native language"; not lacking, like his fellow ministers, "Heaven's last and rarest attestation of their office, the Tongue of Flame"—the gift "that descended upon the chosen disciples at Pentecost" (V, 173). Indeed it is in harmony with this New England holiday (or holy day) that during Dimmesdale's Election Sermon the influence of the Holy Spirit, who is the infinite love that exists between God the Father and God the Son, "could be seen, as it were, descending upon him, and possessing him" (V, 294-295); which is why inspiration had never "breathed through mortal lips more evidently than it did through his" (V, 294) on this day. Hester's attitude toward the Election Sermon is that of Dimmesdale's flock toward his other sermons in that she listens to his dying "'words as if a tongue of Pentecost were speaking'" (V, 229). In truth, she is affected by Dimmesdale's heroic confession—by his Election Sermon—in the same way as some of his parishioners were affected by the sermon he preached the day after his midnight meeting with Hester upon the scaffold—a sermon, therefore, that was also delivered under the

---

[7] *The Heart of Hawthorne's Journals*, ed. Newton Arvin (Boston, 1929), p. 66.

influence of the "vital warmth" (V, 186) of Hester's love.[8] This discourse "was held to be the richest and most powerful, and the most replete with heavenly influences, that had ever proceeded from his lips. Souls . . . were brought to the truth by the efficacy of that sermon, and vowed within themselves to cherish a holy gratitude towards Mr. Dimmesdale throughout the long hereafter" (V, 191).

And just as one of these souls, a young girl, was won by this sermon "to barter the transitory pleasures of the world for the heavenly hope, that was to assume brighter substance as life grew dark around her, and which would gild the utter gloom with final glory" (V, 262), so too is Hester won by the minister's Election Sermon and comes to cherish "a holy gratitude towards Mr. Dimmesdale throughout the long hereafter." And just as this same young girl enshrined Dimmesdale "within the stainless sanctity of her heart, which hung its snowy curtains about his image, imparting to religion the warmth of love, and to love a religious purity" (V, 262), so too will Hester's remembrance of the holy death of Mr. Dimmesdale, enshrined as he already was within the not-so-stainless sanctity of her heart, impart to her love a religious purity, and to her future religious devotion the warmth of love. It is in this way that Dimmesdale's last " 'footsteps . . . leave a gleam along [his] earthly track, whereby the pilgrims that shall come after [him] may be guided to the regions of the blest' " (V, 175).

Hester will, therefore, eventually bring the love within her bosom to God as her most precious offering; and in so doing she will very much resemble those virgins of Dimmesdale's church who were so influenced by his sermons as to become "victims of a passion so imbued with religious sentiment that they imagined it to be all religion, and brought it openly, in their white bosoms, as their most acceptable sacrifice before the altar" (V, 174). *Mutatis mutandis*, the closing lines of Hawthorne's "Graves and Goblins," spoken as they

[8] Hawthorne's description of Hester and Dimmesdale during the midnight scaffold scene, with little Pearl between them and the light of the meteoric *A* surrounding them, is prophetic of that "noon of . . . solemn splendor" when they will be redeemed through love: "And there stood the minister, with his hand over his heart; and Hester Prynne, with the embroidered letter glimmering on her bosom; and little Pearl, herself a symbol, and the connecting link between those two. They stood in the noon of that strange and solemn splendor, as if it were the light that is to reveal all secrets, and the daybreak that shall unite all who belong to one another" (V, 187). Here Pearl and the scarlet letter in the sky are very obviously both symbols of the love that exists between Hester and Dimmesdale; and this love of theirs is the light that is to reveal their secret, and the daybreak that shall unite them in heaven.

are by a young man's ghost, aptly describe the influence Dimmesdale's dying words will have on Hester's heart:

But where is the maiden, holy and pure, though wearing a form of clay, that would have me bend over her pillow at midnight, and leave a blessing there? With a silent invocation, let her summon me. Shrink not, maiden, when I come! . . . in death, I bring no loathsome smell of the grave, nor ghostly terrors,—but gentle, and soothing, and sweetly pensive influences. Perhaps, just fluttering for the skies, my visit may hallow the wellsprings of thy thought, and make thee heavenly here on earth. Then shall pure dreams and holy meditations bless thy life; nor thy sainted spirit linger round the grave, but seek the upper stars, and meet me there! (XII, 77)

Indeed the spiritual fatherhood that Dimmesdale assumes in regard to Hester just before his flight to Heaven is foreshadowed in the first scaffold scene when Hester declares that Pearl must seek a heavenly Father because she will never know an earthly one. It is, of course, no less true that only when Dimmesdale becomes a loving father and religious guide to the love he has begotten in Hester's breast can Pearl, the personification of that love, find a Father in God.

Hawthorne, however, is too acute an observer of the human heart to allow Hester to achieve religious purity immediately after Dimmesdale's death. Only after she meditates for many years on Dimmesdale's last catechetical lesson is the wild, rich nature of her love for him—the wild, rich nature of her child—"softened and subdued, and made capable of a woman's gentle happiness" (V, 309). Only then is Hester able to return to New England, the place of her sin and sorrow, and where is "yet to be her penitence" (V, 310). In thus resuming the scarlet letter, she obeys Dimmesdale's loving injunction: "The law we broke!—the sin here so awfully revealed!—let these alone be in thy thoughts!" (V, 304). It is through Hawthorne's final remarks on Pearl, however, that we learn with certainty that Dimmesdale's heroic example has made Hester heavenly on earth by hallowing the wellsprings of her thought and blessing her life with holy meditations. Indeed, some of the benefits which in this life, according to the Westminster Catechism, either accompany or flow from justification, adoption, and sanctification—"assurances of God's love, peace of conscience, joy in the Holy Ghost, increase of grace, and perseverance therein to the end"[9]—find their

[9] *The New-England Primer, Improved; The Assembly of Divines' Catechism* (Norwich, Conn.: Russell Hubbard, 1812; reprinted by Henry Ford, 1926), p. 43.

allegorical embodiment in the gifts and letters that Pearl sends her mother during Hester's last years in Boston; which is, in truth, the kind of allegorical finish that is almost necessitated by the ripening to maturity of the allegorical child who, at the age of three, "could have borne a fair examination in . . . the first column of the Westminster Catechisms" (V, 138). The letters with strange armorial seals that come to Hester from "some inhabitant of another land" (V, 309) are therefore no other than Hester's assurances of God's love—her "spiritual communications with the better world" in which her redeemed love for the minister now dwells. For Hester, in "the toilsome, thoughtful, and self-devoted years" (V, 310) that make up the end of her life, is very like those "true saintly fathers, whose faculties had been . . . etherealized . . . by spiritual communications with the better world, into which their purity of life had almost introduced these holy personages, with their garments of mortality still clinging to them" (V, 173). Moreover, the articles of comfort and luxury in Hester's cottage, "which only wealth could have purchased, and affection have imagined for her" (V, 310), can be construed as the religious consolations that Hester's love—the richest heiress in the New World—purchases for her. Just as the loss of loved ones by the oldest of Dimmesdale's parishioners, "which would else have been such heavy sorrow, was made almost a solemn joy to her devout old soul, by religious consolations and the truths of Scripture, wherewith she had fed herself continually for more than thirty years" (V, 261), so too is Hester's heavy sorrow after Dimmesdale's death converted into a solemn and religious joy by her never-ending meditation on the truths of Scripture that he so effectively taught her.

Not even yet, however, has the allegory come to an end: the baby garment that Hester, with "a lavish richness of golden fancy" (V, 310), embroiders for Pearl's child indicates, as we have suggested earlier, that Hester's love for Dimmesdale has become religiously fruitful—has borne the fruit of salvation. Consequently when Hester tells the women who bring her all their sorrows that she recognizes "the impossibility that any mission of divine and mysterious truth should be confided to a woman stained with sin, bowed down with shame, or even burdened with a life-long sorrow" (V, 311), her words have for us an irony to which Hester in her holiness and humility is oblivious; for we know that "the divine and mysterious truth" of the redemptive power of love has become the very substance of Hester's life. The irony becomes more marked when Hester tells these women that "the angel and apostle of the coming revelation must be a woman indeed, but lofty, pure, and beautiful; and wise, moreover, not through dusky grief, but the ethereal medium of joy; and showing how sacred love should make us happy, by the truest test of a life successful to such an end!" (V, 311). Indeed, sacred love has made Hester an angel and an apostle to those in sorrow and trouble; and it has made her wise by converting her dusky grief into a solemn joy through her religious consolations and her meditations on the truths of Scripture. In short, Hester has shown how sacred love can "make us happy, by the truest test of a life successful to such an end." Moreover, it is well in accord with the indirectness of Hawthorne's style that Hester should speak these words about sacred love in the last line of the story's next-to-last paragraph, and that she should thereby unwittingly summarize her life and Dimmesdale's by correctly interpreting the living hieroglyphic—the Tongue of Flame—that we have known as little Pearl.

Hester had therefore been right in thinking that "perchance, the torture of her daily shame would at length purge her soul, and work out another purity than that which she had lost; more saint-like, because the result of martyrdom" (V, 104). In the eyes of the reader as well as in the eyes of the townspeople, the scarlet letter should now have "the effect of the cross on a nun's bosom," imparting to Hester "a kind of sacredness" (V, 197). There is now something in Hester's relationship to her child to remind us—and no longer merely by contrast—"of that sacred image of sinless motherhood, whose infant was to redeem the world" (V, 77); for it is no other than Pearl, the incarnation of Hester's love, who has redeemed the world of her mother's heart.

Since Hester's love for the minister has survived his death and followed him to heaven, we must agree with the gossips who believed "that Pearl was not only alive, but married, and happy, and mindful of her mother, and that she would most joyfully have entertained that sad and lonely mother at her fireside" (V, 310). Thus we may legitimately say of little Pearl—the infant who "was worthy to have been brought forth in Eden; worthy to have been left there, to be the plaything of angels, after the world's first parents were driven out" (V, 114)—what Hawthorne says of her literary ancestor Lilias Fay: "The chill winds of the earth had long since breathed a blight into this beautiful flower, so that a loving hand had now transplanted it, to blossom brightly in the garden of Paradise" (I, 502). Truly, Hester, now that her love for Dimmesdale is purified, has achieved a spiritual union with him that blesses only the rare marriage. Earlier in the story, she had deemed herself connected in a union with him, "that, unrecognized on earth, would bring them together before the bar of final judgment, and make that their marriage-altar, for a joint futurity of endless retribution" (V, 103). Her last words to him, "Shall we not spend our immortal life together? Surely, surely, we have ransomed one another, with all this woe!" (V, 303), show that she is finally able to hope that the bar of final judgment will become their marriage altar for a joint futurity, not of endless retribution, but of eternal happiness. Our reading of Pearl's allegorical role ratifies Hester's hope and rejects the possibility that Dimmesdale suggests with his dying words: "It may be that, when we forgot our God,—when we violated our reverence each for the other's soul,—it was thenceforth vain to hope that we could meet hereafter, in an everlasting and pure reunion. God knows; and He is merciful!" (V, 304). God has been merciful: we have seen that throughout Hester's long years of penitence the light of faith has been guiding her to where her love for Dimmesdale already dwells—to what is to be her Eternal Home and Fireside. Hester and Dimmesdale could well have made their own the words that the elderly Mr. Smith in "The Wedding Knell" speaks to his bride, the widow Mrs. Dabney:

"Yes; it is evening with us now; and we have realized none of our morning dreams of happiness. But let us join our hands before the altar, as lovers whom adverse circumstances have separated through life, yet who meet again as they are leaving it, and find their earthly affection changed into something holy as religion. And what is Time, to the married of Eternity?" (I, 51)

There is no doubt, then, that Hester and Dimmesdale are among the few who, "we are glad to say, made earnest efforts to exchange vice for virtue, and, hard as the bargain was, succeeded in effecting it" (II, 374). Love, finding its personification in little Pearl and its symbols in the scarlet letter, the red rose, and the Tongue of Flame, has ultimately defeated Chillingworth, the "black flower" (V, 68) of Fate and the incarnation of Cowardice, Shame, Egotism, Falsehood, and ineffectual Remorse (V, 180). Because the love of Hester and Dimmesdale for one another—"their infant commonwealth" —has been "under a celestial guardianship of peculiar intimacy and strictness" (V, 188), they have made their own the "high and glorious destiny" that Dimmesdale, in his Election Sermon, prophesies for "the newly gathered people of the Lord" (V, 295).

Hawthorne and Nineteenth-Century Perfectionism
Claudia D. Johnson

ONE OF THE MOST prominent members of the Bowdoin College faculty at the time of Nathaniel Hawthorne's attendance was a young philosopher-psychologist named Thomas C. Upham. Horatio Bridge, Hawthorne's college classmate and friend, remembered Upham, who was Professor of Moral and Mental Philosophy during their senior year, as "young, scholarly, gentle, and kind to the students, by all of whom he was much beloved."[1] A few critics have speculated about the influence of Upham's theory of trifaculty psychology on Hawthorne,[2] but another of Upham's convictions, on which he wrote a number of books, has received almost no attention. This was the doctrine of Christian perfection for which Upham, in his day, was as well known as for his psychological theories. The very word, "perfection," however, connotes a belief so far removed from the dark vision of Nathaniel Hawthorne as to render absurd any consideration of the writer's relationship to the doctrine.[3] The word leads one to think that the advocates of per-

[1] Horatio Bridge, *Personal Recollections of Nathaniel Hawthorne* (New York, 1893), p. 53.
[2] Marvin Laser, "'Head,' 'Heart,' and 'Will' in Hawthorne's Psychology," *Nineteenth-Century Fiction*, X (Sept., 1955), 130–136; Leon Howard, *Literature and the American Tradition* (New York, 1960), p. 122; Joseph Schwartz, "A Note on Hawthorne's Fatalism," *Modern Language Notes*, LXX (Jan., 1955), 33–36. Laser and Howard cite the influence of Upham's trifaculty psychology on Hawthorne's work. Schwartz makes the point that the insistence of Hawthorne's educators, including Upham, on freedom of the will contributed to his rejection of orthodox fatalism.
[3] Merle Curti, "Human Nature in American Thought," *Political Science Quarterly*, LXVIII (Sept., 1953), 354–375; Joseph Schwartz, "Nathaniel Hawthorne, 1804–1864: God and Man in New England," *American Classics Reconsidered*, edited by Harold C. Gardiner, S.J. (New York, 1958), p. 141. These two critics reflect the tendency to ignore or to misrepresent perfectionism. Although Schwartz is aware of Upham's influence, he fails to take perfectionism into account, saying only that Hawthorne had no sympathy with the *Unitarian* idea of "human perfectability." Curti concludes, presumably because Upham was a perfectionist, that he had no sense, as did Hawthorne, of the profound depths of evil in the heart.
  The summary of perfectionist doctrine in this paper is made on the basis of primary readings in the following nineteenth-century perfectionist literature: William Arthur,

fectionism thought that, after having been made "perfect," the heart was free from evil. Nothing, however, could be further from the truth. Thomas Upham, Charles G. Finney, John Humphrey Noyes, and other perfectionists were as thoroughly convinced of the evil of the heart as were their Puritan forebears. The journals and the memoirs of perfectionists disclose that their knowledge of the heart's evil came from painful personal experiences. Like John Humphrey Noyes, they were very much aware of "the labyrinth of iniquity" at the bottom of the heart.[4]

Like the Puritans, perfectionists believed that man is, by nature, sinful and requires regeneration. Unlike those early Calvinists, however, the perfectionists taught that after conversion man could experience a second stage of religious growth when he would, for a second time, be the recipient of God's grace. At this time he was "perfected" by partaking of God's love which "purified" his inclinations. Even after purification, however, evil was a powerful force in the perfect man's heart. Noyes, who had an immense impact on nineteenth-century Protestantism through the circulation of *The Perfectionist*, was convinced that being purified in heart did not exempt one from inner experiences with evil. Evil was a part of the carnal self which would not be lost until the body died, and forces of good and evil would war within even a perfect man until he died. One needed only to look at the tempted Christ to understand this warfare:

Our theory of Christian life, while it equips the spiritual soldier with a pure heart and a good conscience at the outset, nevertheless does not discharge him from service. To *keep* his heart pure and his conscience good, in the midst of a world of pollution and accusation . . . will cost him

---

The Tongue of Fire (Toronto, 1857); Jeremy Boyton, *Sanctification Practical* (New York, 1867); J. T. Crane, *Holiness* (New York, 1875); Charles G. Finney, *Attributes of Love: A Section From Lectures on Systematic Theology* (Minneapolis, 1963) and *Memoirs* (New York, 1876); R. S. Foster, *Christian Purity* (New York, 1869); Asa Mahan, *Out of Darkness Into Light* (New York, 1876); John Humphrey Noyes, *Religious Experiences of John Humphrey Noyes* (New York, 1923) and *Salvation From Sin* (Wallingford, Conn., 1866); Phoebe Palmer, *Present to My Christian Friend* (New York, 1853); Thomas C. Upham, *Treatise on Divine Union* (Boston, 1857); *Principles of the Interior or Hidden Life* (New York, 1843), and *Life of Faith* (New York, 1845).

[4] Noyes, "Journal Entry, July 25," *The Religious Experiences of John Humphrey Noyes*, pp. 47–48.

many and sore conflicts with his own corrupted propensities, and with "principalities and powers, and spiritual wickedness in high places."[5]

Thomas Upham in *The Interior Life* also warned that evil would be an even greater force within the soul of the perfected man than it was in other men:

> Thou hast contended with Satan, and hast been successful. Thou hast fought with him, and he has fled from thee. But, O, remember his artifices. Do not indulge the belief that his nature is changed. True, indeed, he is now very complacent and is, perhaps, singing thee some syren song; but he was never more a devil than he is now.[6]

Even though evil would continue to fight within his soul, as long as love sustained the perfected man, he had reason to hope that his victories over evil would be assured. In short, the doctrine of perfectionism was in no sense the conviction that the soul could reach a stage in which it was free from the experience of evil.

This clarification of the perfectionists' beliefs about the evil of the heart, which, contrary to what the term may suggest, is not so radically different from Hawthorne's view, may serve to open for consideration the relationship of Hawthorne to this vital and far-reaching nineteenth-century Protestant movement.

Upham and his fellow perfectionists insisted on three essential characteristics of the perfected man which are relevant to Hawthorne's themes: man had to be guided by love, the transforming principle in the life of the perfected man; he had to live in this life rather than for the hereafter; and he had to be active rather than passive. The perfectionist taught that love was the transforming power of the soul, the indwelling principle which caused the old man locked in inwardness to emerge reborn. Love displaced selfish pride and united men. It propelled a perfected man into the world: perfectionism, by definition, meant the state of man *in this life*, not in the hereafter. One of the Methodist perfectionists, William Arthur, goes so far as to label a man's concern for his salvation as a selfish perversion of the gospel.[7]

Just as love drew the good man into this world, it necessarily

[5] Noyes, *Salvation From Sin*, p. 394.
[6] Upham, *The Interior Life*, p. 394.
[7] Arthur, p. 129.

drew him into fellowship with other men. It made a life of solitude impossible. Introspection was a stage in Christian development, but to prolong seclusion was to be caught in the dead end of selfishness. Asa Mahan, the perfectionist president of Oberlin College, called such inwardness "spiritual paralysis."[8] In Thomas Upham's comments on isolating inwardness one sees the expression of a theme which would be persistently repeated in the works of Nathaniel Hawthorne:

> A being who is supremely selfish is necessarily miserable. . . . Instead of the principle of unity, which tends to oneness of purpose with other beings, and naturally leads to happiness, he has within him the principle of exclusion and of eternal separation. In its ultimate operation, if it is permitted permanently to exist, it necessarily drives him from everything else, and wedges him closer and closer in the compressed circumference of his own personality. . . . This is the true hell and everlasting fire.[9]

The perfect man, therefore, had to ascend from inwardness to union with the world. The man of God who failed in this union abdicated a profound Christian duty, according to Upham:

> The mind, separated from the bonds which link it to others, and falling back upon itself, as both centre and circumference, becomes contracted in the range of its action, and selfish in its tendencies.[10]

Perfectionist doctrine not only insisted upon fellowship in the world; it demanded action in the world. Passivity was a characteristic of the initial religious experience of introspection, but a Christian must move from the passive to an active state. Love, again, was the compelling force. Charles G. Finney, the most prominent evangelist of the second great awakening and an Oberlin perfectionist, wrote of the perfect man:

> . . . the intellectual perceptions never sink so low as to leave benevolence to become a stagnant pool. It is never sluggish, never inactive. . . . It is essential activity itself.[11]

Thus, the good man, according to the perfectionist doctrine, followed a definite mythic development. In order to be converted,

[8] Mahan, p. 117.
[9] Upham, *The Interior Life*, p. 118.
[10] Ibid., p. 193.
[11] Finney, *Attributes of Love*, pp. 110–111.

he descended into the depths of his heart as the Puritans had taught that he must. After having received a clear view of his sins, he was converted. But a man could become entrapped and poisoned in this pious, passive introspection if he were not moved by love. If he were guided by love, he would ascend from inwardness to an active existence on the earth among his fellow human beings. Thomas Upham's student, Nathaniel Hawthorne, saw the perils and possibilities of man in just such terms.

"The Haunted Mind," Hawthorne's sketch of the progress of the mind which descends into inwardness and emerges renewed, mirrors the perfectionists' values as well as their concept of man's spiritual development. In this early sketch, a dreamer in repose isolates himself from the realities of the world in order to descend into his heart, which he subsequently comes to know as an infernal region outside of time, outside of nature, and outside of society, "where the business of life does not intrude" (p. 343).[12] The bed into which the dreamer sinks in "conscious sleep," is no less than a cozy womb until the thought of death breaks in to remind him that the components of this inward world—timelessness, lifelessness, inaction, and isolation—are also the components of death. As he sinks deeper into the tomb of the heart, he is accosted by fiends of his own making and comes to know that to remain forever in this inward inferno is to live forever with fiends. The everyday materials of the real world—book, table, letter—and the influence of love bring the dreamer back to the living world which is now presented in pictures of "gladsomeness and beauty" (p. 348), the last of which is "a brilliant circle of a crowded theatre. . ." (p. 348). Thus the moral history of man's descent and rebirth, as it is portrayed in "The Haunted Mind," is almost identical to that outlined by nineteenth-century perfectionists.

Furthermore, the vision of Hawthorne's major tales and romances is basically perfectionistic in that his characters are measured against the perfectionist possibility. In a few instances his characters reach a greater humanity than they have known before as love displaces self, action displaces inaction, and social concern displaces

[12] Quotations from Hawthorne's short stories are taken from *The Complete Works of Nathaniel Hawthorne* (New York, Sully and Kleinteich, 1882, 1883). Quotations from the novels are taken from *The Centenary Edition of the Works of Nathaniel Hawthorne*.

egoistic isolation. More often, however, his characters fail to ascend from that inwardness which Upham called "a true hell."

Although Hawthorne was strongly convinced that the man who would be regenerated must make a descent into the tomb of the heart, he, like the perfectionists, was just as strongly convinced of the dangers of sustained inwardness. It is not surprising that his characteristic protagonist in the tales is a man who remains in an inner hell, unable to pronounce his brotherhood with other men or to join them in a common struggle. Goodman Brown, the Reverend Hooper, Wakefield, Richard Digby, Adam Coburn, and Roderick Elliston are the protagonists who best exemplify the perfectionist pattern, albeit in Hawthorne's largely negative fashion.

These protagonists are caught in a stage of development which the perfectionists called the descent into the heart. Because each of them meditates within the circle of his own ego, he is removed from the larger world of human society and human passions. The man of adamant physically leaves his village and, shutting himself away in a cave, an image of his own heart, contemplates his righteousness in an evil society. Adam Coburn deserts the village to find shelter in a sect which turns its back on the world and human nature; Wakefield steps aside "from the main business of his life" (p. 163) to seclude himself in disguise; and Goodman Brown leaves his wife and his village not just for a night, but for a lifetime. The Reverend Hooper's veil and Roderick Elliston's bosom serpent are symbolic of the dark obsessive visions which separate them from other men. Neither love nor sympathy touches the Reverend Hooper in his "true hell": "With self-shudderings and outward terrors, he walked continually in its shadow, groping darkly within his own soul. . ." (p. 65). Roderick, too, lives without the love of friends, wife, or God: "Not merely the eye of man was a horror to him; not merely the light of a friend's countenance; but even the blessed sunshine, likewise, which in its universal beneficence typifies the radiance of the Creator's face, expressing his love for all the creatures of his hand" (p. 307). Wakefield, in deserting his wife, loses his place in the universe.

The alternative to gloomy inwardness in each of these tales is the love of a woman who is capable of drawing the self-directed soul back into human society. The Reverend Hooper, however, refuses to lift his veil in order to love Elizabeth. It must always separate him from the world and from love. Richard Digby disregards all of Mary Goffe's pleas that he return with her to the village. Adam Coburn withdraws his hand from Martha's in "satisfied ambition" (p. 476) as he chooses to be a Shaker leader and a brother instead of a lover and father. Although Goodman Brown returns to Faith, he "looked sternly and sadly into her face, and passed on without a greeting" (p. 105). Of these men, only Roderick Elliston is happily reunited with his wife and the society from which he had separated himself.

Like the nineteenth-century perfectionists, Hawthorne often compares the achievement of a higher humanity to growing up, a metaphor which is central to his first two major novels, *The Scarlet Letter* and *The House of the Seven Gables*. The unregenerate man who lingers in inwardness is like a child whose only world is himself, whose primary interest is attending to his own wants, who feels little responsibility for those other than himself, and who, as a stranger in the larger world, sacrifices almost nothing of himself to it.

Indeed, in both of these novels the principal settings suggest the childlike dependency of the characters. The society created by the Puritan elders in *The Scarlet Letter* and the ancestral home place of *The House of the Seven Gables* are both paternalistic shelters from the larger world and reflections of the decay and gloom of the characters who live in them. The most prominent landmarks of the Puritan community are the scaffold, the prison, and the cemetery. The community's most prominent members are stern and somber old men who are incapable of "sitting in judgment on an erring woman's heart and disentangling its mesh of good and evil. . ." (p. 64). The ordinary citizens remain children in this oligarchy.

Dimmesdale is a child not only in his dependence upon the Puritan elders and in his rejection of fatherhood, but in his failure to emerge from the closed circle of his own heart. He is a striking example of the self-centered, unperfected man as he is described on the scaffold under cover of darkness:

In such a case, it could only be the symptom of a highly disordered mental state when a man, rendered morbidly self-contemplative by long, intense, and secret pain, had extended his egotism over the whole expanse of nature until the firmament itself should appear no more than a fitting page for his soul's history and fate. (p. 155)

Hester also knows years of despairing self-contemplation, pride, and self-deception but, in contrast to Dimmesdale, the love which she feels for him and for Pearl turns her affections outward and enables her not only to endure, but eventually to mature into a stronger and more productive member of human society. After she returns to the place of her ignominy to take up the letter humbly and of her own free will, her acts of charity grow from love rather than from concern for her own salvation:

And, as Hester Prynne had no selfish ends, nor lived in any measure for her own profit and enjoyment, people brought all their sorrows and perplexities, and besought her counsel, as one who had herself gone through a mighty trouble. (p. 263)

In short, despite her inescapable gloom, she comes to possess those traits by which the perfected human being was identified.

A similar pattern discloses the values of perfectionism in *The House of the Seven Gables*, where the inhabitants of the patriarchal shelter remain children, each largely wrapped up in his own world, unacquainted with anything outside that world, and unable to act in it. For all of her life Hepzibah has hidden away in her father's house like a child. Because she has never before "put forth her hand to help herself" (p. 52), she is as clumsy as an infant in setting up her shop, in keeping her house, and in trying to establish a relationship with the everyday world of the street beside her house. Clifford, too, is a child devoid of judgment, overwhelmed by his immature emotions, and absorbed almost entirely in himself. Holgrave, although he does not fit the metaphor of immature child as clearly as Clifford and Hepzibah do, is, nonetheless, unregenerate in that he is largely loveless, egoistic, and ill at ease in the world. He has wandered, homeless, from place to place, from profession to profession, unwilling to become sufficiently involved with his fellow creatures "to help or hinder" (p. 216), but only to observe and analyze them.

Phoebe, on the other hand, lives harmoniously with a world in which she is productive and orderly. Shop-keeping and house-keeping are not mysteries to her, and she is capable of giving her love to the unlovely Hepzibah and Clifford. She represents the agency of love which embodies active commerce with the greater world beyond the self.

The issues which occupied perfectionists continued to be apparent in Hawthorne's last major novels. Miles Coverdale is the chief illustration of the unregenerate or unperfected man in *The Blithedale Romance*. His inaction, his preference for the spiritual, and his obsession with the lives of his friends betray a failure to ascend to the living world. The leafy cave to which he retreats during his Blithesdale stay is symbolic of the state of his soul. He is persistently guided by cold curiosity and self-interest rather than by love, and he fittingly ends his life as an unproductive writer and lonely batchelor. Hollingsworth, by contrast, is able to break the circle of his egoistic obsession and to begin reforming himself with the help of Priscilla, his link with the world.

The perfectionistic values which had been the basis for Hawthorne's tales and novels are, in *The Marble Faun*, formulated explicitly as myth in the history of the Monte Benis. The characters in this last major novel are measured against the perfectionist possibility of gaining greater humanity. As the novel opens, each of the four characters is in a state of withdrawal from the active, time-affected world, out of touch with society, and out of sympathy with other people: Donatello in his Arcadia is too animalistic to be called fully human; Hilda lives in an angel's untouchable world; Miriam broods in the dark cave of bitterness; and Kenyon lives in the cold marble world of art. Each must, if he is to reach a higher form of being, first enter a period of self-scrutiny, become fully aware of his own ignominy, and, as Donatello finally does, emerge from inwardness to commit himself in love to other mortals.

After he has committed murder, Donatello begins to brood about the ugliness and mortality of his soul. It is Kenyon who warns him of the dangers of sustained inwardness:

"Believe me," said he, turning his eyes upon his friend, full of grave and tender sympathy, "you know not what is requisite for your spiritual growth, seeking, as you do, to keep your soul perpetually in the unwholesome region of remorse. It was needful for you to pass through that dark valley, but it is infinitely dangerous to linger there too long; there is poison in the atmosphere, when we sit down and brood in it, instead of girding up our loins to press onward." (p. 273)

In order to grow, the soul must take a new direction. The perfectionist hope of a greater life for a man who dedicates himself in love to humankind is reflected by Kenyon and then by the narrator as they anticipate Donatello's emergence from remorse. Kenyon advises him to avoid the life of seclusion and to make his new life among men:

"But, for my own part, if I had an insupportable burthen—if, for any cause, I were bent upon sacrificing every earthly hope as a peace-offering towards Heaven—I would make the wide world my cell, and good deeds to mankind my prayer." (p. 267)

Donatello seems to respond to Kenyon's humanism:

. . . when first the idea was suggested of living for the welfare of his fellow-creatures, the original beauty, which sorrow had partly effaced, came back elevated and spiritualized. In the black depths, the Faun had found a soul, and was struggling with it towards the light of heaven. (p. 268)

That Donatello does eventually achieve what the perfectionists would call a higher humanity is supported by the growth of a mature love for Miriam and by the awakening of a moral sense which leads him to deliver himself up to the world for judgment.

Thus from the earliest published tales to the last major novel, Hawthorne demonstrated that he shared with nineteenth-century perfectionists a timeless moral concern, which had caught the attention of his Puritan ancestors, of how man rises above his natural state to a finer humanity, a greater manhood. Like both Puritan and perfectionist, Hawthorne believed that it was necessary for man to begin by making a journey into his own foul heart. Only when he faced the awful truth that he was the worst of sinners could he begin to grow in love. Man's ultimate concern, however, could not continue to be his own soul nor his own salvation in the hereafter, but the well-being of his brothers on this earth. The arrow of his soul's compass had to be moved outward by love rather than inward, for although contemplation and seclusion were necessary stages in man's development, the complete man had to emerge from seclusion to become an active participant in society. The Hawthornian character who fails to emerge continues to be obsessed and bedeviled. The possibility of regeneration is usually represented by the love of a woman who is invariably a link with society.

Hawthorne found these concerns interesting and useful to the end of his life because he was both Puritan and democrat, convinced of the dangerous inner hell of the soul at the same time that he was caught up in the high possibilities of nineteenth-century society, and because he could not dismiss either the past or the present, either the light or the dark of human nature.

The combination of seventeenth-century Puritanism and nineteenth-century progressivism, which has confused or intrigued Hawthorne's critics, is no other than the religious mind of the age as it was mirrored in the perfectionism of Hawthorne's Bowdoin professor, Thomas C. Upham, and others. Both recognized the dark, forbidden mystery of the soul below, which had to be experienced and transcended in love, and the active, growing world of human relationships above, in which salvation had to be achieved.

Hawthorne's Public Decade and the Values of Home
Terence Martin

BETWEEN 1850 and 1860 Nathaniel Hawthorne lived the most public years of his life. The early part of the decade evidenced what was for him a virtual burst of creative energy. To recall: within four years he produced three of his major romances and demonstrated his versatility with children's books and a campaign biography of Franklin Pierce. Additionally, following the advice of James T. Fields, he endeavored to gain maximum financial advantage from the widening importance of his name and appeared before the public with new editions of previously published tales. In all, nine separate books—new, reissued, or repackaged—appeared under Hawthorne's name between 1850 and 1853. It was, indeed, in the words of Roy Harvey Pearce, a time of "flourishing self-confidence."[1]

If, in these years, Hawthorne presented himself to the public, the middle years of the decade saw the public presenting itself to him. From the time he assumed his post as United States Consul at Liverpool, he received a steady stream of callers—merchant seamen with grievances, American citizens seeking legal, financial, or perhaps emotional help, exiles in search of assistance. Overwhelmed at first by the "rascally set of sailors" who crowded "pirate-like" into the entry of his office, he responded with a greater involvement in the affairs of others than he had formerly had occasion to show.[2] The years 1853 to 1857 brought Hawthorne into direct contact with distress and inhumanity. They also introduced him to England and to an idea of homecoming that he would later seek in vain to articulate in fiction.

In Italy during the last years of the decade, Hawthorne met artists and poets as a peer, visited cathedrals and museums as an

[1] "Historical Introduction," in *True Stories from History and Biography*, Centenary Edition (Columbus, Ohio, 1972), p. 287.
[2] Randall Stewart, ed., *The English Notebooks by Nathaniel Hawthorne* (New York, 1941), p. 3.

amateur critic, and perceived the mighty dimensions of the past as an American. He was now the man of letters, of established reputation, gathering force for a romance which would embody some significant aspect of his European experience. *The Marble Faun* (1860) marks the conclusion of Hawthorne's public decade; in his Preface he adopts a characteristic stance of trepidation but has the casual authority of a man who has seen something of the world. There is an eventful difference between the author who would offer "The Gentle Boy" or "The Gray Champion" to the public as the fruits of an uneasy solitude and the author who can say that his "Romance was sketched out during a residence of considerable length in Italy, and has been rewritten and prepared for the press in England."[3] As much as anything could, the decade had made Hawthorne a cosmopolite.

As *The Marble Faun* reveals, however, Hawthorne had been challenged and unsettled by Italy. Rome, especially, held an attraction with revolutionary implications for him. For he had carried abroad an idea of home that served the specific requirements of his imagination. In England he acquired a second (related) idea of home that extended his sense of history without transforming the capacities of his imagination. Finally, in Italy, a third idea of home took hold of his consciousness, one that he had perforce to repudiate even as he wrenched fiction out of his experience.

I

Recorded in his *English Notebooks* and fashioned later into the sketches of *Our Old Home* (1863), Hawthorne's descriptions of England demonstrate the manner in which he assimilated what he saw. Although the attitudes of individual Englishmen occasionally annoyed him, an American, Hawthorne felt, "has a singular tenderness for the stone-encrusted institutions of the mother-country."[4] English scenes give him the persistent feeling of "having been there before" (p. 63), so that he walks the streets of old Boston like someone "who has a right to be there" (p. 156). At ease in history, he is

---

[3] *The Marble Faun: or, The Romance of Monte Beni*, Centenary Edition (Columbus, Ohio, 1968), p. 2.
[4] *Our Old Home: A Series of English Sketches*, Centenary Edition (Columbus, Ohio, 1970), p. 60. Subsequent references to this edition will appear in the text.

able to pass judgment on aspects of the present because the past of England is also his. The results of Puritan iconoclasm, for example, evoke a bemused tolerance which softens the violence of a previous century. The manner in which nature has domesticated stone fences calls forth approval. And the "homelike atmosphere" (p. 213) of his residence in the suburbs of London gives him a feeling of personal comfort not unlike that of the Old Manse years before.

Hawthorne's years in England thus extended his sense of home into an idea of homecoming. But they did more than that: when Hawthorne appraises London, "the dream-city of my youth" (p. 215), the idea of homecoming gives way to the experience of being at the center of human activity. London, he writes, contains "the central spot of all the world (which . . . we may allow to be somewhere in the vicinity . . . of St. Paul's Cathedral)" (p. 214). Greenwich Observatory accentuates this feeling of centrality; as he sets his watch by the dial-plate on the wall of the Observatory, Hawthorne feels "it pleasant to be standing at the very centre of Time and Space" (p. 223). London draws him from the periphery to the center—of place, time, and space—establishing thereby a uniqueness to which he must, and can, defer. He found the real London, he says, better than the city of his youthful dreams, and he "acquired a home-feeling there, as no where else in the world" (p. 215).

It is worth noting, however, that Hawthorne's most complete acceptance of London is to be found in *Our Old Home* and not in his earlier notebook entries. Only after he had been to Italy did he emphasize the magnetic centrality of London. Only after he had lived in Rome did he describe London as incomparable. From the vantage point of the Thames he bids us look back upon roofs, steeples, towers, columns, "and the great crowning Dome—look back, in short, upon that mystery of the world's proudest city, amid which a man so longs and loves to be; not, perhaps, because it contains much that is positively admirable and enjoyable, but because at all events the world has nothing better" (p. 255).

The troubled opening sentence of chapter thirty-six of *The Marble Faun* provides a striking contrast to this reconciled praise of London. It is a monumental sentence, by far the longest Hawthorne ever wrote; in waves of detail he struggles to express the assault of Rome on a temperament nourished in and by New England. He enumerates the ugliness and hypocrisy of Rome so enervating both to body and spirit—the "alley-like" streets, the "cheerless" firesides, the bug-ridden beds, the "rancid butter," the "pretense of Holiness and the reality of Nastiness." But Hawthorne's aggregation of details, concrete, startling, with the bite of experience behind them, turns out over three hundred words later to be a massive concession. For when we have known at first hand the languor and trickery of Rome, and departed, "hating her with all our might," we are astonished to discover, "by-and-by, that our heart-strings have mysteriously attached themselves to the Eternal City, and are drawing us thitherward again, as if it were more familiar, more intimately our home, than even the spot where we were born!"

Hawthorne expressed his divided and swirling feelings about Rome before he extolled London as the best of the world's cities, before he said that London gave him a "home-feeling" as did no place "else in the world." In the later years of his public decade, Rome had engaged Hawthorne as London never did. It was the "imperial" city, the "City of all time, and of all the world."[5] Yet, in his French and Italian notebooks, Hawthorne repeatedly bemoans "the dreariness, the ugliness, shabbiness, un-home-likeness of a Roman street."[6] Another notebook entry at the time of his leaving Italy catches the ambivalence of his feelings: he wishes never to see

> any of those objects again, though no place ever took so strong a hold of my being as Rome, nor ever seemed so close to me and so strangely familiar. I seem to know it better than my birthplace, and to have known it longer; and though I have been very miserable there . . . , and disgusted with a thousand things in its daily life, still I cannot say I hate it, perhaps might fairly own a love for it. But life being too short for such questionable and troublesome enjoyments, I desire never to set eyes on it again.[7]

The illness of his daughter Una in Rome caused Hawthorne considerable personal anguish. Beyond that, however, Rome came to represent to him the antithesis of his New England sense of home, all the more forcibly to be resisted because submitting to it would require a radical shift in vision, in faith, in personality. He seems later to have stressed the homelikeness of London as a way of tempering the claims of Rome.

[5] *The Marble Faun*, p. 111.
[6] *Passages From the French and Italian Note-Books*, Riverside Edition (Boston, 1883), p. 59.
[7] Ibid., pp. 506–507.

Hawthorne had gone abroad in 1853 with a sense of home so developed, so ingrained, that he could grumble about it and sport with it, even as he relied on it. Out of his felt assumptions about New England and his investigations into New England history had come fiction that bore a particular imaginative signature. His years in England and those in Italy gave him as a man two additional senses of home, one congenial, one fraught with a feeling of attraction and repulsion. But Hawthorne the man remained Hawthorne the artist. And the importance of such biographical considerations is that we might come to see more clearly how and why his European homes failed to satisfy his artistic needs. Framing Hawthorne's public decade are *The Scarlet Letter* and *The Marble Faun,* his classic romance and his most ambitious but least satisfactory one. To consider certain qualities of each of these romances (along with aspects of representative tales) in the context of his European experience is to understand something of the meaning of home for Hawthorne's imagination.

II

When Henry James catalogs the items of high civilization that were missing in the United States of Hawthorne's time, he lists social phenomena which supported the texture of his own fiction. But Hawthorne, as James concedes, was part of the culture in which he worked: accustomed to a lack of density in his world, he could breathe, and draw sustenance from, a rarefied social atmosphere.

There is a good deal of truth in James's observations. To press the matter further, however, is to see that Hawthorne, plagued by what he calls the American insistence on actualities, deliberately courts in his work a thinness and sparseness far greater than that of his own day. Tales such as "The Hollow of the Three Hills" and "The Birthmark," for example, are set in vague, a-social worlds. The mode of reality is that of the fairy tale converted to the purposes of the moral fable; consequently, such tales lack social furnishing even as they defy history. But Hawthorne's historical tales likewise thrive on sparseness: he consistently moves his most characteristic fiction back toward the beginnings of the colonial experience in America and lets his imagination take advantage of what he finds—and does not find —there.

Hawthorne's descriptions of a Puritan meetinghouse and of a

cathedral may serve to illustrate the importance of a *démeublé* historical artifact to him. Plain on the outside, the meetinghouse in "The Gentle Boy" is "rude" in its interior, with a "low ceiling," "unplastered walls," "naked wood work," an "undraperied pulpit," and, in place of pews, "rows of long, cushionless benches."[8] Beyond the fact of historical accuracy, which leads Hawthorne to seat the adult men and women on opposite sides of the single aisle, the very lack of churchly furnishings, inviting the rhetorical negatives, makes the meetinghouse functionally accessible to Hawthorne's fictive imagination—which is to say that in such an "unadorned" setting (as he terms it) the actions of his characters can command full attention. In *Our Old Home,* he uses the "one set of phrases" which, he believes, adequately describe "all the Cathedrals in England, and elsewhere": "an acre or two of stone-flags for a pavement; rows of vast columns supporting a vaulted roof at a dusky height"; "stained glass" windows, a "massive organ," the "Bishop's throne, the pulpit, the altar" (p. 147). The consequence, as Hawthorne goes on to say, is that in cathedrals "the sermon is an exceedingly diminutive and unimportant part of the religious services." The "magnificence of the setting quite dazzles out what we Puritans look upon as the jewel of the whole affair" (pp. 226-227).

The difference—iconic density and iconoclastic sparseness—between cathedral and meetinghouse is obvious. And the meaning of that difference is equally clear: in a cathedral setting, amid splendor that expresses the significance of the past, the importance of human action, specifically the human word, is lessened, even minimized. Hawthorne's ideal seems to be the Puritans' first "house of worship," described in "Main Street" as "naked, simple, and severe," infused, however, with an "enriching" faith that makes "of these new walls, and this narrow compass, its own cathedral."[9] The best cathedrals take their metaphorical structure from the human spirit. Only in such a house of worship could Arthur Dimmesdale's sermons possess their compelling power. In a European cathedral, the Reverend Mr. Hooper might pass unnoticed behind a veil of incense.

For Hawthorne, sparseness, in virtually every form, was preferable to denseness. In his fiction it allowed him to emphasize the

---

[8] *Twice-Told Tales,* Riverside Edition (Boston, 1882), pp. 96–97.
[9] *The House of the Seven Gables and The Snow Image,* Riverside Edition (Boston, 1883), p. 449.

importance of the human character. In his life it allowed him to respond to human situations more fully than he could otherwise. His experience with beggars is a case in point. When an elderly widow from a foreign land came begging at the Old Manse in 1842, Hawthorne took occasion to write in his notebook that he had never knowingly refused his "mite to a wandering beggar." With so much "want and wretchedness in the world," one may "safely take the word of any mortal" who asks assistance. "It is desirable," he continues, "that such persons should be permitted to roam through our land of plenty, scattering the seeds of tenderness and charity—as birds of passage bear the seeds of precious plants . . . without ever dreaming of the office which they perform."[10]

Hawthorne had doubtless seen very few beggars at this contented point in his life; faced with one, he can indulge himself with a rush of sentiment. He heightens the importance, the human-ness, of the widow and proceeds to consider her life as if she were to be a character in a romance. When, in England, he came into contact with numerous beggars, he learned to distrust them and to withhold his "mite," at times with a guilty conscience. In Italy, inundated with beggars, he reacted with a drastic change in attitude. "This kind of vermin," Hawthorne writes of paupers in *The Marble Faun,* "infested the house of Monte Beni worse than any other spot in beggar-haunted Italy"; beggars become "pests"—"human ones."[11] Such remarks cannot be attributed exclusively to that fashionable abstraction we call a *narrator,* thereby exempting Hawthorne from complicity. These are Hawthorne's feelings, as clear in *The Marble Faun* as they are in his notebooks when he reports that the "multitude of beggars in Italy makes the heart as obdurate as stone."[12] Understandable as this language may be for anyone who has found his capacity to give bankrupted by overwhelming and insistent poverty, it is a far cry from what Hawthorne wrote about the foreign widow in 1842. Confronted by one beggar, he could not only respond but could emphasize her importance to others. Confronted by delegations of beggars, he not only turns hard-hearted but relegates them to the status of "vermin." Once again, the human element, so crucial

---

[10] Claude M. Simpson, ed., *The American Notebooks,* Centenary Edition (Columbus, Ohio, 1972), p. 353.
[11] *The Marble Faun,* pp. 241, 306.
[12] *French and Italian Note-Books,* p. 240.

to his life and art, is made possible only by scarceness or sparseness.

Even sportively, in comparing English and American women, Hawthorne finds a way to award the prize to sparseness. After several years' residence in England, he confesses in *Our Old Home,* the beauty of English women has come to appeal to his "deteriorated" taste. American women, in contrast to their English sisters, seem to possess a "certain meagreness, (Heaven forbid that I should call it scrawniness!) a deficiency of physical development, a scantiness, so to speak, in the pattern of their material make, a paleness of complexion, a thinness of voice." Because he must half-acknowledge that English women are the "finer animals," he resolves, "much the more sturdily," to praise American women as "angels": "It would be a pitiful bargain to give up the ethereal charm of American beauty in exchange for half a hundred-weight of human clay!" (p. 334).

To say that Hawthorne's American fiction is bereft of cathedrals, multitudes of beggars, and fat women is only to make the serious point that Hawthorne, needing a context of sparseness or thinness in order to appreciate the importance of the human character, deliberately courts "thin" settings which accentuate the human drama to be played out. Concomitant with this tendency, as I have suggested, is his need to feel that although his tale might be drenched with what history there is, not much history exists behind it. Only with a sense of being imaginatively near the beginning can Hawthorne tell us, in the second paragraph of *The Scarlet Letter,* that the founders of any new colony "have invariably recognized it among their earliest practical necessities to allot a portion of the virgin soil as a cemetery, and another portion as the site of a prison." He has the authority to record the fact that the Puritans laid out the "first burial-ground" around the grave of Isaac Johnson and that it "became the nucleus of all the congregated sepulchres in the old church-yard of King's Chapel." Imaginatively at the beginning, present in a history that has broken with the past, he can refer to the *first* burial ground and even to the first *death* as he leads us into the new, thin, atmosphere of *The Scarlet Letter.* In Scotland, he looked into a churchyard and "saw that the ground was absolutely stuffed with dead people" (*Our Old Home,* p. 205). That kind of perception—of density and of age impossible to circumvent—would forever stultify Hawthorne's creative impulse.

In Rome, as one might expect, the "massiveness" of the past precludes any attempt to get to a beginning. Indeed, in *The Marble*

Faun the dimensions of the past outreach description: Rome invites one to look not at but through successive stages of history, "through a vista of century beyond century," through alternating phases of barbarism and civilization, "through a broad pathway of progressive generations," until, finally, "you behold the obelisks . . . , hinting at a Past infinitely more remote than history can define." In comparison with that "immeasurable distance," concludes Hawthorne, "your own life is as nothing." What a cathedral does to a sermon, the Roman past does to all individual activity. As a consequence of its "weight and density," our concerns become "but half as real, here, as elsewhere."[13]

With no chance to sift back through history and get to a beginning in *The Marble Faun,* Hawthorne operates under a severe handicap. He tries to give a sense of beginning-ness by reenacting more explicitly than is his wont the story of man's fall from innocence, but the past of Rome stands between him and the fulfilled meaning of his subject. Only in *The Marble Faun* does a past loom thick *behind* the setting of a Hawthorne story. Representative of the historical tales, "Young Goodman Brown" has barely enough past to give meaning to the action taking place. Replete with Hawthorne's persistent concerns, the sketch "Main Street" traces the growth of a community "from infancy upward" and follows that growth only through the life span of John Massey, the "first-born of Naumkeag."[14] *The Blithedale Romance,* very much the story of a beginning, requires the absence of all but a few biographical threads. In *The House of the Seven Gables,* Hawthorne's most time-bound American romance, the thin line of a family past informs the developing contours of a story that reaches toward a new start at the end. And in *The Scarlet Letter* there is virtually nothing behind the Puritans with whom Hawthorne deals; he is so close to a beginning that the death of Governor Winthrop can be converted to the purposes of the romance. At its characteristic best, we may say, Hawthorne's imagination seeks out and creates a beginning (hence sparse, thin) moment in history—out of which much comes tumbling forward but behind which, quite logically, there is very little. In *The Marble Faun,* Hawthorne cannot employ this basic strategy.

Set against the world of *The Marble Faun,* the world of *The*

---

[13] *The Marble Faun*, quotations drawn from pp. 410 and 6.
[14] *The House of the Seven Gables and The Snow Image,* pp. 439, 450. Hawthorne also focuses on Roger Conant, "the first settler of Naumkeag," in this sketch (p. 443).

Scarlet Letter seems wondrously empty. At bottom, what is missing in Hawthorne's Boston is iconography—with all that icons can imply about the expressive nature of the past. Because of the Puritan insistence on directness of worship, because of their *anti*-iconic bias, Hawthorne is able to appropriate a point in time *prior* to icons. Thus, in the marketplace of Boston is the scaffold, the formal and public place for the revelation of sin. In the marketplace of Perugia, by way of contrast, is the statue of Pope Julius III with his hand outstretched in benediction. At noon, Hester Prynne stands on her "pedestal of shame," the absolute center of attention. At noon, too, Miriam and Donatello meet penitentially at the foot of the Pope's statue, while the people in the bustling square pay no more attention to them than to cast admiring glances at Miriam's beauty. Hawthorne's scene in *The Marble Faun* is effective; he makes good use of his "bronze pontiff." But in *The Scarlet Letter* he has been able to put a human character rather than a statue on a pedestal and thereby set a hidden human action directly at the center of his romance. That Hester and Pearl may remind one flickeringly of Madonna and Child enforces the human priority inherent in Hawthorne's setting, as does his statement (toward the end of the romance) that Hester "stood, statue-like, at the foot of the scaffold."[15] At a time "when the professional character was of itself a lofty pedestal," Arthur Dimmesdale is in effect worshipped by his parishioners, who revere him as Romans might venerate the statue of a saint—and thus make his self-serving penance all the more possible. Dimmesdale's final sermon evokes a shout of apotheosis from all assembled in the marketplace: "Never, on New England soil," writes Hawthorne, "had stood the man so honored by his mortal brethren as the preacher."[16] Prior to icons at this fictive moment, the human character in *The Scarlet Letter* compels a total focus of attention from the community and from the reader.

Hawthorne goes one masterful step farther in *The Scarlet Letter*. Possessed of a pre-iconic world, he creates an icon out of the Puritans' punishment for adultery. And in the way his heart can respond to a single beggar, his imagination can respond to a single icon. Rome, Hawthorne might say, is "absolutely stuffed" with iconography, and although his description of Hilda in St. Peter's Cathedral has the

---

[15] *The Scarlet Letter*, Centenary Edition (Columbus, Ohio, 1962), p. 244.
[16] Ibid., pp. 249–250.

charm of a temptation resisted, he balks at the sheer number of statues, crosses, shrines, and grottoes in Italy. His frequent recourse to the techniques of the sketch in *The Marble Faun* suggests a problem of assimilation. In *The Scarlet Letter,* however, with no such problem besetting him, Hawthorne presides over the creation of an icon—which, as he claims in "The Custom-House," has survived the world that brought it into being.

By means of that scarlet A, a literal object, so he would have us believe, Hawthorne leads us back into a world barren of icons. The letter, as we know, dominates the romance. When Hester stands on the scaffold, all eyes are "concentered" on the A. Arthur Dimmesdale finds it fixed at the center of his meditative life. Roger Chillingworth pursues it obsessively. Even the suit of armor in Governor Bellingham's mansion, one of the few things brought into the romance from the past, mirrors it back for all to see. But this icon—standing alone, grounded in a historical moment which Hawthorne can visualize as a beginning—enhances rather than diminishes the importance of the human individual. Moral in nature and meaning, it becomes protean and omnipresent, heuristic and elusive, yet dramatically sacrificial in that each character can embody it, and by so doing, humanize it.

III

When Hawthorne went abroad in the 1850's he wrote extensively in his notebooks, first in England, then in Italy. With great insight he portrayed persons, manners, institutions. Along with *The Marble Faun* and *Our Old Home,* these notebooks demonstrate that he acquired a sense of home in England and that later, in Italy, Rome appealed to him as a place more familiar than the spot where he was born. Such sentiments signified much to a man who put a consummate value on home, whose work dramatized the importance of heart and hearth, whose original sense of New England as home had engendered fiction of high order. Retrospectively, Hawthorne saw London as the central city of the world and developed a perilous love-hate feeling with regard to Rome. New England, London, Rome: with full awareness of his different attitudes toward each, we may say that these were the three homes of Nathaniel Hawthorne.

But Hawthorne abroad was faced with a world to which he could not bring a strategy for writing fiction that had been more than twenty years in the making. For the first time in his career, a sense of home was not easily in the service of his imagination. In London he may have experienced a feeling of centrality, but in New England he could acquire a sense of being near a beginning. In Rome he could find many icons, but in New England he could respond to one forged out of his imagination. His inability to complete *The Ancestral Footstep*—and, later, *Dr. Grimshawe's Secret*—stems, I should think, not only from his failing powers as an artist during the years of the Civil War but also from his attempt to impose life-long creative habits on a history he could not "thin out," to work toward a beginning he could not possess imaginatively. His difficulties with *The Marble Faun* are compounded by his feeling that present day Rome "seems like nothing but a heap of broken rubbish."[17] The density of the Roman past evokes Hawthorne's most archetypal plot. But Hawthorne the artist does not live by plot alone, and when Kenyon asks Hilda to guide him home at the end of the romance one senses that there is no alternative, and one is told that *home* is New England.

Capable of so much after a long, quiet struggle into life, Hawthorne's imagination could not experience another parturition during his years abroad. After beginning his public decade with a flurry of achievement, he came to confront a world that—no matter how broadening, how enticing, how challenging—did not fulfill the conditions for his special kind of fiction. With all its limitations, New England remained Hawthorne's imaginative home. *The Scarlet Letter* testifies to its sustaining quality.

[17] *The Marble Faun*, p. 110.

Hawthorne's Coverdale: Character and Art in *The Blithedale Romance*
James H. Justus

I

WHEN HE DECIDED to draw heavily upon his experiences at Brook Farm for *The Blithedale Romance,* Hawthorne aggressively confronted for the first time in his fiction the abundant materials of the present. Although his letters and notebooks reveal an urgency to define, work within, and preserve a synecdochic present—"that narrow strip of sunlight which we call Now"—his third extended fiction was the closest Hawthorne was ever to come to the beef-and-beer substantiality which he saw and admired in novelists like Trollope.[1] A work that traditionally has been, with the exception of James's and Howells's high regard, the least admired of his major productions, *Blithedale* has always seemed something of an anomaly in the canon of American Romances.

Its characters, sketchily developed like those in most of Hawthorne's works, seem less dependent than usual upon figural types and tend to function independently of their vaguely assigned allegorical roles. It is Hawthorne's only major fiction whose dialogue consistently reproduces the authentic ring of actual speech. Because of its time and place, though they are no more "removed" than those of *The House of the Seven Gables,* this work exploits contemporary events rather than historical legends. Finally, with a first-person point of view, used otherwise for only a few undistinguished sketches, Hawthorne succeeds in making Miles Coverdale one of the most

[1] In their different ways Arlin Turner and Frederick C. Crews have confirmed the deep autobiographical nature of this book; and from the time of its publication there has been no dearth of readers who, taking lightly the author's ambiguous disavowals in the preface, prefer to see *Blithedale* as a *roman à clef.* See Arlin Turner, "Autobiographical Elements in Hawthorne's *The Blithedale Romance,*" *University of Texas Studies in English,* XV (July, 1935), 39–62, and *Nathaniel Hawthorne: An Introduction and Interpretation* (New York, 1961), pp. 79–81; Frederick C. Crews, *The Sins of the Fathers: Hawthorne's Psychological Themes* (New York, 1966), pp. 198–205, passim. I stress not the origins of Coverdale but the manifestations of his character and talent in his own narrative.

interesting and complex I-narrators in our nineteenth-century literature.

II

It is curious that *Blithedale* is such a dispassionate document. Despite its subject, it lacks the fire and thunder appropriate to the widespread hyperbolism of reformist New England. Hollingsworth's moral enthusiasm before his break with Coverdale is low-keyed for a man who is described as "forever fiddling on a single string," and the early Zenobia is as much a chattering dilettante as Coverdale. It is almost as if Hawthorne had taken the fervent reformers of his time, who from most accounts turn out to be impassioned creatures of both mind and tongue—almost their own caricatures of reformers —and scaled them down into characters less sensational, less melodramatic, less visceral than their general counterparts in real life.

One critic believes that Hollingsworth is "an unimpressive monomaniac" and Zenobia is "an unconvincing feminist" because of Hawthorne's inept characterization.[2] More to the point is Hawthorne's necessity for giving over the duties of characterization to his artist-narrator, whose skill at painting such portraits is not equal to the bias which nourishes them. Hawthorne's subject of course is not reform, and Miles Coverdale is not the spokesman for a specific reform movement. Yet Coverdale is convincing in his revealed ambivalences toward reform and reformers; his earlier faint praise of Hollingsworth and his admiration for the New Woman cannot conceal Coverdale's perverse psychic thrill in seeing both finally get their comeuppance. In this complex work, the nature of reform and the nature of the narrator are mutually reinforcing aspects of Hawthorne's vision.

As a document, *The Blithedale Romance* directly confronts the question, livelier perhaps in antebellum Massachusetts than elsewhere, of "How shall a man live?" It exploits the competing claims for saying how, from such pseudo-sciences as mesmerism and spiritualism to such serious concerns as social theory and humanitarianism. Indeed, it touches upon choices demanded by a reformist culture: material grubbing or spiritual transformation? labor or leisure? commerce or art? urban or rural values? patchwork revision or radical

---

[2] Rudolph Von Abele, *The Death of the Artist: A Study of Hawthorne's Disintegration* (The Hague, 1955), p. 83.

reform? dilettantism or ideology? The generating energies in this narrative emerge from what Hawthorne's Concord neighbor Emerson referred to variously as "The Present Age," "The Times," or "The Mind and Manners of the XIX Century." Here, the truths of the human heart are tested by the explicitly social and cultural ferment of reform, the most characteristic signature of American life in the 1840's and 1850's. In no other of his fictions does Hawthorne encompass such a remarkable spectrum of life-styles of his time; *Blithedale* is his "Mind and Manners of the XIX Century," his one romance that at least aspires to the form of the novel.

The pivot in this romance-novel is Coverdale. The bits and pieces of the story of the Blithedale brotherhood form the substance of Coverdale's story; these same bits and pieces, augmented by the ramifying implications of the urban past and the conflict of influences both personal and ideological in Coverdale,[3] form the substance of Hawthorne's story. If Coverdale is an embarrassingly peripheral actor in the romance of Blithedale, Hawthorne makes him the leading performer in *The Blithedale Romance*. That Coverdale, as narrator, is not entirely to be trusted in the tale he tells is by now generally accepted, but Coverdale's limitations follow from the contextual fact that the elusive and disjointed events which Coverdale relates are totemistic events whose importance lies in the valuations he puts on them.[4] The character of this narrator finally cannot be abstracted from the form which he encloses (the story he tells), but, more crucially, he cannot be abstracted from the form which encloses him (the story which Hawthorne tells).

Whereas this minor New England poet writes of a failed communal enterprise, Hawthorne writes of a failed human being—and

---

[3] Leo B. Levy is the only critic to stress societal change as an important context for the fate of Hawthorne's characters. Coverdale, he observes, stands midway between the forces of a newly mechanized society and an older rural America. See *"The Blithedale Romance:* Hawthorne's 'Voyage Through Chaos,'" *Studies in Romanticism*, VIII (Autumn, 1968), 1–15.

[4] In "A New Reading of *The Blithedale Romance*," *American Literature*, XXIX (May, 1957), 147–170, Frederick C. Crews finds Coverdale a morally deficient narrator; in *Sins of the Fathers*, he finds crippling Oedipal compulsions as well. William Hedges argues for a Coverdale who learns from his experiences in "Hawthorne's *Blithedale:* The Function of the Narrator," *Nineteenth-Century Fiction*, XIV (March, 1960), 303–316. Kelley Griffith, Jr.'s "Form in *The Blithdale Romance*," *American Literature*, XL (March, 1968), 15–26, and Nina Baym's *"The Blithedale Romance:* A Radical Reading," *JEGP*, LXVIII (Oct., 1968), 545–569, are the two most pertinent studies which concentrate on the narrator as Hawthorne's subject. See also Louis Auchincloss, *"The Blithedale Romance:* A Study in Form and Point of View," *Nathaniel Hawthorne Journal*, II (1972), 53–58.

does so both as romancer and novelist. Coverdale explores the weaknesses of egotists, faithless lovers, proud businessmen brought low, females both liberated and parasitic, grubby Yankee farmers, and spiritualist charlatans, all of whom undercut the high purposes of Blithedale; Hawthorne explores the process by which a man who shrinks from the taint of human imperfection dooms himself irrevocably to a life of sterile complacency.

The mannerisms which so annoy Coverdale's friends are not only the traits of a self-indulgent Boston gentleman; they are also symptoms of an unfulfilled poet whose life in the city has been as comfortably conventional as his verse. Psychologically, Coverdale is never far away from his urban quarters, which he alludes to several times, and the society which shapes his tastes and values. If his good life suggests dilettantism, the tenacity with which he mentally clings to it suggests the need for emotional anchoring. His bout of chills and fever at Blithedale, following his exposure to the unseasonable weather, is a physical equivalent of the emotional strain involved in the transition. In a new and untried society, he recalls the stable charm of what he has left behind:

My pleasant bachelor-parlor, sunny and shadowy, curtained and carpeted, with the bed-chamber adjoining; my centre-table, strewn with books and periodicals; my writing-desk, with a half-finished poem in a stanza of my own contrivance; my morning lounge at the reading-room or picture gallery; my noontide walk along the cheery pavement, with the suggestive succession of human faces, and the brisk throb of human life, in which I shared; my dinner at the Albion, where I had a hundred dishes at command . . . ; my evening at the billiard-club, the concert, the theatre, or at somebody's party, if I pleased:—what could be better than all this?[5]

The man whose comfort is made secure by "a good fire burning in the grate" and a closet stocked with champagne and claret must adjust to plain tea from "earthen cups" before a more unrestrained fire of peat, pine, and oak in a country fireplace.

---

[5] *The Blithedale Romance and Fanshawe*, Centenary Edition (Columbus, 1964), p. 40. All other extensive quotations from *Blithedale* are from this edition and are incorporated in the text.

III

Miles Coverdale begins his last chapter with a conventional tack: "It remains only to say a few words about myself." What follows, however, is gratuitous, since the entire story has been more a self-dramatization than an account of a failed communal experiment. What the reader learns of the founding and disbanding of Blithedale is thin, curiously inert, generalized; any sense of a thickly textured life comes primarily from the minutely recorded stages of the narrator's personal relationships.

Amiable as he is, Coverdale displays revealing deficiencies both as a man and as an artist, and those deficiencies matter. While Hawthorne was always too ambivalent about the artist ever to equate the good man and good artist, both kinds of flaws in Coverdale coincide in such a way that they not merely round out the portrait of one character but also signal Hawthorne's abiding interest in both the implications of the cold heart in human affairs and in the possibilities and limitations of art. From his own account, two aspects of Coverdale can be isolated for analysis without damaging the overall texture of his narrative: his attitude toward Hollingsworth (which suggests his frailty as a man) and his use of Zenobia as symbol (which establishes the aesthetic boundaries of his art). Coverdale's judgment that he has made "but a poor and dim figure in [his] own narrative," like so many evaluations which he makes earlier, is untrue. Though the springs of action for most of the principals in the story remain hidden, those of Coverdale do not. For all his flaws he is the most familiar, the most knowable character in the book.

Coverdale's declaration of love for Priscilla at the end of his narrative may not be as jejune as earlier readers took it to be, but it indicates a spiritual impoverishment more profound than some readers now are willing to grant.[6] Prior to his "Confession," Coverdale gives no indications that he looks upon the seamstress as anything more than a vacuous encumbrance, a patronizing attitude betraying a social and intellectual snobbery. Throughout the narrative, however, he has been attracted to both Zenobia—for her sexuality, her intelli-

---

[6] Ellen E. Morgan, for example, argues convincingly that Coverdale's passion for Zenobia is psychologically displaced by Priscilla in the "confession," but concludes curiously that Coverdale is "finally not a failure, but . . . a man capable of a profoundly moving lover's obsession." See "The Veiled Lady: The Secret Love of Miles Coverdale," *Nathaniel Hawthorne Journal*, I (1971), 169–181.

gence and passion, and her "mystery"—and Hollingsworth—for his masculine authoritativeness and his magnetism; he has even been drawn briefly, Coverdale admits, to the despicable Westervelt. But all are finally irrelevant in the matter. "Miles Coverdale's Confession" covertly acknowledges an inability to love, a radically disabling flaw which cripples him both as man and artist. His unimpressive substitutes for love, on which he expends considerable energy, are a peevish antipathy for masculine power and an exaggerated emphasis on feminine passion. Those substitutes are a direct outgrowth of his disappointing relationships with Hollingsworth and Zenobia.

Critics usually take Hollingsworth's scheme to rehabilitate criminals at face value (which is to say at Coverdale's valuation)—at best a single-minded, abstract, "partial" reform of the kind which both Emerson and Hawthorne distrusted, and at worst one that is grandiose, self-serving, dishonest, and possibly illegal. Although Hollingsworth's language in Chapter 15 is egocentric and absolutist, as befitting the radical reformer, much of the extremist tone is a result of Coverdale's mediating consciousness. After Hollingsworth rejects Coverdale's proposal to put some of Fourier's principles to work at Blithedale, Coverdale uses the incident to charge his friend with a lack of "real sympathy with our feelings and our hopes"; and he characterizes Hollingsworth's philanthropic reform with such terms as "one channel," "prolonged fiddling upon one string," and "his lonely and exclusive object in life." But Hollingsworth rejects the Fourieristic system because he believes it to be based on "the selfish principle—the principle of all human wrong, the very blackness of man's heart, the portion of ourselves which we shudder at, and which it is the whole aim of spiritual discipline to eradicate" (p. 53).

And though his own scheme may be overly sanguine, its principle is unselfishness.[7] It concerned, Coverdale reports, "the reformation of the wicked by methods moral, intellectual, and industrial, by the sympathy of pure, humble, and yet exalted minds, and by opening to his pupils the possibility of a worthier life than that which had become their fate" (p. 131). Since even in the narrator's paraphrase the project sounds more admirable than heinous, to discredit it Coverdale falls back on what "most people thought": that it was "imprac-

[7] Zenobia's evaluation of Hollingsworth ("It is all self!"), though understandable, is not necessarily the complete story; moreover, the rage is directed toward Hollingsworth the man and would-be husband rather than Hollingsworth the philanthropist.

ticable." But Hollingsworth rightly assesses the impracticableness of Blithedale, which is, he says, "a wretched, unsubstantial scheme . . . on which we have wasted a precious summer of our lives" (p. 130). As reforms go, Hollingsworth's is considerably more tangible and less self-serving than the Blithedale experiment, which Coverdale defends in language that betrays an unsupportable position even as it reveals the abstraction of his commitment.

The man who in April calls Blithedale a "counterfeit Arcadia" and who with his "customary levity" admits that he has little purpose in life other than to "make pretty verses, and play a part, with . . . the rest of the amateurs, in our pastoral," is the same man who in August exclaims that the community is now "beginning to flourish." Hollingsworth disagrees: "It is full of defects—irremediable and damning ones!—from first to last, there is nothing else! I grasp it in my hand, and find no substance whatever. There is not human nature in it!" (p. 132). Coverdale's adherence to the idealism of Blithedale is escapist, and Hollingsworth's invitation to "strike hands" with him promises this minor poet no more "languor and vague wretchedness" but "strength, courage, immitigable will—everything that a manly and generous nature should desire!" (p. 133). From Coverdale's perspective, the temptation is evil, but from the reader's it has all the marks of a healthy alternative for "an indolent or half-occupied man."

What Hollingsworth offers to Coverdale is what Coverdale, given his coldness and abstraction, cannot accept: a tangible brotherhood, disinterested devotion, generous cooperation, purpose, and above all, love. Coverdale admits, "I stood aloof." It is the stance that damns.[8] Blithedale is a sham, but as long as it is detached from what Hollingsworth calls "human nature," as long, that is, as it is safely idealized, Coverdale can pretend to a new life of courage and purpose. A few days after the "crisis" in the potato patch, Coverdale, with "intolerable discontent and irksomeness," lays down his hoe, says farewell to the pigs, and takes his first leave of Blithedale.

If Coverdale's failure as a man is crystallized in his "tragic passage-at-arms" with Hollingsworth, his failure as an artist is confirmed by

[8] For a contrary view, see "The Politics of Blithedale: The Dilemma of the Self," *Studies in Romanticism*, XI (Spring, 1972), 138–146, by John C. Hirsch, who believes Coverdale's rejection proper because to accept Hollingsworth's offer would mean the "veritable extinction of self"—the philanthropist's plans involve the "reassertion of a society ruled by precept from without where individual members are less important than social order."

his last meeting with Zenobia, a scene marked by his inability to redeem his superficial and derivative art with insight and charity. After Hollingsworth's rejection of Zenobia, only Coverdale witnesses her convulsive weeping. Regaining her composure, she adopts what is by this time her usual brittle and deflating attitude toward him: "Ah, I perceive what you are about! You are turning this whole affair into a ballad. Pray let me hear as many stanzas as you happen to have ready!" (p. 223). The words are an echo of her remark to Coverdale on their first evening, when he surmises that Priscilla has come to join the community to pay homage to the well-known feminist. "Since you see the young woman in so poetical a light," Zenobia says, "you had better turn the affair into a ballad" (p. 33). After projecting a romantic literary ballad, which becomes a fanciful condensation of the narrative of *Blithedale,* Zenobia turns from fanciful chatter to a more down-to-earth explanation. By "tokens that escape the obtuseness of masculine perceptions," she declares Priscilla not a death-dealing snow-maiden but a poor seamstress from the city come for "no more transcendental purpose" than to do Zenobia's miscellaneous sewing. The "affair" which might be turned into a ballad is not one of thwarted sexual love between an exotic woman and a rugged philanthropist, but a sisterly love that carries with it moral responsibility. If it is a kind of love which lies beyond Coverdale's "obtuse" perceptions, its violation of course lies even further. By her betrayal of Priscilla, Zenobia sins against the human heart in ways far more serious than her frustrated passion for Hollingsworth could ever do. That remorse over her betrayal of Priscilla for her own gain (love, money, or both) might have impelled her to take her own life never occurs to Coverdale.

The repartee between Zenobia and Coverdale on her final evening is a grim replay of this earlier scene, and her manner is an intensified version of her earlier bantering and edged wit. She utters a "sharp, light laugh." She ranges from mild irony to scornful sarcasm to haughty solemnity to calm security; but throughout the exchange, Coverdale notes that she is also "laughing" or "smiling" and remarks on the strange way in which her mind seemed "to vibrate from the deepest earnest to mere levity." It is clearly the portrait of a woman only partly in control of her emotions; but it is also a glimpse of a woman sufficiently alert to her confidant's limitations to allow him (indeed, to encourage him) to interpret her grief as simplistically as he, with his "obtuseness," is inclined to do. Thus, Zenobia collaborates with Coverdale on a little ballad about herself, the point of which is the way the world conspires against the woman "who swerves one hair's breadth out of the beaten track." Coverdale interprets this specifically as Zenobia's love for Hollingsworth and generally as the dangers of the passions which overcome the intellectual, liberated woman. Though he protests that her interpretation has "too stern a moral," it is nevertheless the one he adopts.

If the moral is "too stern," it is also irrelevant. *The Blithedale Romance* is remarkably free of evidence that the world punishes this feminist for her activities. As in other works of Hawthorne, the source and means of punishment here are more profoundly spiritual than those at the service of the world. (The same is true for Hollingsworth, whose public scheme for the reformation of criminals must be painfully internalized to cope "with a single murderer.") Though we hear much of Zenobia's activism in the cause of women's rights—which would presumably distort her humanity just as Hollingsworth's philanthropy is said to distort his—what Hawthorne dramatizes is feminine spirit, not ideological advocacy. And in the most explicitly "feminist" chapter in the book, "Eliot's Pulpit," Zenobia's statements on women's rights pale into vagueness when set beside Coverdale's own conciliating, extravagant vision of a matriarchy in which the submissive male "would kneel before a woman-ruler!"

Coverdale's limited understanding of both friends is betrayed by his language. Hollingsworth's challenge provokes Coverdale to self-torturing envy. Whereas in the earlier chapters the narrator speaks merely patronizingly of his friend, after "A Crisis" he drops even the pretense of good will. The diction grows excessive, even virulent: *odious, loathsomeness; great, black ugliness of sin; trample on considerations; squalid.* After Zenobia's death, his conduct toward Hollingsworth is dictated by what Coverdale believes to be "all the evil" of which the philanthropist is guilty; his taunts are those of a harpy. Coverdale's "ballad" about Zenobia, the kind which might have reclaimed a genteel, minor Romantic, turns out to be simply another work about the passionate heroine who, "defeated on the broad battlefield of life," falls on "her own sword, merely because Love had gone against her." Even Westervelt, at her grave, knows better than this. The world, concludes Coverdale, should throw open "all its avenues to the passport of a woman's bleeding heart" (p. 241). The vision is derivative just as the language which describes it is shabby. But Coverdale's failure of perception here, antecedent to his failure as artist, should come as no surprise. Much earlier, with his narrator's arrival at Blithedale, Hawthorne has prepared the reader for this moment. His new friends, particularly Zenobia, understand that Coverdale will be poet in residence, which means a continuation of his role as romantic poet now put to the service of the brotherhood; Coverdale, however, apparently expects that his new life will be the source for an art that will be qualitatively different from his previous work.[9] Perhaps now, he says to Zenobia, he will write something deserving the name of poetry—"true, strong, natural, and sweet, as is the life which we are going to lead—something that shall have the notes of wild-birds twittering through it, or a strain like the wind-anthems in the woods" (p. 14). If this remark does nothing else, it establishes Coverdale as a thoroughly undistinguished talent of Mainstream Romantic. Although Hawthorne protects his readers from knowing at first hand any of his protagonist's productions, the implications are clear. The new experience should result in work more ambitious and more significant than the mechanical competence which finally attracts the attention of Rufus W. Griswold. Now to be tested are the depth and breadth of Coverdale's artistic powers, and the crucial question has implications both personal and aesthetic. Can this creator of trivial art show himself to be more than trivial? Can he in fact create something better than trivial art? The results are not promising. If there is tragedy attendant upon Zenobia's fate, it takes shape, outside and beyond the range of Coverdale's perceptions. If there is tragedy attendant upon Hollingsworth's abortive scheme for the reformation of criminals, its resonances are heard despite Coverdale's assessment of the man.

Coverdale's "romance," then, is one of the thinner kinds. It is compounded of soaring passions—most of them misdirected and coming to grim fruition. Two linked ironies emerge—that a self-confessed idler whose lack of purpose has rendered his life "all an emptiness" should denounce and hound someone else whose errors have dried up his "rich juices," and that the rich potentialities of artistic re-

[9] Terence Martin stresses the narrator's search for a role, a search seen largely in theatrical imagery that reinforces the position of Coverdale as spectator. See *Nathaniel Hawthorne* (New York, 1965), pp. 151-157.

newal should wither to the point where Coverdale can divert the tragedy of Zenobia into conventional nineteenth-century melodrama.

IV

The Blithedale Romance stands as its own critique of Coverdale. As a memoir, it contains the testing of himself as a man; the memoir itself is the test of Coverdale the artist. He fails the first test, and only ironically does he pass the second. A bittersweet narrative, not wind-anthems or onomatopoetic songs about twittering birds, is Coverdale's ultimate response.

If Coverdale's focus in his narrative is blurred by a multiplicity of subjects (Hollingsworth, Zenobia, Old Moodie, his own routine urban life as well as his one ambivalent adventure in communal living), Hawthorne's focus on Coverdale is as sharp, intense, and composed a bit of portraiture as that provided by other first-person narratives of the nineteenth century. One of the remarkable accomplishments of *Blithedale* is Hawthorne's novelistic exploration of a theme most commonly seen in those tales written as romances, allegories, or exempla. Coverdale, a man whose emotional deficiency isolates him from the human mainstream, joins the ranks of Wakefield, Ethan Brand, Roger Chillingworth, Aylmer ("The Birthmark"), and Giovanni ("Rappaccini's Daughter"); but unlike them, he seems to exist in an actual and multidimensional society which asserts its own claims beyond the rather rigid ones he chooses to acknowledge. Hawthorne allows his protagonist entry into a wide area of contemporary life, the pleasing urbanities of society in the city, the not-so-pleasing physical demands of life in the country, the low-powered lyceum entertainments in the villages. Though in writing his memoir Coverdale thinks and acts as the romancer, Hawthorne renders the context in which Coverdale moves with the kind of circumstantial detail, the observations of commonplace reality, which occur more often in Hawthorne's notebooks than in his fiction.

Readers find Coverdale as unsatisfactory as do most of his fellow participants in the Blithedale brotherhood, and for much the same reasons: his reticence to commit himself humanly to others and his dilettantish curiosity. Both his reticence and his curiosity are expressions of a man whose frustrated search for meaning leads him to the dubious comfort of "conjectured" reconstructions of events and their significance.

Coverdale's insufficiency as man or artist cannot be justified or wished away, but lurking about this narrator is something more than mere obtuseness or inexcusable behavior. Many of Hawthorne's protagonists—saints and sinners alike—suffer from spiritual rigidity, obsessiveness, isolation, and the cold heart which threatens their moral survival; but unlike most of them, Coverdale displays a sense of humor, a tonic irony directed toward himself as well as others, a distancing perspective which permits disclosure of those ambivalences pulling him from one inadequate footing to another. With these characteristics Hawthorne extends the complexities only suggested by his customary quasi-allegorical figures into a narrator more fictively realistic. The gain is substantial. For this character whose dilemma is neither so domestic as Wakefield's nor so apocalyptic as Ethan Brand's, Hawthorne succeeds in projecting a situation that is understated, bland, and modern in its horror onto a consciousness singularly unequipped to perceive the horror. That very disparity allows Hawthorne to lavish his full creative attention on a character who, despite an irritating and acerbic ineffectuality, stands revealed as pathetic.

For all the annoying complacency in which he cloaks himself, Coverdale still possesses a certain frail honesty which makes his failures humanly, even poignantly, understandable. The reader is not surprised, for example, when he asserts, on practically the last page of his narrative, that he would still be willing to die for a just cause provided "the effort did not involve an unreasonable amount of trouble," because this is precisely the attitude he reveals in Chapter 1, when he expresses a willingness to do Old Moodie a favor if it involves "no special trouble" to himself. Early or late, Coverdale never disguises his arid emotions. What gives this account both its chill and its pathos is the realization that at its end nothing has changed. Even more pathetic, however, is the realization that Coverdale fails to understand his limited nature; his experiences, though traumatic, contribute nothing to his potential self-knowledge. It is a horrifying self-portrait of a man whose divided sensibilities are never harmonized, whose purposelessness is never replaced by purpose, and whose inability to love continues to be trivialized by fantasy.

Except for the final chapter, Coverdale seems not to see his narrative as a confession. But in its larger perspective, Hawthorne surely means for his readers to see it as such. This protagonist is not an Underground or Superfluous Man. Those Russian figures, alive as they are to every suggestion of suffering, grope messily and blatantly for some meaning to their separated lives. Coverdale, however, covers his tracks, throwing off pursuit by the civility of his personality, and presumes that sickness is to be found in souls other than his own. His document, for all its veneer of control and self-sufficiency, is confessional, and its complexity comes not from Coverdale's bland exposition but from Hawthorne's manipulation of his narrator's character.

The key to that character is Coverdale's idealism. Behind the aloofness, behind the witty and abrasive language, stands the man of good will who insists that the ideal represented by the Blithedale experiment is one to which he once genuinely subscribed. Moreover, at the end of the narrative he strongly suggests that of that little band of reformers, only he has remained faithful to its high undertaking. The adventure is a crucial one for Coverdale; and both the substance and the style of his account bespeak the poignant efforts of a man struggling to redeem himself morally and aesthetically. Alone of the major characters, including even the frail and ill-used Priscilla, Coverdale engages in no real deceptions, has no past worthy of concealing, offers no covert reformist schemes as alternatives to the community; but despite those admirable, if negative, virtues, he is concerned exclusively with ideal relationships. He is unprepared to accept, or at first even to acknowledge, the imperfect human context in which the ideal must realize itself if it is to realize itself at all. The idea of brotherhood, like a high and certainly cloudy romance, continues to attract him more than a decade after the collapse of Blithedale. As Hawthorne makes clear, however, the *idea* of brotherhood is not sufficient for redemption. Hollingsworth and Zenobia come to experience the full human implications when idealism and factuality clash, which is another way of saying that they attain a tragic self-awareness denied Coverdale.

Coverdale's very inability to do full justice to his Blithedale fellows ironically allows a self-concentration—the disclosure of character broader and richer than is possible in the portrayal of Hollingsworth, Zenobia, and Priscilla. Hawthorne's choice of a first-person narrator provides an obvious but functional hiatus of information at several crucial moments throughout the narrative. Zenobia, for example, tells

Coverdale that he has returned to Blithedale "half an hour too late" to witness a climactic scene between her and Hollingsworth, and Coverdale with some chagrin admits the missed opportunity:

And what subjects had been discussed here? All, no doubt, that, for so many months past, had kept my heart and my imagination idly feverish. Zenobia's whole character and history; the true nature of her mysterious connection with Westervelt; her later purposes towards Hollingsworth, and, reciprocally, his in reference to her; and, finally, the degree in which Zenobia had been cognizant of the plot against Priscilla, and what, at last, had been the real object of that scheme. On these points, as before, I was left to my own conjectures. (pp. 215-216)

Considering the consummate effectiveness of the final scaffold scene in *The Scarlet Letter,* it is somewhat surprising that Hawthorne should pass up an opportunity to dramatize what would normally have been its counterpart in this work. Technically, of course, Hawthorne limits himself: to supply information unavailable to Coverdale would violate point of view, even with the latitude generally enjoyed by the romancer. He as well as his narrator must remain content with Coverdale's "conjectures." But why should Hawthorne deliberately delay his narrator's arrival for the key scene thirty minutes too late? Dramatized or not, this is the climactic moment in the action, the moment from which Zenobia's death and funeral and Hollingsworth's remorse inevitably follow. A simple adjustment, coming so late in the narrative, would have necessitated no radical changes in plot progression or character development. The answer lies in consistency of characterization. If Hawthorne had finally given his narrator full access to those subjects about which he had been "feverish" for several months, a vital aspect of Coverdale's character—mischievous curiosity—would have been mitigated. By keeping Coverdale in ignorance Hawthorne maintains the careful ambivalence with which he imbues his narrator from the beginning. Disallowing him the final and most important revelations is a deft tactic. It not only sustains the too-little-too-late aspect of Coverdale with which the reader has come to be so familiar; it also marks an innovative imagination at work—in its tidy culmination, the romance form is in this case skewed just enough to deprive both narrator and reader of full gratification. Both must be content with the "conjectures" of one limited man whose partial view is not only self-evident but also self-admitted.

It is tempting to sympathize with Hollingsworth's impatience with Coverdale's fashionable airs or with Zenobia's exasperation when she accuses him of "Bigotry; self-conceit; an insolent curiosity; a meddlesome temper; a cold-blooded criticism . . . ; a monstrous scepticism . . ." (p. 170). But the reader knows Coverdale better than his friends know him, and for all his flaws, he is not quite a monster.[10] He is, to be sure, a "frosty bachelor" who takes too keen an interest in indulging his curiosity; and coupled to his ineffectual and rigid idealism is a mannered style which paradoxically establishes him as a frivolous dabbler among solemn socialists. When he is not being the abrasive wit, he is the moralistic meddler. His customary moral posture is a little silly, but, more important, it is also sad. It dooms him from any further emotional growth, either in or out of Blithedale. The personal renewal promised by the new life is aborted, and with it goes the chance for artistic renewal. Thus, Coverdale will recast his Blithedale experiences according to both what he knows (which is limited enough) and what he feels—pity and exasperation in dangerous proportions.

What Hawthorne achieves in this work is a sense of the human costs of failure, the pathos of weakness, without any diminishment of his own tough-minded standards for the conduct of life. In no other work does he succeed so well in dramatizing emptiness and purposelessness; in no other work does he sacrifice so many of the comfortable conventions of allegory or moral apologue or legend for the more difficult challenges of the realistic memoir, exchanging (in currently fashionable terms) telling for showing. Coverdale looks forward to James's emotional cripples (Marcher of "The Beast in the Jungle," Winterbourne of *Daisy Miller,* or Acton of *The Europeans*) and beyond them—to the desperate expatriates of Fitzgerald's and Hemingway's fiction and to the hollow men of Eliot's earlier poems.[11]

---

[10] It is surely a misplaced emphasis to suggest, as readers occasionally do, that Coverdale's speculative detachment destroys Blithedale and that his spoiler instincts aggravate and hasten the personal tragedies of Zenobia and Hollingsworth. The latter two characters pursue destruction out of the strength of their own wills. And common sense, as well as the logic of the narrative, says that Blithedale must fail with or without Coverdale. Its presumptuous example of the higher possibilities for living, directed at crass society at large, is articulated by physical withdrawal from that society (though, significantly, not to the point of disdaining agricultural competition).

[11] Roy R. Male sees Coverdale as the fictive ancestor of such modern intellectuals as Prufrock and Robert Penn Warren's Jack Burden. See *Hawthorne's Tragic Vision* (Austin, 1957), pp. 151–155. John C. Stubb remarks that to achieve a fusion of the comic and the tragic, "Hawthorne had to invent the Jamesian narrator before James" (*The Pursuit of Form:*

In permitting Coverdale virtually to construct his self, his voice, his configuring nuances, Hawthorne releases the ironic possibilities of a narrating intelligence who unconsciously steps beyond the limits which, as a romancer, he consciously observes.

A Study of Hawthorne and the Romance, Urbana, Ill., 1970, p. 136). See also Nicholas Canaday, Jr., "Community and Identity at Blithedale," *South Atlantic Quarterly,* LXXI (Winter, 1972), 30–39.

Beyond Convention: The Dynamics of Imagery and Response in Hawthorne's Early Sense of Evil

David Downing

EARLY in his career Hawthorne modeled his tales according to conventional literary structures. He combined the popular gothic and romantic conventions of his day with the more rigid doctrines of his cultural and familial ancestry, rooted in the Calvinist belief in the natural depravity of man. Puritan typology even offered itself as a kind of literary model: the minister's duty (like the writer's?) was to read and decode the sensible world as a system of signs revelatory of God's works and intent. Despite the pressure of these conventions, however, Hawthorne created his own unique vision. In this essay I shall examine two stories which serve for Hawthorne as tentative explorations that will later propel him beyond the limits of traditional forms.[1]

In "The Hollow of the Three Hills," Hawthorne uses conventional symbolic representations such as darkness, desolation, and witchcraft. Within this external framework, he creates an experience of evil that includes a series of perceptual impressions lacking in formal or objective detail, but which nevertheless have more far-reaching consequences than the predominant gothic terror. Narrative action and plot have been reduced to a bare minimum. A beautiful young woman afflicted with a strange "untimely blight" seeks the aid of

---

[1] Among studies of Hawthorne's tales I have found the following particularly helpful in this essay: Nina Baym, *The Shape of Hawthorne's Career* (Ithaca, N.Y., 1976), pp. 15–83; Stanley Brodkin, "Hawthorne and the Function of History: A Reading of 'Alice Doane's Appeal,'" *The Nathaniel Hawthorne Journal 1974*, ed. C. E. Frazer Clark, Jr. (Englewood, Col., 1975), pp. 116–128; Clinton S. Burhans, Jr., "Hawthorne's Mind and Art in 'The Hollow of the Three Hills,'" *Journal of English and Germanic Philology*, LX (April, 1961), 286–295; Frederick Crews, *The Sins of the Fathers: Hawthorne's Psychological Themes* (New York, 1966), pp. 3–60; Kenneth Dauber, *Rediscovering Hawthorne* (Princeton, N.J., 1977), pp. 47–86; Prabhat K. Pandeya, "The Drama of Evil in 'The Hollow of the Three Hills,'" *The Nathaniel Hawthorne Journal 1975*, ed. C. E. Frazer Clark, Jr. (Englewood, Col., 1975), pp. 177–181; Ely Stock, "Witchcraft in 'Hollow,'" *American Transcendental Quarterly*, XIV (Spring, 1972), 31-33.

American Literature, Volume LI, Number 4, January, 1980. Copyright © 1980 by Duke University Press.

a decrepit old woman steeped in the lore of witchcraft. The nocturnal meeting begins at sunset in the "mathematically" symmetrical hollow between three hills. The ritual incantations of the aged crone precipitate three hypnotic or hallucinatory visions of the life of the young woman. The whole story consists of little more than the metaphorical filling up of the stagnant hollow with the successive visions of the woman's loneliness and separation beginning with a domestic image of the bereaved parents and ending with the funeral march of the abandoned child she has apparently left to die.

Beyond the initial suggestion of adultery, Hawthorne supplies us with no specific reasons for the woman's strange losses. His fictional world, however, actively engages the reader in the poetics of distance and immediacy. By approaching his subject through the distance of conventional tropes—an "untimely blight" has stricken the "natural bloom" of the young woman—Hawthorne skirts the subconscious depths of his material and leaves us with a genuine interpretive problem. But he also employs rhythm and imagery in new and significant ways that enable him to fuse a coherent experience out of nonspecific materials. The images of decay and infestation, with their necessarily bodily meanings, function as metaphors for bodily and psychical processes, and the narrative rhythm intensifies the imagery by a gradual buildup and fusion of the energies conveyed by the various images in the three visions. The rhythm depends not just on the symmetrical geometry of the scenes, but on the emotional intensification carried over from scene to scene: from decay and sorrow to madness to isolation and death.

The narrative rhythm itself has a double function which illustrates the aesthetic dilemma. The rhythm defends against a prolonged probing of individual lives, but it also energizes one's reading experience so as to prevent what Hawthorne could see as the dangerous urge to systematically dissect meanings merely to find a single source for the woman's "untimely blight." Given the symbolic framework of "Hollow," Hawthorne teases us to employ the theological construct of natural depravity as an interpretive tool. But the text resists this closure—it represents a form of disengagement from the text which, if extreme, amounts to an unnatural separation of the individual from the larger cultural history in which we are all involved. Within this story we cannot even draw clear boundaries between individual characters—the separate voices of the mob join in unison; we cannot be sure who is actually having or creating the visions: the old woman's magic, the young woman's dreaming, a combination of the two, or some power controlling both. The point is that all contribute, and we need not make those separations.

Hawthorne's only attempt to come to terms with such boundaries within the world of the hollow occurs in a superficial way in his description of the setting. The "almost mathematically circular" shape of the hollow provides for a separation or juxtaposition of natural and unnatural. Like the concavity of a lens, the hollow vale focuses on the "putrid waters" of a stagnant pool so contaminated with the "powers of evil" as to push the beauty of the natural world far to the periphery: the rich colors of the sunset gild the three hill-tops, but only "a paler tint stole down their sides" into this vortex of human depravity. Within the hollow, however, boundaries dissolve. The decayed body of the old crone fuses with the decayed waters of the pool. Traditional images of darkness and moonlight reinforce the sense of the hollow as the heart; the shape of the hollow suggests a woman's sexual organs. The source of emotional and sexual power is dead and decaying, its blood turned to the bile-green waters of the infested pool. As conventional boundaries dissolve, the vision of evil becomes generalized to include the young woman, the entire village, and, in turn, the entire human race. The strange "untimely blight" of the young woman may then suggest a youthful foreshadowing of the "withered, shrunken, and decrepit" aspects of the old crone.

Hawthorne fuels the story with the underlying fantasy of yielding to the old crone: the mother figure, whose body, heart, and sexual organs have decayed, engulfs the guilt-ridden daughter. All taboos against evil have been broken, and fear of drowning in the deadly pool propels the hallucinatory vision. Hawthorne recognizes the solipsistic dangers of the internalized fantasy (it leads to meaningless idiosyncrasy), and he seeks to relate it to more external, cultural conditions. He links the terrifying vision of isolation with a socially acceptable vision of home life.

In the first vision, we are given a glimpse of the young woman's parents, now old and broken by sorrow. The home and hearth appear as a distinct space, totally separated from the poisonous world of the hollow: "Those strangers appeared not to stand in the hollow depth

. . ." (p. 5)[2] But the "appearance" is little more than just that. Although the young woman is surely an outcast and may not return home, the similarities between home and hollow may be more important than the literal separation. The old couple is described in words similar to those used to describe the old crone: they are "aged," "broken and decayed." They are broken not only by the dishonorable daughter, but by "other and more recent woe." If they are bound to a moral code as Hawthorne knew most Puritans to be, then the rigid code may make it difficult for the parents to ever forgive the errant daughter. In this way they may contribute directly to the daughter's forced isolation. While "their voices were encompassed and re-echoed by the walls of a chamber," those walls surrounding the world of the hearth can hardly be experienced as secure boundaries. The echoing walls may be the echoing hollow which actually houses the vision, and the voices easily blend with the lonely breeze between the hills. The woeful separation of the old couple appears of a piece with the woeful separation of the young woman.

We have no way of establishing more definite connections, but the presence of decay provides enough energy to carry us into the second vision—the gothic heart of the story. Following (as if beneath the surface) the sorrowful mourning of the parents, the narrator plunges into this chaotic ménage of primal explosions, a passage which would become entirely chaotic and undeveloped except for several key images and phrases within the paragraph. Evil for Hawthorne will repeatedly be associated with bizarre passions and frenzied laughter. Consider the following passage:

Shrieks pierced through the obscurity of sound, and were succeeded by the singing of sweet female voices, which, in their turn, gave way to a wild roar of laughter, broken suddenly by groanings and sobs, forming altogether a ghastly confusion of terror and mourning and mirth. Chains were rattling, fierce and stern voices uttered threats, and the scourge resounded at their command. (p. 6)

The diabolical nature of this "wild scene" is associated with the release of unbound passions, but under specific conditions. Although the women hear a mob whose passion is unbounded and limitless, they are literally bound with rattling chains, threats, and commands.

[2] Nathaniel Hawthorne, *Selected Tales and Sketches,* ed. Hyatt Waggoner (New York, 1970), p. 6. All subsequent citations of Hawthorne's work are from this edition.

Indeed, as a literal account, the scene embodies an image of an external authority exercising its power by controlling the mob with such brutal means. Hawthorne will later enlarge and intensify such physical images of repression. Hollingsworth's "barrel-chested," "iron countenance" has its precursor in the iron chains. As an image, the rattling chains function in a way similar to the "mind-forged mannacles" in William Blake's poem, "London": external authorities exercise their control over both mind and body, and such culturally reinforced repressions of bodily experience produce disease and terror in London as well as in America.[3] The sporadic mixture of frenzied merriment and raging terror in Hawthorne's vision may reflect the disorganization of the rebellion and revenge against the controlling powers. Possibly it is disorganized because of the psychological imbalance produced by just those repressive powers represented in the story and thus in the culture.

When we examine this second vision more closely, we find that it also contains a rather simplistic division in the gothic imagery. The shrieks, wrath, sobs, and hysteria are juxtaposed against the "singing of sweet female voices," the "soft and dreamy accent of the love songs," and the "manly and melodious voice" of her bereaved husband. We have a sense of transition in which "the love songs ... died causelessly into funeral hymns." Hawthorne is trying to create a fictional experience which clarifies his own intuitive knowledge of the senseless loss of natural love consequent upon the perversion of these passions into death and terror.

Just as the voices of the aged parents blended with the wind in the hollow, so too the voices of this mob join in unison with the "fitful, and uneven sound of the wind." The third vision thus concludes with the inevitable sense of doom and death in the funeral march of the abandoned child. Here the two worlds blend even more fully: the social convention of the funeral cannot be clearly separated from the asocial perpetration of evil and death as experienced in the hollow where the body has likewise decayed. The young woman does not even raise her head to differentiate the two worlds. Perhaps she too has died and the funeral is her own. The wind in the hollow now seems to physically shake the very coffin in the vision. Incorporated

---

[3] Just like Hawthorne's story, Blake's poem begins by observing "marks of weakness, marks of woe" and concludes with blood, disease, and death. See: *The Poetry and Prose of William Blake,* ed. David V. Erdman (New York, 1970), pp. 26-27.

in this final image is the wife, daughter, and mother who has wronged the parents, betrayed the husband, and abandoned the child. Hawthorne supplies us with no details as to how or why the woman committed such abominable acts. The specifics are lost. But we do not lose the generalized sense of brutality. Indeed, it appears to be not just the woman who has "sinned against natural affection," but the whole culture itself. However undeveloped, this story shows Hawthorne working to describe a culture which he intuitively senses has produced a great deal more pain than pleasure.

Hawthorne concludes "The Hollow of the Three Hills" with the "withered crone, chuckling to herself . . . 'Here has been a sweet hour's sport!'" (p. 7) The gothic sarcasm seems consistent with the story's more conventional representations of evil delight in the suffering of others. But a significant aspect of Hawthorne's sense of evil involves just such a sadistic inversion of pain for pleasure. The old woman's total lack of sympathy for the plight of the suffering woman characterizes her inability to feel the natural flow of emotions in her "decayed" body and in her "diseased" imagination. The young woman's pain may serve as an unconscious mirror image of the crone's own youthful pain which she has now blocked from feeling by rigidly suppressing and converting it into sadistic delight. Disease and decay of the body are the inevitable consequences of such emotional twisting.

In "Alice Doane's Appeal," Hawthorne associates Leonard Doane's "diseased imagination" with the evils of incestuous jealousy and fraternal murder. And just as the witch in "Hollow" seemed to have control of the young woman, we find that a wizard in "Alice Doane's Appeal" has control of Leonard. Can we take Hawthorne seriously? He describes the wizard in "Appeal" as "a small, gray, withered man . . . senseless as an idiot and feebler than a child to all better purposes." (p. 130) The caustic humor of a world controlled by the reckless buffoonery of this wizard serves on one level as a reactionary antidote to the transcendentalists' humorless spiritualism. But the story itself reveals Hawthorne's awareness that such manipulating of the plot to make the wizard appear as the evil scapegoat solely accountable for psychological perversion of all sorts will hardly produce a satisfying response in his nongothic readers. Indeed, the shifts and breaks in this story reveal significant aspects of Hawthorne's ironic portrayal of himself struggling to create a more fully resonant fiction.

Hawthorne's understanding of the biopsychological nature of evil resists purely symbolic representation. He begins to reject the conventional notion of evil as merely a metaphysical given and represents it more as a cultural creation, at least insofar as it relates to the unnatural control of emotions conditioned by a culturally based fear of the body. In "Appeal" Hawthorne tries to account for the sources of the wizard's power in an otherwise unnecessary descriptive passage of the "town glittering in icy garments." (p. 134) "The creation of wizard power" Hawthorne attributes to a freezing of the emotions and heart. This image functions as an isomorphic metaphor—the qualities of "icy garments" correspond to an armoring of the physical body so as to prevent sensual relief in natural sexual forms. Nightmare and a barrage of destructive forces result, as in the hysterical mob in "Hollow" and in the march of the dead and accursed souls in the paragraph following the "fantastic piece of description" of the frozen city in "Appeal." While Hawthorne undoubtedly uses the wizard to defuse the threatening and unmanageable incestuous plot between Alice and her two brothers, he also suggests that the wizard's source of power derives from the "frigid glory" of the whole village—a village in which any one of the inhabitants might, at a given historical moment such as the witch hangings, be capable of becoming a witch or wizard. Thus: "One looked to behold inhabitants suited to such a town glittering in icy garments, with motionless features, cold sparkling eyes, and just sensation enough in their frozen hearts to shiver at each other's presence." (p. 134)

Hawthorne's self-conscious awareness of the limitations of such an image in an undeveloped fictional context can be seen in his hedging, in his calling it fantastic, as if he would even prefer to shake off the more serious implications while confessing that it's all a bit silly and extravagant. Such descriptive exuberance might succumb to being just another in the list of gothic extremes of the original story "Alice Doane," which lacked both depth and originality. But Hawthorne does not really prefer the silly gothicism, and even his sarcastic hedging takes a serious turn when Hawthorne portrays himself as a narrator struggling from out of the gothic and into the psychological and historical: on the premise that "our history had been very imperfectly written," the stated intention of "Appeal" is to explore the "universal madness" of "guilt and frenzy . . . which . . . consummated the most execrable scene that our history blushes to record." (p. 127)

The major advance of "Appeal" over "Hollow" is that while the latter remains tied to "those strange old times, when fantastic dreams and madmen's reveries were realized among the actual circumstances of life" (p. 3), the former story joins the gothic horrors of incest and murder with the historical horror of the actual hangings on Gallows Hill in the 1692 witch hunt. Indeed, the importance of this story lies in Hawthorne's understanding of a key psychological parity at the heart of both gothic and historic extremes of cruelty.

Hawthorne incorporates within this story the self-reflexive quest for a fiction capable of deeply moving, even changing, his actual readers. A narrator portrayed as a young writer leads two young ladies to Gallows Hill where he reads them a gothic tale he has written about incest and murder. Ironically, the search for fictional intensity thrives on the repressed wish for power and control over his audience, and Hawthorne comes close to a manipulative, wizardly control of emotions and events. He parodies this effect by having his narrator attempt to control and heighten the response of the ladies by not only fictionally but also literally moving them about, directing them first to Gallows Hill, then to a grave, then to the woodwax on the hill. For example, as the fictionalized narrator reads the account of Alice and her brother approaching the graveyard of "the murdered man who was buried three days before" (p. 134), the narrator simultaneously leads the two ladies "to a new made grave." Hawthorne and his fictionalized narrator seem to merge when it becomes unclear who voices the final sentence: "suddenly there was a multitude of people among the graves." Hawthorne would like to fuse the gothic graves with the literal graves around which the narrator is standing. And he partially succeeds with this control: his audience of two remains silently captive, and the narrator proceeds into the gothic vision arising from the grave.

This vision corresponds to the gothic vision in "Hollow," and again we find the sadistic inversion of pleasure for pain when the accursed souls look at each other "with glances of hatred and smiles of bitter scorn, passions that are to devils what love is to the blest." (p. 136) The narrator ends this "apparition" with the confession that it was "too shadowy for language to portray." The specifics of the gothic plot would become unmanageable for him to explore further, and we are left with the quick summary of the plot ending with Alice's appeal to her brother Walter. As the narrator admits: he "dare not give the remainder of the scene except in very brief epitome." (p. 136)

Hawthorne toys with the narrator's limitations (his need to avoid something) through the melodramatic irony of these admissions. We are left with the suggestion that language need not be so "shadowy," that it could do a better job than the obscure visions the narrator has thus far offered us. But here is an instance when it becomes difficult to determine just where Hawthorne stands in relation to his text. The aesthetic distance verges on collapse as the author may be identifying a little too closely with his narrator. The irony threatens to break down into literal confession, and the narrator quickly drops the gothic plot. The only achievement of the "brief epitome" has been silence and perhaps momentary awe on the part of the ladies. In frustration, the narrator steps outside his narrative to point out that the nearby woodwax "had sprouted originally from . . . Walter's . . . unhallowed bones." The ladies suddenly break into laughter.

The narrator recognizes these failures of the gothic contrivance, but he also understands the underlying connections embedded in both the gothic and the historic plots, whereas the ladies' conventional expectations defend against the threatening perceptions. By acquiescence to social conventions and to such "acceptable" and "proper" literary taste, their "gentility" so limits their own responsiveness that they rigidly avoid or deny close contact with unpleasant experiences. As a result, the narrator feels "a little piqued that a narrative which had good authority in our ancient superstitions, and would have brought even a church deacon to Gallows Hill, in old witch times, should now be considered too grotesque and extravagant for timid maids to tremble at." (p. 137) But recovering from his justifiable frustration and now inspired by the literal "indistinctness" of twilight, the narrator gives up the "icy splendor" of the gothic tale and entrances his two listeners with an imaginative description of the actual hangings themselves as they might have taken place on Gallows Hill. And sure enough, this fictionalized account "reaches the seldom trodden places of their hearts." Even though it here attains to a somewhat gothic sentimentality, Hawthorne has been searching for a natural power in the "well-spring of tears," a power diametrically opposed to the wizardlike denial of emotional warmth and vulnerability.

The historical actuality provides clear and resonating connections with the culture of the young ladies. Their response no longer ends in gothic mystery—for this can be laughed away. Nor can they glibly deny the psychological underpinnings of both Leonard's individual hysteria and Salem's mass hysteria. They can feel the common criminality of these hysterias: both Alice and those who were hanged during the witch hunt were victimized by a disturbed people. And the experience of death, the senseless killing of innocent bodies, becomes the final undoer of the genteel defenses of the narrator's two lady companions. Now they too have a sense of the guilt which they may share as the present-day upholders of the society which once committed such atrocities.

The failures of the gothic tale have provided the grounds for the success of the historic tale. "Appeal" hangs not only on a structural parallel between the tales, but also on an emotional fusion in the tone and content of the two plots. The gothic terror carries over from one to the other, although the moment of mirth between the two tales breaks the gothic extravagance down into a kind of muted glow or emotional residue which blends into the subjectivity represented by the twilight: natural phenomenon such as "the crimson west" and the breeze become personified "as if responsive to" the mood of the ladies. The story has been working towards this responsiveness where artificial boundaries between past and present dissolve: "Twilight over the landscape was congenial to the obscurity of time." (p. 137) As contexts change from gothic to present/historical, the image of twilight functions with aesthetic precision. It accurately reflects a phenomenological quality of the natural world: at dusk, boundaries do become hazy. But also, the insight and response which emerge from the ensuing historic plot are both sharp and powerful.

We may account for this apparent contradiction between sharply felt insights and hazy boundaries by reconsidering the case of the young women. As twilight descends, the boundaries between their inner experience and the outside world become more permeable. Hawthorne uses the words "blend" and "intermingled" to describe this condition: "An indistinctness had begun to creep over the mass of buildings and blend them with the intermingled tree-tops . . ." (p. 137). The human artifacts (buildings) blend with the natural world (tree-tops). The blending applies equally well to individual psychologies. Conventional boundaries no longer hinder the flow of energies represented by the glow of twilight. The women's need to maintain the artificial defenses of sociability decreases proportionally because these defenses are useful only when the external social world is clearly visible and defined. We find evidence for the connection between twilight and subjectivity in the overall changes the women will undergo at this time of day: their personal identities simply have more room to expand (or grow) when defensive borders become hazy rather than rigid. Concomitantly, their vulnerability to the forces in the outside world increases. The twilight represents not only a haziness but a readiness to take in experience, especially affective, emotional experience which cannot be easily intellectualized and defined. The narrator proceeds to call upon his own "share of feeling and fancy" to relate the historical "facts."

Hawthorne thus suggests that genuine historical vision occurs only when one becomes vulnerable to the entire emotional and psychological context involving the intermingling of boundaries between the experience of one's present and the historical past. Theoretically stated, the fullness of subjective responsiveness (unarmored experience) provides the preconditions for objective knowledge and critical insight. The quality of fullness or receptivity may be as natural as the twilight, yet, paradoxically, we rarely find it in Hawthorne's characters or in his fictional world. In this story, however, Hawthorne begins to imagine a kind of responsiveness, beyond convention, in which one can dialectically move between inside and outside, subjective and objective, without severely interfering with or short-circuiting the perceptions via one's idiosyncratic defenses, wishes, or fantasies. Given these conditions, the tone of Leonard's declamatory rant as he tells his story to the wizard corresponds to the frenzied intensity of the mob leading the condemned to the gallows. Hawthorne's portrayal of the Puritan superstitious intolerance revives the original intensity of the harmless nineteenth-century genteel intolerance of literary extremes reflected in the two women's defensive superficiality.

The violence in both plots derives from a noticeable impairment of judgment: the natural reasoning and perceptive powers of human beings have been severely maligned by the world in which they live. Leonard's judgment becomes impaired when Walter Brome's hints of a vile seduction drive Leonard's incestuous jealousy to a demonic intensity. Walter serves as the catalyst which ignites Leonard's unconscious upheaval, but the original impairment of Leonard's judgment occurs long before, in a childhood trauma: Leonard recalls the dim memory of his father murdered during an Indian raiding party. Historical forces thus play a part in controlling and violating Leonard's life before he can ever defend himself or understand what has happened.

The apparition of his father's murder emerges during Leonard's confession to the wizard of his murder of Walter Brome. As the dead Walter lay at his feet, the childhood vision of his dead father overwhelms Leonard ". . . with the sensation of one who struggles through a dream. . . . Me thought I stood a weeping infant by my father's hearth; by the cold and blood-stained hearth where he lay dead." (p. 132) The struggle with the dream is a struggle with the dark powers of the unconscious which threaten to overwhelm him. Leonard tries ineffectually to control the upsurge of violent and destructive impulses. He turns to the wizard: the one person least likely to help him. His hysterical frenzy increases until he becomes vulnerable to deception. As Stanley Brodkin suggests: "he is . . . unable to distinguish between a gust of wind and the wizard's laugh which mocks the 'indubitable proofs' (p. 132) of Alice's guilt, proofs which the wizard knows are unreal."[4]

The "indubitable proofs" parody the "spectral evidence" of the witchcraft trials where the hallucinatory visions of young children who claimed to be afflicted by witches acquired the legal status of "spectral evidence." Merely on the basis of their unprovable claims, nineteen people were condemned by the law to be hung on Gallows Hill. That the demonic deceptions of these children could be accepted as adequate proofs of an individual's guilt parallels Leonard's demonic deception at the hands of the wizard. But whereas Leonard— neither as a fatherless child nor as a disturbed adult—has no one to trust, no supporting culture or folklore to fall back on, the disturbed children of Salem found their visionary powers idolized by the "dis-

[4] Brodkin, pp. 120-121.

eased imagination" of the entire culture. The sexual and Oedipal confusions Hawthorne outlines at the core of even such an imperfectly rendered character as Leonard provide insight into similar sexual and Oedipal confusions in the members of any culture afflicted by a disturbance comparable in nature to that of the witchcraft craze.[5] Leonard's sexual hallucinations become fixated on individual members within the family, whereas the sexual hallucinations of the young children of the witchcraft craze, supported by a folklore, could reach outside the family and fixate on any member of the culture.

Either way, fixation is a measure of unresponsiveness. The wizard, Leonard, and both children and adults in the Puritan society have all become immune to the natural flow of sympathy for the suffering of others. The cost of this immunity reverberates throughout the story. The extremes of death and pain magnify a disturbance more intrinsic to their epistemology than a momentary breach in the cultural values which are supposed to eliminate these forces. The normal Puritan dependence on the visible signs of the natural world as evidence of God's presence opposed the replacement in 1692 with immediate, invisible, "spectral evidence" without recourse to provable natural signs. In Hawthorne's story, however, we may experience the more fundamental connection between these two modes (verbal typology vs. sudden intuition), in any culture which places as much, if not more, credibility on another world besides (or beyond) our bodily existence. In this sense the visible evidence supporting the "words" of the ministers is not all that different in kind than the invisible evidence of the "words" of the afflicted children. They both point towards a world we can neither see nor feel nor touch with our senses.

Responsiveness to the potential qualities in Hawthorne's text may depend on an openness to the physical world as experienced through our bodies. From the symbolic presence of the "vile and ineradicable weed" which "blasted the spot" on Gallows Hill with "a physical curse," the story moves quickly to the murdered corpse of Walter Brome and the hysteria of Leonard Doane. These initial sensations of bodies being menaced (Leonard's, at least emotionally, beginning

---

[5] Among studies of witchcraft I have found the following two sources particularly helpful in this essay: H. R. Trevor-Roper, *The European Witch-Craze of the 16th and 17th Centuries* (Harmonsworth, Eng., 1969); Larzer Ziff, *Puritanism in America* (New York, 1973), pp. 229–250.

with his father's murder) provide the affective grounds for our reading experience. Through the activity of critical insight, we are led to a critique of the underlying values of the patriarchal society which establishes the conditions for both Indian raids and witch hunts.

From the reverse direction, we find that as Hawthorne plunges deeper into the seemingly invisible world of words and language, he finds himself carried deeper into his own body and his own culture. He does not always like what he finds, but he employs various ways to communicate those dark insights without letting them destroy either himself or his art. As we have seen in these two early stories, and throughout his writing during the 1830's, Hawthorne draws heavily on the material of his native history so as to redirect his literary plunge away from his solipsistic self-consciousness. "Hollow" and "Appeal" focus on Puritan America, but it is only natural that he would also turn to the most significant series of events in American history culminating in the Revolution of 1776. The nature of the psychological insights embedded in the early stories help to illuminate the more complex and successful stories such as "My Kinsman, Major Molineux." We can more easily understand why the familiar Oedipal and sexual dimensions are not just Hawthorne's limiting obsessions but reflect actual dimensions of the psycho-historical moment.

Nathaniel Hawthorne and His Mother:
A Biographical Speculation

Nina Baym

EVERY student of Nathaniel Hawthorne's work and life knows that he wrote *The Scarlet Letter* because he lost his job at the Salem Custom House. He told the world so in his autobiographical preface to the story, "The Custom-House," and all later biographers have followed his lead while filling out the details.[1] But the sequence of events Hawthorne chronicles in the preface explains no more than how he came to be free to write, and offers no factual basis for understanding what he wrote. To be sure, his angry and defiant heroine might express some of his own humiliation and rage. To write a story which favored the outcast so heavily against the establishment might have been an act of sweet revenge on the author's powerful enemies.

I

But such connections are remote. The essence of Hester's character and story (not to mention Dimmesdale's) is untouched. Why did Hawthorne pick a woman protagonist? Why a lone woman? Why a mother? To the extent that we seek biographical explanations for such choices we are probably always limited to surmise rather than certain knowledge. But it seems fair to say that the biographical accounts we now have do not offer hypotheses which engage with these questions.

Another event occurred in Hawthorne's life at the same time, exactly, that he was dismissed from the Custom House. On 30 July 1849, only six days after the new surveyor was appointed, his mother died. Her health had long been fragile, but she had lived to be sixty-

---

[1] See Hubert H. Hoeltje, "The Writing of *The Scarlet Letter*," *New England Quarterly*, 27 (1954), 326–46, and Stephen Nissenbaum, "The Firing of Nathaniel Hawthorne," *Essex Institute Historical Collections*, 114 (1978), 57–86.

nine years old. She was residing in Hawthorne's house (as were his two sisters, both unmarried) when she succumbed to a sudden, relatively brief illness which took the author by surprise. He was greatly affected by her death, coming near to a "brain fever" after her burial on 2 August. Six days later he was writing for the first time of leaving Salem, "this abominable city," forever, as indeed he was to do after finishing *The Scarlet Letter*. By early September he had recovered from his illness and begun *The Scarlet Letter,* working with an intensity that almost frightened his wife, and with a speed that brought the book to completion before the year ended. He was inspired as he had never been before, or was to be again.[2]

Common sense suggests that a work following so immediately on the death of a mother, featuring a heroine who is a mother (and whose status as a mother is absolutely central to her situation), might very likely be inspired by that death and consist, in its autobiographical substance, of a complex memorial to that mother. But one looks virtually in vain for a biographical analysis of *The Scarlet Letter* which pursues such a suggestion.[3] One looks in vain for a reliable, comprehensive account of Hawthorne's mother and his relationship with her. Instead, we have a longstanding and unreliable tradition about her which persists despite a quantity of countervailing evidence. This tradition permits critics to accuse her of a grotesque, pernicious role in his life or, alternatively, to deny her any role at all.

Mark Van Doren, one of the few skeptics, described the situation well: "His mother has long been the subject of a sentimental legend which no evidence supports. She is supposed, soon after her husband's death, to have shut herself away not only from the world but from the Mannings [her natal family] and her own children. There are hints of a darkened room where she takes her meals alone, says nothing, and mourns 'in a Hindoo seclusion' the irreparable sadness

---

[2] Arlin Turner, *Nathaniel Hawthorne, A Biography* (New York: Oxford, 1980), p. 208; Julian Hawthorne, *Nathaniel Hawthorne and His Wife* (Boston: Houghton Mifflin, 1884), I, 353-54 (henceforth cited parenthetically).

[3] Jean Normand, *Nathaniel Hawthorne: An Approach to an Analysis of Artistic Creation,* tr. Derek Coltman (Cleveland: Case Western Reserve Univ. Press, 1970), and John Franzosa, " 'The Custom-House,' *The Scarlet Letter,* and Hawthorne's Separation from Salem," *ESQ*, 24 (1978), 5-21, find the biographical significance of the romance to reside in the maternal figure of Hester, as I do. But both subsume this figure into larger, abstract schemes, Jungian and quasi-Freudian respectively, and ignore biographical detail.

of her lot. It appears on the contrary that she was an excellent cook, an attentive mother, and an interesting talker about things past and present. Her son's childhood letters to her, a number of which survive, are addressed to no such awful stranger as the legend suggests."[4] Van Doren could have added that some of her letters also survive, showing an active, outward-looking disposition and betraying no hint of reclusiveness. But despite evidence accumulated and publicized by such scholars as Norman Holmes Pearson, Randall Stewart, Manning Hawthorne, and (recently) Gloria Ehrlich, the legend persists in newer biographies.[5] Thus when we look for Hawthorne's mother we have to make our way past a legend constructed, it seems, to deny access.

It is not hard to understand why the legend has persisted. It has Hawthorne's own authority behind it, as well as the endorsement of his wife, his sister-in-law, and his son. For those seeking a reason for Hawthorne's supposed lifelong feelings of gloom and alienation, both the maternal rejection and her example of seclusion seem to provide clues. Such early biographers as George Woodberry, Lloyd Morris, Herbert Gorman, Robert Cantwell, and Newton Arvin depended heavily on the legend to explain the oddities of Hawthorne's imagination and his fiction. To other biographers seeking (for various reasons) to connect Hawthorne to the father he never knew and the father's family he had nothing to do with, her alleged absence allowed them to follow their preferences by writing her out of his life altogether. Among such biographers one must include Randall Stewart, Hubert Hoeltje, Arlin Turner, and James R. Mellow.

It is not especially difficult to understand the motives of Hawthorne's surviving family in transmitting to the public a misrepre-

---

[4] Mark Van Doren, *Nathaniel Hawthorne* (New York: Sloane, 1949), p. 9.

[5] Norman Holmes Pearson, "Elizabeth Peabody on Hawthorne," *Essex Institute Historical Collections*, 94 (1958), 256–76; Randall Stewart, "Recollections of Hawthorne by His Sister Elizabeth," *American Literature*, 16 (1945), 316–31; Manning Hawthorne, "Hawthorne's Early Years," *Essex Institute Historical Collections*, 74 (1938), 1–21; "Parental and Family Influences on Hawthorne," *Essex Institute Historical Collections*, 76 (1940), 1–13; "Nathaniel Hawthorne Prepares for College," *New England Quarterly*, 11 (1938), 66–68; "Maria Louise Hawthorne," *Essex Institute Historical Collections*, 75 (1939), 103–34; "Nathaniel Hawthorne at Bowdoin," *New England Quarterly*, 13 (1940), 246–79; "A Glimpse of Hawthorne's Boyhood," *Essex Institute Historical Collections*, 83 (1947), 178–84; Gloria Ehrlich, "Hawthorne and the Mannings," *Studies in the American Renaissance 1980* (Boston: Twayne, 1980), pp. 97–117.

sentation of his mother. The misrepresentation operated to their advantage, as we shall see; and in any case they would not have been likely to go against a story originating with Hawthorne himself. It is very puzzling, however, to make out Hawthorne's own motives in this case. But it is important to try to do so, for every conscious misrepresentation points to something hidden. Hawthorne seems to have been trying to hide not merely the actual role that his mother had played in his life, but the fact that she had a role at all. Such a denial—completely unnecessary in those innocent pre-Freudian days—only suggests that her role must have been very large indeed.

The legend made its first appearance of record in his early love letters to Sophia Peabody, where he writes of his mother's and sisters' eccentric reclusiveness, and the morbid atmosphere in their house, which he calls "Castle Dismal." (The phrase later became a favorite of Sophia's.) Later he resisted Sophia's urgings that he make their engagement known by citing "the strange reserve, in regard to matters of feeling, that has always existed among us. We are conscious of one another's feelings, always; but there seems to be a tacit law, that our deepest heart-concernments are not to be spoken of."[6]

These sentences have carried a good deal of weight with biographers who have taken them at face value instead of observing their highly literary character. They need to be examined for the equivocations of their rhetoric—the unallowable equation of an engagement with deepest, private heart-concernments, for example. And, while asserting the existence of "a strange reserve" these lines imply a group of people deeply attuned to one another's moods and hence, possibly, an understanding beyond the need for speech. In any event, people who are always conscious of one another's feelings must be in more or less constant contact. A particular irony of this letter is the way Hawthorne offers up its obfuscation to Sophia as exemplary of how he can gush out freely to her and to her only.

In fine, what we seem to have here is an instance of a lover's strategy, to claim that nobody understands him and thereby appear both more needy and more interesting in the beloved's eyes, all the

---

[6] *Love Letters of Nathaniel Hawthorne* (Chicago: Society of the DOFOBS, 1907), II, 78 (henceforth cited parenthetically).

while giving her the pleasure of enacting the heroine's role in his romantic drama. "Mine ownest," he wrote her on 4 October 1840, addressing her as though they were already married, "Here sits thy husband in his old accustomed chamber, where he used to sit in years gone by. . . . Sometimes (for I had no wife then to keep my heart warm) it seemed as if I were already in the grave, with only life enough to be chilled and benumbed . . . till at length a certain Dove was revealed to me, in the shadow of a seclusion as deep as my own had been. . . . So now I begin to understand why I was imprisoned so many years in this lonely chamber, and why I could never break through the viewless bolts and bars" (*Love Letters,* I, 223-24).

Sophia's limpid, unsophisticated imagination accepted the lover's hyperbole as literal truth, as Hawthorne expected—for he was aware of, and attracted to, the transparent sensibility which seemed the very opposite of his own. "I tell thee these things," he wrote, "in order that my Dove, into whose infinite depths the sunshine falls continually, may perceive what a cloudy veil stretches over the abyss of my nature" (*Love Letters,* II, 79). Her simple sincerity guaranteed that she would mistake the veil for the abyss. And, as a result of her mistake, she transmitted the legend through conversations and letters until it became an article of family faith.

Sophia was apparently not the only one to whom Hawthorne talked in this vein in the years before his marriage. When Julian Hawthorne was preparing a biography of his parents in the early 1880s he asked Elizabeth Peabody, Sophia's sister, to write up her recollection of Hawthorne during the period of his courtship. (Peabody had sought Hawthorne out after the publication of *Twice-Told Tales* and had introduced him to her sister Sophia.) Her memories can be questioned, since they pertain to a period almost fifty years behind her; but the statements she attributed to Hawthorne resemble those he wrote to Sophia. He is represented as saying, " 'We do not live at our house, we only vegetate. Elizabeth [Hawthorne's older sister] never leaves her den; I have mine in the upper story, to which they always bring my meals, setting them down in a waiter at my door, which is always locked.' 'Don't you even see your mother?' said I. 'Yes,' said he, 'in our little parlour. She comes and sits down with me and Louisa [Hawthorne's younger sister] after tea—and sometimes Louisa and I drink tea together. My mother and Elizabeth each take their meals in their rooms. My mother has never sat down to table with anybody, since my father's death.' I said, 'Do you think it is healthy to live so separated?' 'Certainly not—it is no life at all—it is the misfortune of my life. It has produced a morbid consciousness that paralyzes my powers.'"

Peabody then goes on to describe the reclusive widow Hawthorne who, through Julian Hawthorne's biography, found her way into the common understanding of Hawthorne's life. But in the very same description she comments on the widow in a manner that undercuts her own account. "Widow Hawthorne always looked as if she had walked out of an old picture, with her ancient costume, and a face of lovely sensibility, and great brightness—for she did not *seem* at all a victim of morbid sensibility, notwithstanding her all but Hindoo self-devotion to the manes of her husband. She was a person of fine understanding and a very cultivated mind."[7] It takes no great acumen to observe that Elizabeth Peabody could not have known how the widow "always" looked, or characterize her fine and cultivated sensibility if she had seldom left her bedroom. Indeed, the revealing phrase "she did not *seem* at all a victim of morbid sensibility" shows that Peabody's theories of Elizabeth Hathorne did not mesh with her memories.

Julian Hawthorne was a shrewd and tactful man who doubtless perceived discrepancies in the material he had before him. However, given the filial respect which was his announced motive in writing *Nathaniel Hawthorne and His Wife,* he could not contradict views of events maintained by his parents. He transmitted much of Elizabeth Peabody's account, and building from its description of the widow's reclusiveness, he attributed Hawthorne's alienated temperament to the mother's unnatural behavior. Hawthorne "was brought up," Julian wrote, "under what might be considered special disadvantages. His mother, a woman of fine gifts but of extreme sensibility, lost her husband in her twenty-eighth year; and, from an exaggerated, almost Hindoo-like construction of the law of seclusion which the public taste of that day imposed upon widows, she withdrew entirely from society, and permitted the habit of solitude to grow upon her to such a degree that she actually remained a strict

---

[7] Pearson, "Elizabeth Peabody on Hawthorne," pp. 266–68.

hermit to the end of her long life, or for more than forty years after Captain Hawthorne's death. . . . It is saying much for the sanity and healthfulness of the minds of these three children, that their loneliness distorted their judgment, their perception of the relation of things, so little as it did" (*Hawthorne and His Wife,* I, 4–5).

Only a few pages further on, Julian approves Widow Hawthorne's views on education, and credits her with shaping her son's literary sensibilities by encouraging him to read poetry, romance, and allegory. And he prints recollections by other informants which contradict the legend implicitly. But ultimately he fails to engage with the inconsistencies in his narrative. He needs the widow's morbidity for his thesis, which is that Hawthorne was saved as man and artist through his marriage to Sophia. The story that Julian's father had invented as an ardent lover is respectfully promulgated by a dutiful son.

Perhaps the damage done to Elizabeth Hathorne's reputation resulted inadvertently from Hawthorne's campaign to win Sophia. But, unquestionably, there is malice and hostility expressed toward her in the particular legend Hawthorne devised. In some obscure manner she is held accountable for Hawthorne's incarceration in the Castle Dismal. In the fairy-tale structure of the legend (a variant of "Beauty and the Beast," perhaps) she is allocated the role of the enchanter whose evil spell must be undone by the greater power of Sophia's beneficence. While the structure is demonstrably out of keeping with known facts, it might well be an accurate, though necessarily figural, dramatization of Hawthorne's inner reality. If so, then its representation of the mother as absent actually masks an oppressive sense of her presence in his psychic world. But, known facts do not permit us to characterize Elizabeth Hathorne as domineering and possessive. The presence that is symbolized, then, is the presence of Hawthorne's own deep attachment to his mother.

II

Elizabeth Clarke Manning was born in 1780, the third of nine children of Miriam Lord (b. 1748) and Richard Manning (b. 1755). The other children were Mary, b. 1777; William, b. 1778; Richard, b. 1782; Robert, b. 1784; Maria, b. 1786; John, b. 1788 Priscilla, b. 1790; and Samuel, b. 1791: a total of five boys and four girls, all surviving to adulthood. The Mannings were a close-knit and late marrying family who lived together in a large plain wooden house on Herbert Street in Salem. The head of the family, Richard Manning, began his working life as a blacksmith and progressed to owning a stagecoach line. Through this and other enterprises, including land investments, he built a comfortable estate.

Although none of the Manning children attended college— Nathaniel Hawthorne would be the first of the line to do so—there was considerable interest in education among them, and all (including Elizabeth) received some schooling. As adults, they were avid readers. Their religious views inclined toward the liberal, as they belonged to the Unitarian church. (Elizabeth and her sister Mary joined the Congregational Church in 1806, however.) Elizabeth was the first to leave the Manning household, marrying Nathaniel Hathorne—as the name was then spelled—on 2 August 1801, when she was twenty-one years old. Hathorne, a sea captain, was five years older than she, and had probably known her for some time because he lived across the back fence in a house on Union Street, where she moved upon marriage. There is evidence of a courtship of some duration: on a voyage two years earlier Nathaniel had written couplets to his "dear Betsey." The notebook in which these verses were inscribed became in time the property of his son, who copied over one of his father's amatory couplets: "In the Midest of all these dire allarms/I'll think dear Betsey on thy Charms."[8]

The household to which Elizabeth moved was presided over by Nathaniel's mother, a widow; and his two unmarried sisters also lived there. He and his brother Daniel, also a seafaring man, lived at home when they were on shore, which was seldom. He left for sea very shortly after his marriage and was away when Elizabeth bore her first child on 7 March 1802, a daughter also named Elizabeth though commonly called Ebe.

The date of Ebe's birth was barely seven months after that of her parents' marriage. The significance of this seven-month's child has escaped notice, or at least mention, by virtually all of Hawthorne's biographers. But it could hardly have escaped the notice of the

---

[8] James R. Mellow, *Nathaniel Hawthorne in His Times* (Boston: Houghton Mifflin, 1980), p. 13.

three women with whom Elizabeth was now domiciled, nor could it have been insignificant to them. Perhaps they were models for the hostile chorus of women at the beginning of *The Scarlet Letter*. For, as the historian Carl N. Degler reminds us, "bridal pregnancies" in nineteenth-century America appear to have been quite rare—well under ten percent—and, as evidence of sexual relations outside marriage, led to social stigma which "fell like a hammer" on the errant.[9] Certainly among conservative segments of Salem society, including quite probably the old-fashioned and pious Hathornes, Elizabeth would have been harshly judged. The daughter Ebe grew up into a strikingly independent, only partially socialized woman, much as though she had been exempted from normal social expectations by those entrusted with rearing her. It is not improbable that Hawthorne's depiction of the wild Pearl had as much to do with his memory of Ebe as a child, as it did with his observations of his own daughter Una.

Nathaniel Hathorne Jr. was born on 4 July 1804; his father was again away at sea. A third child, Maria Louisa (called Louisa) arrived on 9 January 1808, barely two weeks after the father had again set sail, this time on what proved to be his last voyage. Early in the spring of that year he died of a fever in Surinam. He left Elizabeth a widow at the age of twenty-eight, with children aged six and four and an infant of a few months. In seven years of married life he had spent little more than seven months in Salem, and had been absent from home at the births of all his children. We need hardly look further for sources of the image of a socially stigmatized woman abandoned to bear and rear her child alone.

However, Elizabeth did not have to deal with her harsh lot alone, although support did not come from the Hathornes. Only a few months after receiving word of her husband's death she returned permanently to the Mannings. It was only prudent for her to do so, since the Hathornes were not well off and she had inherited nothing from Nathaniel. The Mannings were lower on the social scale than the Hathornes but they were prospering, and the family included several vigorous men to look after its interest and conduct its business.

[9] *At Odds: Women and the Family in America from the Revolution to the Present* (New York: Oxford, 1980), p. 20.

In addition, there is evidence of bad feeling between Elizabeth and her husband's family. Aunt Peabody in her recollection to Julian Hawthorne wrote that Elizabeth "was not happily affected by her husband's family—the Hawthornes being of a very sharp and stern individuality—and when not cultivated, this appeared in oddity of temper."[10] Peabody's syntax is defective here but her intent is to characterize the Hathornes as people who had, through want of cultivation, let a naturally stern individualism turn to oddness and eccentricity. It may well be that they, rather than Hawthorne's mother, went in for solitude. In any event, after she left them Elizabeth Hathorne made little effort to keep up contacts, notwithstanding their continued proximity. Nor is any effort at relationship recorded from their side. On an occasional Sunday young Nathaniel went over and read the Bible in his grandmother's parlour, and the difference between that household of sharp and stern eccentrics, and the cooperative Mannings, must have been imaginatively striking.

The failure of the Hathornes to pursue a relationship with Elizabeth seems stranger than her defection from them, because in losing her they lost grandchildren who bore their name. But perhaps Elizabeth's misstep had disqualified her children as Hathornes in their eyes. Perhaps they viewed her as a social interloper, a female conniver using a woman's age-old trick to entrap a husband. Perhaps their old-fashioned piety led them to perceive her as sinful and fallen. Perhaps the causes of the falling-out were banal. But however it came about, it is impossible that Nathaniel Hawthorne could have absorbed any other perspective on this rift than that of his mother. Through his later readings in New England history he came to associate the early Puritans with the Hathornes, and this association may go far to explain the severity with which he turns their judging natures back on themselves. The Puritans versus a defenseless woman equalled the Hathornes versus his mother. If his mother herself suffered some sense of guilt or shame under the judgment, then her psychological turmoil filtering into her son's consciousness might linger to provide a model for Hester's complex ambivalences. In any event, I should suppose that some heightened response to her situation underlies the poignant depiction of Hester's duress in *The Scarlet Letter*.

[10] Pearson, "Elizabeth Peabody on Hawthorne," p. 268.

Of course much would have been beyond his childish understanding. He would have to be old enough to mesh a knowledge of wedding and birth dates with a knowledge of biological processes before he could relate his mother's guilt, her children, and her separation from the Hathornes in one logical structure. But the aura of mystery—of the uncanny—that accompanies so many "adult doings" in his fiction from "My Kinsman, Major Molineux" to *The Marble Faun* may be an expression of just that deeply-impressed early sense of bewilderment.

As he became more knowing, Hawthorne may have come to feel some guilt himself—guilt over siding with his mother, if she was indeed in the wrong; and guilt over carrying the name of people (perhaps sharing their traits) who had repudiated his mother for the sin of bearing children. *He* was one of those children, and when later in his life he was reading New England history and found a variant spelling of the paternal name—Hawthorne instead of Hathorne— his adoption of that orthography may have been a gesture of counter-repudiation.

Elizabeth's return to the Mannings has been seen as the first step in an intensifying withdrawal, but in fact the Mannings were much more in the world than the Hathornes, and there were enough of them to be a world in themselves. In 1808 the entire clan was intact at Herbert Street. This means that ten people were living there, ranging from Mrs. Manning who was then sixty years old to Samuel who, at age seventeen, was only eleven years older than Hawthorne's sister Ebe. These numbers alone explain Hawthorne's subsequent appetite for solitude; he must have had almost none of it in his boyhood. The addition of Elizabeth and her three children to the Herbert Street group brought the total living in that house to an incredible (by our modern middle-class standards) fourteen.

The three children were apparently regarded as a joint family charge, and their futures were discussed and determined upon by all. After the senior Manning died in 1813, and Richard settled in Raymond, Maine, to manage family property there, the business head of the Mannings became Robert, while Mary ran the household. Given the limited biological understanding of the child, young Hawthorne probably never missed his dead father consciously, and since there were male heads of the Manning household in abundance he probably never grasped, at any level, the fact that he was lacking a father until he was beyond childhood. At the best, this lack could only have been grasped intellectually, for in his emotional world he had several. The evidence is that he missed not one more father, but a home which might be presided over by his *mother* without the intervention of any other adult. For a while this seemed likely: Elizabeth considered settling near Richard in Maine and running her own farm. She actually tried this way of life, on and off, for six years, and though Hawthorne often had to stay behind in Salem for his schooling, he was anxious for her to make Raymond her permanent residence.

"I hope, Dear Mother," he wrote from Salem on 19 June 1821, "that you will not be tempted by any entreaties to return to Salem to live. You can never have so much comfort here as you now enjoy. You are now undisputed mistress of your own House. Here you would have to submit to the authority of Miss Manning. If you remove to Salem, I shall have no Mother to return to during the College vacations. . . . If you remain where you are, think how delightfully the time will pass with all your children around you, shut out from the world with nothing to disturb us. It will be a second garden of Eden."[11] Two elements of Hawthorne's imagery are noteworthy. First, Raymond was at that time not a garden but a forest setting (although, perhaps not insignificantly, a rose bush grew before Elizabeth Hathorne's door).[12] Ever after, Hawthorne visualized Eden not as a garden but a forest, albeit that vision was often obscured by subsequent grief and loss in his fiction. Too, the "first" Garden of Eden had no children in it, while Hawthorne's second Eden conspicuously lacks an Adam. If Hawthorne secretly casts himself in Adam's role, then he is his mother's son and lover both. For him, Eden is a benign matriarchy.

A year earlier he had written his mother expressing reluctance to go to college and, more generally, to grow up. "Oh how I wish I was again with you, with nothing to do but go a gunning. But the happiest days of my life are gone. Why was I not a girl that I might have been pinned all my life to my mother's apron."[13] Given the

[11] Manning Hawthorne, "Nathaniel Hawthorne at Bowdoin," p. 87.
[12] Manning Hawthorne, "Nathaniel Hawthorne Prepares for College," p. 77.
[13] "Nathaniel Hawthorne Prepares for College," pp. 69–70.

conspicuous gun image, Hawthorne is not complaining about his gender, but about social rules that force a boy out of the Garden of Eden into the cold patriarchal world while permitting a girl to remain enclosed in the maternal paradise. The search for the lost *mother,* rather than the lost father, underlies much of the story patterning in his mature fiction, as does the scheme of flight from the patriarchy. The idea of the matriarchy retained a powerful hold on his imagination throughout life, and he could only view patriarchal social organizations—the only kind he knew, though others could be imagined—with enmity.

The enmity may owe its origins precisely to Elizabeth's return to Salem. Hawthorne may have been hurt and angry that his mother disregarded his wishes in favor of her siblings' entreaties. He may have resented her failure to conform her life to his plans; a residue of bitterness may have indeed affected his relation to her after he graduated from Bowdoin and had to come back to Herbert Street instead of Raymond. But he could fault the Mannings too. Hawthorne was glad enough to leave Herbert Street when he was married, but in fact he never felt at home again.[14] Home was mother.

By 1825 the Manning family had suffered from time and circumstance. Only six were still living at Herbert Street when Hawthorne came back from Bowdoin, although some of the others were domiciled close by. Briefly, the senior Richard Manning had died in 1813, his son Richard had gone to live in Maine, and John had disappeared the same year (presumably lost at sea). Maria died in 1814. Priscilla married in 1817 and Robert in 1824; both moved out but remained in Salem. When Hawthorne was married in 1842 the household had been so far depleted as to consist only of his mother and two sisters. Mrs. Manning died in 1826, William went into bachelor quarters, and Samuel died in 1833. At the time that Hawthorne was stressing his solitude to the Peabody sisters, Mary was still living at Herbert Street, but she died in 1841. Robert died in 1842.

For some reason, the probable cumulative effect of all these deaths

---

[14] Nathaniel Hawthorne, *English Notebooks,* ed. Randall Stewart (New York: Modern Language Association of America, 1941), p. 23; *French and Italian Notebooks,* ed. Thomas Woodson (Columbus: Ohio State Univ. Press, 1980), p. 570. Subsequent references to Hawthorne's works citing the Centenary Edition published by the Ohio State Univ. Press will be parenthetically included in the text, noting volume and page number of the edition.

on Hawthorne has never been appreciated, possibly because he said and wrote little about them. Whatever effect they had on him, however, they must have been disastrous for Elizabeth, who had made her whole life within the family circle. It is useful to remember that when Hawthorne was married she was mourning for the sister to whom she had been closest, and was soon to lose a brother. If she seemed somewhat reclusive in the years when the Peabody sisters came to know her, it may have been merely because she was sad. Or because she did not change with her changing world—she was approaching the age of sixty, and may have seen no way to fill the void that her departing siblings created. She did remain close to her surviving sister Priscilla (Mrs. Dike) and to Robert's widow, Rebecca.

In the years that Hawthorne was living at Herbert Street after graduation, he may well have been the obscurest man of letters in America (as he poetically characterised himself) but he certainly could not have been the most solitary. He may indeed have had to resort to such devices as taking meals in his room and locking his door in order to get some writing done in that busy house. Still, he walked and visited, went on trips with his uncle Samuel, worked on a magazine in Boston (with help from Ebe). He shared his literary plans and agonized over his failures with his mother and sisters. Ebe selected books for him from the Salem Athenaeum. The three knew about his anonymous first novel *Fanshawe,* although Sophia never learned of it. Ebe was able partly to reconstruct, many years later, the early aborted projects for framed collections of short stories. All three women helped him to collect copies of the pieces printed in *Twice-Told Tales* and to prepare the manuscript for publication.[15] Louisa made him a shirt when he went to Brook Farm, while Elizabeth sewed buttons on his trousers and rejoiced in Osgood's flattering portrait of her son that he had made for her. Louisa, who carried on most of the correspondence with him while he was at the farm, bemoaned the infrequency of his letters and visits in a manner that suggests ordinary family intimacy.[16] That Hawthorne was much petted and greatly adored he implicitly admits (Castle Dismal notwithstanding) in a letter to Sophia gently

---

[15] *Hawthorne and his Wife,* I, 123–25; Stewart, "Recollections of Hawthorne by His Sister Elizabeth," pp. 323, 327–28.

[16] Mellow, pp. 185–86.

chiding her for having taken offense at something he had written earlier: "Dearest, I beseech you grant me freedom to be careless and wayward—for I have had such freedom all my life" (*Love Letters*, I, 43).

When Hawthorne fell in love with Sophia Peabody late in 1838 he was thirty-five years old. No evidence survives as to whether his mother and sisters had hoped that he would marry, or wished him to remain single, or simply hoped for his happiness whatever he did. Given their general fondness, the last is the most likely possibility. Certainly, however, they never expected him to *conceal* an attachment, and when he finally announced his engagement a scant month before his wedding, Ebe at least was angered beyond the ability to forgive or to rejoice in his happiness. She wrote to Sophia as follows:

Your approaching union with my brother makes it incumbent upon me to offer you the assurances of my sincere desire for your mutual happiness. With regard to my sister and myself, I hope nothing will ever occur to render your future intercourse with us other than agreeable, particularly as it need not be so frequent or so close as to require more than reciprocal good will, if we do not happen to suit each other in our new relationship. I write thus plainly, because my brother has desired me to say only what was true; though I do not recognize his right so to speak of truth, after keeping us so long in ignorance of this affair. But I do believe him when he says that this was not in accordance with your wishes, for such concealment must naturally be unpleasant, and besides, what I know of your amiable disposition convinces me that you would not give us unnecessary pain. It was especially due to my mother that she should long ago have been made acquainted with the engagement of her only son.[17]

To some degree, Ebe never forgave her brother for his deviousness. "We were in those [early] days almost absolutely obedient to him," she wrote to Julian. "I do not quite approve of either obedience or concealment" (*Hawthorne and His Wife*, I, 124–25). And, despite her comment about Sophia's amiable disposition, she never warmed to her brother's wife. "I might as well tell you that [Sophia] is the only human being whom I really dislike," a late letter to relatives said. "Though she is dead, that makes no difference.

[17] Turner, p. 141.

I could have lived with her in apparent peace, but I could not have lived long; the constraint would have killed me."[18] Perhaps Hawthorne's having chosen so timid and conventional a woman caused Ebe to reassess his character.

But Elizabeth responded in a different way, as Hawthorne wrote to Sophia:

> Sweetest, scarcely had I arrived here, when our mother came out of her chamber, looking better and more cheerful than I have seen her this some time, and enquired about the health and well-being of my Dove! Very kindly too. Then was thy husband's heart much lightened; for I knew that almost every agitating circumstance of her life had hitherto cost her a fit of sickness; and I knew not but it might be so now. Foolish me, to doubt that my mother's love would be wise, like all other genuine love! . . . Now I am very happy—happier than my naughtiness deserves. It seems that her heart was troubled, because she knew that much of outward as well as inward fitness was requisite to secure thy foolish husband's peace; but, gradually and quietly, God has taught her that all is good, and so, thou dearest wife, we shall have her fullest blessing and concurrence. (*Love Letters*, II, 93-4)

Despite his mother's loving acceptance, Hawthorne's concealment had done her a great wrong, and he knew it. His little boy's confession of naughtiness refers to more than that concealment, however. He was also confessing the naughtiness of his involvement with Sophia to his mother. And, too (what he did not confess), there was the naughtiness of the way in which he had misrepresented her and his relation with her, to the Peabody sisters (and perhaps to others as well). In fact, I surmise that it was his complex sense of acting in bad faith toward Elizabeth that led him to desire concealment; and then that this concealment became another act of bad faith, in a chain of the sort that Hawthorne's fiction sets out so knowingly. Indeed, for the rest of his life Hawthorne was caught by that act of bad faith since he was never able to rectify it except in the oblique language of his fiction.

And I suspect that there was yet more than the lies about Castle Dismal and solitary meals that burdened Hawthorne's conscience. The constellation of images in which he represented his case to Sophia suggested, as I have said above, that Sophia was to save him

[18] Turner, p. 142.

from and substitute for his mother. The image of the one woman annihilates the image of the other; on the inner stage, where the image is the person, to let Sophia rescue him is to kill his mother. No evidence exists to suggest that Sophia or Elizabeth regarded each other as rivals; the narrative Hawthorne projected derives (to the extent that it is sincere) from his own emotions and not fact. The narrative suggests—what the belated adolescent quality of his romance with Sophia tends to confirm—that his attachment to Elizabeth was so deep and pervasive that he experienced his love for another woman as doing some kind of violence to her, as a killing infidelity. At the same time, if Hawthorne blamed her for his long years of "enchantment" in the Herbert Street house while the world of adult sexual relationships passed him by, then he must also assuredly have *wanted* to kill her to gain his freedom. And so on, through the complex layers of the heart that Hawthorne knew so well.

Doubtless, Sophia caught no glimmer of these depths in his talk of naughtiness, but we can see that she was not entirely satisfied with his explanations because she later worked out a tale which made Ebe (conveniently) the culprit in the concealment. Obligingly, though in revealing language, Julian transmitted her explanation: Ebe, wishing to come between the two lovers, let Hawthorne know that "news of his relation with Miss Sophia would give [Elizabeth] a shock that might endanger her life." As a loving son, Hawthorne was naturally "not prepared to face the idea of defying and perhaps 'killing' his mother" (*Hawthorne and His Wife,* I, 196-97). This story does not withstand a moment's scrutiny. Ebe could not have forestalled the announcement of an engagement which she didn't know about; her blunt nature was incompatible with concealment; and, of course, Hawthorne knew how his mother was likely to react as well as Ebe did. But, if *Ebe* had not persuaded Hawthorne that his engagement would kill his mother, he had probably persuaded himself.

However, Elizabeth declined to be killed, and hence not even a temporary break in her relations with Hawthorne actually took place. Granted, she did not attend his wedding; but there are other explanations for this than hostility. During his sojourn at the Old Manse he had more than one occasion to return to Salem, and inevitably he stayed at Herbert Street, dining and chatting with his mother and sisters. (See *Love Letters,* II, 107, 114, 120–21, 126–27, 155–56.) When he returned with Sophia and his child Una to Salem upon being appointed to the Custom House, he took up residence in Herbert Street while looking for his own home. He did this as a matter of course. The stay lasted several months—longer than anticipated—and seems to have produced tension. But we must remember that Sophia never became a favorite with the three women, nor did she greatly care for them. For example, we find her writing to her mother in January of 1846 that "on many accounts it would be inconvenient to remain in this house. Madame Hawthorne and Louisa are too much out of health to take care of a child, and I do not like to have Una in the constant presence of unhealthy persons. I have never let her go into Madame Hawthorne's mysterious chamber since November, partly on this account, and partly because it is so much colder than the nursery, and has no carpet on it" (*Hawthorne and His Wife,* I, 307–08). A woman who regarded her husband's closest female relatives only as babysitters, described them as "unhealthy persons," and kept her child out of grandmamma's room for many weeks because it lacked a carpet, cannot be imagined to have encouraged family intimacy. It seems clear that a major goal on Sophia's part was to preserve the autonomy of her own new family.

Nevertheless, when a house (on Mall Street) that finally suited them was found, it was determined that Elizabeth, Ebe, and Louisa should join them permanently. The house, Sophia wrote to her mother, fortunately had a suite of rooms "wholly distant from ours so that we shall only meet when we choose to do so. Madame Hawthorne is so uninterfering, of so much delicacy, that I shall never know she is near excepting when I wish it; and she has so much kindness and sense and spirit she will be a great resource in emergencies. . . . It is no small satisfaction to know that Mrs. Hawthorne's remainder of life will be glorified by the presence of these children [Julian had been born] and of her own son. I am so glad to win her out of that Castle Dismal, and from the mysterious chamber, into which no mortal ever peeped till Una was born and Julian—for they alone entered the penetralia. Into that chamber the sun never shines. Into these rooms in Mall Street it blazes without stint" (*Hawthorne and His Wife,* I, 314). One wonders how Sophia knew so much about Elizabeth's room if none but the little children had ever entered it, or what opportunties the widow would have had to show her kindness, sense, and spirit if she herself never left it. Indeed, Sophia's obtuseness is equalled only by her complacency (or is some complex defensiveness working itself out here?). What sort of rescue would it be for "Madame Hawthorne" if her lot was to wait in her chamber until called on for help in an emergency?

However, Elizabeth Hathorne had her own kind of spunk, it seems. She made her presence known after all. She began to cook items of food for Hawthorne that he had loved as a boy, and even to carry bowls of coffee to him in his study as he sat writing. Though Sophia was appalled, Hawthorne made no objection. Sophia unbent so far, finally, as to obtain from Elizabeth a recipe for an Indian pudding of which her husband was especially fond.[19]

Hawthorne's feelings about his mother in the years after his marriage are not recoverable, for he spoke of these personal matters only to Sophia and then necessarily in a highly oblique language designed as much to veil as reveal. Sophia regularly read his journal and therefore he had to compose his entries with her expectations in mind. Nevertheless, we can be sure that the threatened loss of his position at the Custom House after the election of 1848 must have been particularly horrifying because he had assumed responsibility for his mother's welfare and undertaken to make a home for her "remainder of life." While he could be sure that the surviving Mannings would provide for her (as they did for Ebe and Louisa after Elizabeth's death), the question was not her physical or even psychological welfare but his own.

Certainly, then, her sudden serious illness and death at just the moment when he became unable to provide for her must have seemed profoundly significant to a man who felt so strongly the force that the inner life exerted on the outer world. It is in the context of a host of like thoughts, which he could not articulate plainly, that we must read his extraordinary journal entry penned the day before his mother died:

I love my mother; but there has been, ever since my boyhood, a sort of coldness of intercourse between us, such as is apt to come between

---

[19] Louise Hall Tharp, *The Peabody Sisters of Salem* (Boston: Little, Brown, 1950), p. 185.

persons of strong feelings, if they are not managed rightly. I did not expect to be much moved at the time—that is to say, not to feel any overpowering emotion struggling, just then—though I knew that I should deeply remember and regret her. Mrs. Dike was in the chamber. Louisa pointed to a chair near the bed, but I was moved to kneel down close by my mother, and take her hand. She knew me, but could only murmur a few indistinct words—among which I understood an injunction to take care of my sisters. Mrs. Dike left the chamber, and then I found the tears slowly gathering in my eyes. I tried to keep them down; but it would not be—I kept filling up, till, for a few moments, I shook with sobs. For a long time, I knelt there, holding her hand; and surely it is the darkest hour I ever lived. Afterwards, I stood by the open window, and looked through the crevice of the curtain. . . . I saw my little Una of the golden locks, looking very beautiful; and so full of spirit and life, that she was life itself. And then I looked at my poor dying mother; and seemed to see the whole of human existence at once, standing in the dusty midst of it. (*Centenary*, VIII, 429)

Though constrained to repeat the legend of coldness since boyhood (which his boyhood letters so decisively refute), and to finish this entry with an expression of hope in the afterlife suitable for Sophia's eyes, Hawthorne nevertheless permits the depths of his grief to come to light. Connecting Una to his mother through himself, and making this linked chain of three comprise the whole of human existence, he effectively expunges Sophia from the record, makes Una his mother's child, and hence makes his mother both wife and mother to him. But these were not his last words on the subject. His real tribute to her, and to her influence, was to come in *The Scarlet Letter*.

III

The Scarlet Letter obviously cannot be called a work of autobiography or even biography as we use these terms to refer to recognizable literary genres.[20] But this discussion is meant to demonstrate the way in which it, along with "The Custom-House," contains autobiographical and biographical material (his mother's biography) and is engendered specifically by Hawthorne's experience of his

---

[20] William C. Spengemann, in *The Forms of Autobiography: Episodes in the History of a Literary Genre* (New Haven: Yale Univ. Press, 1980), makes *The Scarlet Letter* a sort of ultimate "self-reflexive" autobiographical statement, but in his definition autobiography need not refer to any real-life happenings.

mother's death. It is not inaccurate to describe *The Scarlet Letter* as Hawthorne's response to his mother's death. This response is composed of a number of elements difficult to extricate separately from the one dense texture of the romance. The fact that the woman it writes about is dead is paramount, for her death provides the motive for writing and also the freedom to write. The consciously articulated intentions of *The Scarlet Letter*, one might say, are to rescue its heroine from the oblivion of death and to rectify the injustices that were done to her in life, and both of these intentions take death as their starting point.

It is possible, within the elegiac frame of the work, to point to several autobiographical and biographical strands, some pertaining to the mother herself, some to the mother and son, and some to the son alone. First, *The Scarlet Letter* makes a noble attempt to realize the mother as a separate person with an independent existence in her own right; such an attempt represents the son's very belated recognition that his mother was a human being with her own life and consciousness, something more than a figure in his own carpet. As a youth of seventeen begging his mother to live in Maine, Hawthorne had his own Garden of Eden in mind, but he never doubted that his ideal would be hers also, and that a life shut off from the world with her children would content her. Perhaps as a mature man he began to know better.

Yet, in realizing the separate individuality, he must make Hester a mother, for that is what Elizabeth inescapably was not only as part of his reality but as part of hers also. So he tries to understand what motherhood might mean for a person who does have, as all human beings do, a sense of independent existence. The way in which Pearl both impinges on and defines her mother's selfhood vividly dramatizes the claims that children make on their mothers.

Yet even as he strives to provide Hester with an independent existence as the center of her own world, Hawthorne maintains a double focus. Events in *The Scarlet Letter* never work themselves free of the constant voice of the narrator. We are always aware that the character Hester depends for her reality on the act of narrative generosity which is creating her. Here, Hawthorne reverses the biological relation of mother and child and becomes the creator of his mother. It seems to me that such a reversal not only underlies all representational art, but also responds to a specific set of wishes in the particular author writing at this particular time—the wish to be free of lifelong dependency on maternal power, the wish to have one's mother all to oneself (even if that possession can be attained only after death).

But—another twist in the cable—Hester's instant-by-instant dependence on the narrator-author is reversed again in the testimony of "The Custom-House" where "Hester" is defined as a creative force *outside* the romance which is responsible for his inspiration and his ability to write about her. Thus there is a transcending symbiosis of symbol and artist, mother and son—each created by the other and each dependent on the other for artistic life: the artist dependent on the image which inspires him, and the image dependent on the artist for representation.

There is, finally, an inevitable gap between the image and the being who has inspired it and whom it represents; the image is the refraction of the mother's influence in the son's psychic world. And so the work becomes an ambitious attempt to give his mother her own reality and bring to life her image in his mind as well and somehow to keep these distinct. Mediating between the two intentions of biography and autobiography, Hawthorne as narrator creates a structure in which the identities of the two subjects alternately assert themselves independently and then merge into a larger unity. The unity is best symbolized in the icon of mother and child—Divine Maternity—which is thrust on our attention in the first scaffold scene of *The Scarlet Letter*.

Beyond this complex personal intention, Hawthorne is also concerned to make his romance a public document, and hence much of the work of his text goes into generalizing, extending, and depersonalizing the meaning of his core images. The maternal symbol at the heart of *The Scarlet Letter* is contained within a sophisticated narrative structure, and this structure is distanced from the reader by the prefatory "Custom-House" essay. The personal meanings of the romance are processed though a sequence of narrators (the narrator of "The Custom-House" is not identical to the narrator of *The Scarlet Letter*) who are deeply aware of what, in "The Custom-House," Hawthorne refers to as the reader's right—the reader's right not to have unwanted confidences forced upon him.

Some of the resemblances between Hester's and Elizabeth's stories will, I hope, already be evident from the account provided of her life: the questionable circumstances of their children's births, their repudiation by those assigned society's judging function, the absence of spouse and abandonment of the child entirely to the mother. Facing down Hester's critics and overcoming presumed reader resistance to her, Hawthorne goes beyond forgiveness to complete acquittal. The chief agency of Hester's exoneration is Pearl. Although the narrative perspective is resolutely adult, it silently privileges Pearl's point of view toward her mother over all the others. Her very existence is the narrative's first and last fact, and it legitimizes the act of her mother which engendered her. We cannot doubt that Pearl has a right to be, and hence cannot fault the mother for bringing her into existence.

Essentially, too, Pearl is her mother's child only. Though society and Hester are aware that a man participated in the act, Pearl has no sense of this necessity and hers is the view that the reader is forced to adopt. That is, we know that Hester has had a lover but we never really "know" that Pearl has a father. Through Pearl and because of her, then, Hester takes precedence over Dimmesdale and over the society which tries to put him and his cohorts at the organizing center of the fictional world. The world of the romance is organized around her. Matriarchy prevails. Autobiographically speaking, Hawthorne identifies himself once and for all as his *mother's* child.

To be sure, Hester pays a high price for her legitimation, the price of confinement within her motherhood for most of her life. Throughout the romance she is virtually never separated from Pearl; the image she represents, we remember, is inextricably linked to maternity rather than selfhood or even womanhood. The brookside scene in the forest, for all its multiple possibilities of interpretation, dramatizes at some basic level the need of the child to possess the mother all to herself. Pearl recognizes at once through the mother's changed appearance, as Hester blossoms out into relation with Dimmesdale, that the mother is no longer merely and entirely her mother. She cannot abide this. Imperiously she requires that Hester reassume motherhood as her sole reality before she will return to her. The "A" at this point means only maternity: the complex, bewildering, and ambiguous set of events which have set Hester's course for life are ultimately reduced to the "sin" of having given birth to a child.

The tensions between Hester's motherhood and personhood, between the needs of her own life and the needs of her child, between the person herself and the figure in the son's tale, are resolved at a higher level of the story than Pearl's perceptions. The narrator, taking the roles of her prophet, son, and lover simultaneously, creates an image now responsive to its own rhythms and now to the rhythms of the two beings who impinge on her—Pearl, her figured child, and the author-narrator who in many respects is her child grown up. The image to which both subscribe, and within which they enclose Hester, is the Garden of Eden, the benign matriarchy.

One is reminded not only of Hawthorne's adolescent letters but of a lengthy passage from "Main Street," which is the only tale we are sure that Hawthorne meant to include along with *The Scarlet Letter* in the larger collection he was originally planning. "Main Street" is a rapid survey of New England history and it begins before the patriarchy comes to impose its civilization on western soil, with the timeless land existing under the rule of a woman:

> You perceive, at a glance, that this is the ancient and primitive wood,—the ever-youthful and venerably old,—verdant with new twigs, yet hoary, as it were, with the snowfall of innumerable years, that have accumulated upon its intermingled branches. The white man's axe has never smitten a single tree; his footstep has never crumpled a single one of the withered leaves, which all the autumns since the flood have been harvesting beneath. Yet, see! along through the vista of impending boughs, there is already a faintly-traced path. . . . What footsteps can have worn this half-seen path? Hark! Do we not hear them now rustling softly over the leaves? We discern an Indian woman—a majestic and queenly woman, or else her spectral image does not represent her truly—for this is the great Squaw Sachem, whose rule, with that of her sons, extends from Mystic to Agawam. That red chief, who stalks by her side, is Wappacowet, her second husband, the priest and magician. (*Centenary*, XI, 50–51)

The white man—adulthood for the race—has arrived, and the happy days of mother-rule retreat to legend and imagination. But within imagination their existence is powerful and pervasive. *The Scarlet Letter* is Hawthorne's testimony to the existence of that inner world ruled over by a woman. The woman in that inner world could never die.

The Scarlet Letter is the only one of Hawthorne's long romances whose origin can be attributed to a specific autobiographical impulse. Alerted by the kinds of concerns it manifests, one can perceive certain biographical implications in the others, however. Although there is not a trace of the Squaw Sachem in *The House of the Seven Gables,* this is a quintessential family story whose deepest meaning resides, ultimately, precisely in her absence. For it tells a tale of the submersion of individual identity and the total loss of happiness and freedom in a male-ruled household. The reason why the alternatives of Pyncheon and Maule can provide no resolution to the excesses of the other is that each remains in essence a patriarchy. Eliminating Pyncheon, the hero Holgrave has nothing to substitute but—himself. One can interpret the families of Pyncheon and Maule as Hathorne and Manning respectively, the run-down aristocrats and the rising laborers, and recall that neither permitted Elizabeth to be mistress in her own house. From another vantage point, the Pyncheon house can be seen as an amalgamation of *both* Hathorne and Manning into a composite figure of hated family oppression, an overwhelming symbol of patriarchal usurpation. In sum, the repudiation of father and fathers imaged forth as a minor point in *The Scarlet Letter* as it defended Hester's priority here becomes the central autobiographical statement.

In this context Phoebe can be only Sophia, as indeed we are asked to understand by other indications (Hawthorne frequently called Sophia Phoebe). Her role in the rescue, or failed rescue, plot is only superficial, however. She is fundamentally unequal to the other powers in the story and at crucial points in the narrative is shown to be susceptible to victimization by them. Hawthorne, I think, is here beginning to realize, or at least to signify, that Sophia was having far less efficacy in his life than he had originally imagined.

That the simplicity of Sophia's imagination was more and more seeming like shallowness rather than infinite depths is more overtly suggested in *The Blithedale Romance* and *The Marble Faun.* In both romances the hated male rulers are abetted, albeit without much awareness, by female figures whose task is to supplant or discredit a more matriarchal or maternal type. (It must be granted that in *The*

Blithedale Romance the matriarchal type is badly flawed, and is so to a lesser degree in *The Marble Faun,* so to speak truly no possibility for any restoration of the matriarchy is seriously entertained in either romance.) In *The Blithedale Romance* this dovelike supplanter appears at the beginning as part of the degraded urban complex which the narrator-protagonist wishes to reject for a pastoral ideal. The proper Arcadian values are established at once when the narrator finds Zenobia ruling over Blithedale, but her initial matronly and queenlike authority is systematically undercut and discredited by the collusion of all the other characters until she is driven to suicide. The dove is left in command of the field. But the survivors of the battle are merely the walking wounded, and her lifelong task is to nurse and guard them—a parody of matriarchy, making *Blithedale* in some sense the dark inverse of *The Scarlet Letter.*

Something similar happens in the tortured symbolism and obscure narrative line of *The Marble Faun,* where Kenyon's election of Hilda, the dove transmuted into a steely virgin, is equivalent to retreat from the complexities of an adult world. Hilda's cutting simplifications and platitudes masquerade as a world view which the sculptor, finding himself unable to deal with the implications of adult relations between the sexes, gladly espouses. The babyland to which Kenyon and Hilda are returning at the end of the romance is nothing like the ageless forest presided over by the Indian Queen who, disguised in this romance as Venus, has been rejected by Kenyon on the campagna in favor of Hilda. But Hawthorne does not blame Sophia.

Toward the close of his literary career Hawthorne, working up his English essays for publication, inserted a passage into "Outside Glimpses of English Poverty" for which there is no notebook source:

Nothing, as I remember, smote me with more grief and pity . . . than to hear a gaunt and ragged mother priding herself on the pretty ways of her ragged and skinny infant, just as a young matron might, when she invites her lady-friends to admire her plump, white-robed darling in the nursery. Indeed, no womanly characteristic seemed to have altogether perished out of these poor souls. It was the very same creature whose tender torments make the rapture of our young days, whom we love, cherish, and protect, and rely upon in life and death, and whom we delight to see beautify her beauty with rich robes and set it off with jewels. (*Centenary,* X, 283)

The image goes beyond the gaunt and ragged mother, beyond the young matron, and even beyond Elizabeth Hathorne to the archetype, the Magna Mater enthroned in a blaze of jewels in her son's imagination. Even at this late date the imagination remains centrally possessed of and by her image. Elizabeth had been dead for fourteen years. Hawthorne would be dead within a year himself. In this ardent image, he indicates that her presence will survive with him to the end.

The Scarlet Letter and Revolutions Abroad
Larry J. Reynolds

WHEN Hawthorne wrote *The Scarlet Letter* in the fall of 1849, the fact and idea of revolution were much on his mind. In "The Custom-House" sketch, while forewarning the reader of the darkness in the story to follow, he explains that "this uncaptivating effect is perhaps due to the period of hardly accomplished revolution and still seething turmoil, in which the story shaped itself."[1] His explicit reference is to his recent ouster from the Salem Custom House, his "beheading" as he calls it, but we know that the death of his mother and anxiety about where and how he would support his family added to his sense of upheaval. Lying behind all these referents, however, are additional ones that have gone unnoticed: actual revolutions, past and present, which Hawthorne had been reading about and pondering for almost twenty consecutive months. These provided the political context for *The Scarlet Letter* and shaped the structure, characterizations, and themes of the work.

I

ROME YET UNCONQUERED! FRANCE TRANQUIL. LEDRU-ROLLIN NOT TAKEN. THE HUNGARIANS TRIUMPH! GREAT BATTLE NEAR RAAB! THE AUSTRIANS AND RUSSIANS BEATEN. CONFLICTS AT PETERWARDEIN AND JORDANOW. SOUTHERN GERMANY REPUBLICAN. BATTLE WITH THE PRUSSIANS AT MANHEIM. RESULT UNDECIDED. These are the headlines of the *New York Tribune* for 5 July 1849; and because they are typical, they suggest the excitement and interest gener-

---

[1] *The Scarlet Letter*, ed. William Charvat, Roy Harvey Pearce, and Claude Simpson (Columbus: Ohio State Univ. Press, 1962), p. 43. Hereafter cited parenthetically in the text.

ated in America by the wave upon wave of revolution that swept across Europe during the years 1848 and 1849. In Naples, Sicily, Paris, Berlin, Vienna, Milan, Venice, Munich, Rome, and nearly all the other cities and states of continental Europe, rulers and their unpopular ministers were overthrown, most notably Louis Philippe and Guizot in France, Ferdinand I and Metternich in Austria, and Pope Pius IX and Rossi in the Papal States.[2] Meanwhile revolutionary leaders such as Lamartine, Kossuth, and Mazzini became heroes in American eyes as they tried to institute representative governments and alleviate the poverty and oppression that precipitated the revolutions.

By the fall of 1849, all of the fledgling republics had been crushed by conservative and reactionary forces, and this fact explains in part why the influence of the revolutions upon *The Scarlet Letter* in particular and the American literary renaissance in general has been overlooked. Unlike the American Revolution (whose influence has received thorough study), the revolutions of 1848–49 came to naught, making them appear inconsequential in retrospect. In addition, the excitement generated in America, while intense, was short lived and soon forgotten; national attention soon turned to the turmoil generated by the slavery issue, which obscured Europe's role as the previous focus of this attention. A third explanation for the neglect is that studies of the literature of this period have tended to focus on native themes and materials. Concomitantly, reference works such as James D. Hart's *Oxford Companion to American Literature* and John C. Gerber's *Twentieth Century Interpretations of "The Scarlet Letter"* have provided chronological indexes that correlate only American history with the lives and works of American authors, despite the fact that the major newspapers of the day devoted three-fourths of their front-page coverage to European events.

Although the European revolutions all failed, from the spring of 1848 to the fall of 1849, the American public displayed its interest and sympathy by mass gatherings, parades, fireworks, proclamations, speeches, and constant newspaper coverage, which

---

[2] Useful overviews of the revolutions of 1848–49 are provided by *The Opening of An Era: 1848 An Historical Symposium*, ed. François Fejto (1948; rpt. New York: Howard Fertig, 1966) and *The Revolutions of 1848–49*, ed. Frank Eyck (New York: Barnes & Noble, 1972).

swelled with the arrival of each steamer.[3] Members of the American *literati*, Hawthorne's friends among them, also responded with ardor. To celebrate the French Revolution, Lowell wrote two poems, "Ode to France, 1848," in which he linked American Freedom with the fires burning in the streets of Paris, and "To Lamartine, 1848," in which he sang the praises of the poet-statesman who headed the new provisional government. Evert Duyckinck, Hawthorne's editor at Wiley & Putnam's, declared himself *"en rapport"* with the French Revolution;[4] and S. G. Goodrich, Hawthorne's former publisher, who witnessed events in Paris, wrote an enthusiastic account for the *Boston Courier*. Emerson, who visited Paris in May 1848, expressed reservations about the posturings of the mobs in the streets but was impressed by Lamartine and sympathized with the social activists. "The deep sincerity of the speakers," he wrote, "who are agitating social not political questions, and who are studying how to secure a fair share of bread to every man, and to get the God's justice done through the land, is very good to hear."[5]

Margaret Fuller, who served as one model for Hester, became, as is well known, more intently engaged in the European revolutions than any of her countrymen. As a witness to the rise and fall of the Roman Republic, she wrote impassioned letters to the *New York Tribune* praising the efforts of her friend Mazzini, describing the defense of Rome, and pleading for American support. "The struggle is now fairly, thoroughly commenced between the principle of democracy and the old powers, no longer legitimate," she wrote in the spring of 1849. "Every struggle made by the old tyrannies, all their Jesuitical deceptions, their rapacity,

---

[3] A comprehensive study of the American response to the revolutions has yet to be published; however, the specialized studies of Elizabeth B. White, *American Opinion of France, from Lafayette to Poincaré* (New York: Knopf, 1927), Arthur James May, *Contemporary American Opinion of the Mid-Century Revolutions in Central Europe* (Philadelphia: Univ. of Pennsylvania Press, 1927), and Howard R. Marraro, *American Opinion of the Unification of Italy, 1846–1861* (New York: Columbia Univ. Press, 1932), when placed side by side, cover most of the salient features of this response, as it revealed itself publicly.

[4] Letter to George Duyckinck, 18 March 1848. All of the letters from the brothers Duyckinck are quoted with the kind permission of the Duyckinck Family Papers, Rare Books and Manuscript Division, The New York Public Library, Astor, Lenox and Tilden Foundations.

[5] *The Letters of Ralph Waldo Emerson*, ed. Ralph L. Rusk, IV (New York: Columbia Univ. Press, 1939), 73–74.

their imprisonments and executions of the most generous men, only sow more dragon's teeth; the crop shoots up daily more and more plenteous." When the battle of Rome was fought, Fuller served tirelessly as a nurse and watched the warfare surrounding her. "Men are daily slain," she wrote on June 21, "and this state of suspense is agonizing. In the evening 't is pretty, though terrible, to see the bombs, fiery meteors, springing from the horizon line upon their bright path, to do their wicked message." After the French had invaded the city, she wrote, "I see you have meetings, where you speak of the Italians, the Hungarians. I pray you *do something*. . . . Send money, send cheer,—acknowledge as the legitimate leaders and rulers those men who represent the people. . . ."[6]

As Hawthorne was defending himself from the attacks of the Salem Whigs and battling to be reinstated as surveyor, the developments in Italy received a predominant amount of American attention. On June 20, the *Boston Daily Advertiser* reported that the French, in order to restore the power of the Pope, were marching on Rome with 80,000 men, and it quoted Mazzini's declaration that "We shall fight to the last against all projects of a restoration." The following day, alongside of Hawthorne's public letter to Hillard, this same newspaper reported Garibaldi's arrival upon Neapolitan territory and printed Louis Napoleon's lengthy speech explaining his government's support of the Pope. During the next two months, as Hawthorne ceased careering through the public prints in his decapitated state, accounts of the defeat of the Roman revolutionaries made their way to the United States, where they were greeted by most with sadness or outrage.

Although Margaret Fuller's former devotee Sophia Hawthorne (in her dutifully childlike manner) expressed approval of the republican successes in Europe as they were occurring in 1848,[7] her husband most likely shared neither her optimism nor the enthu-

---

[6] *At Home and Abroad, or Things and Thoughts in America and Europe*, ed. Arthur B. Fuller (1856; rpt. Port Washington, N.Y.: Kennikat, 1971), pp. 380, 381, 409, 421.

[7] In a December 1848 letter to her mother, Sophia declared, "What good news from France! . . . There seems to be a fine fresh air in France just now. . . . it is very pretty when the people do not hurt the kings, but merely make them run. Since Prince Metternich has resigned, I conceive that monarchy is in its decline," quoted in Julian Hawthorne, *Nathaniel Hawthorne and His Wife*, I (1884; rpt. n.p.: Archon Books, 1968), 331.

siasm of their literary friends, particularly Fuller. In fact, the book that he wrote in the wake of the revolutions in 1849 indicates that they reaffirmed his scepticism about revolution and reform and inspired a strong reactionary spirit which underlies the work.

Revolution had been a fearful thing in Hawthorne's mind for some time, even though he found the ends it wrought at times admirable.[8] Violent reform and the behavior of mobs particularly disturbed him,[9] as the final scene of "My Kinsman, Major Molineux" makes clear. This story may celebrate the beginnings of a new democratic era, as some have suggested, but it cannot be denied that Molineux is presented as a noble victim of a hellish mob. "On they went," Hawthorne wrote, "like fiends that throng in mockery round some dead potentate, mighty no more, but majestic still in his agony."[10] Similarly, in "The Custom-House" sketch, Hawthorne presents himself as the victim of another "bloodthirsty" mob, the Whigs, who, acting out of a "fierce and bitter spirit of malice and revenge," have struck off his head with the political guillotine and ignominiously kicked it about. This presentation, humorous in tone but serious in intent, gives *The Scarlet Letter* its alternate title of "THE POSTHUMOUS PAPERS OF A DECAPITATED SURVEYOR" and foreshadows the use and treatment of revolutionary imagery in the novel proper.

This imagery, of course, is drawn from the French Revolution of 1789, which was at the forefront of Hawthorne's mind for several reasons. First of all, the spectacular excesses of that revolution provided the language and metaphors used by conservatives to de-

---

[8] See Celeste Loughman, "Hawthorne's Patriarchs and the American Revolution," *American Transcendental Quarterly*, 40 (1979), 340–41, and John P. McWilliams, Jr., " 'Thorough-Going Democrat' and 'Modern Tory': Hawthorne and the Puritan Revolution of 1776," *Studies in Romanticism*, 15 (1976), 551.

[9] Hawthorne's reservations about the behavior of revolutionary mobs can also be seen in his sketches "The Old Tory" (1835) and "Liberty Tree" (1840). His manuscript "Septimius Felton" contains some of his final thoughts on the subject. "In times of Revolution and public disturbance," he writes, "all absurdities are more unrestrained; the measure of calm sense, the habits, the orderly decency, are in a measure lost. More people become insane, I should suppose; offenses against public morality, female license, are more numerous; suicides, murders, all ungovernable outbreaks of men's thoughts, embodying themselves in wild acts, take place more frequently, and with less horror to the lookers-on." See *The Elixir of Life Manuscripts*, ed. Edward H. Davidson, Claude M. Simpson, and L. Neal Smith (Columbus: Ohio State Univ. Press, 1977), p. 67.

[10] "My Kinsman, Major Molineux," in *The Snow-Image and Uncollected Tales*, ed. J. Donald Crowley (Columbus: Ohio State Univ. Press, 1974), p. 230.

scribe events in 1848–49. In a letter to the *New York Courier and Enquirer*, Bishop Hughes, a supporter of Pope Pius IX, denounced the revolutionaries of Rome and claimed, "They have established, according to what I regard as the truest accounts, a reign of terror over the Roman people, which they call a government." Alluding to Margaret Fuller, Hughes added that "no ambassador from foreign countries has recognized such a republic, except it be the female plenipotentiary who furnishes the *Tribune* with diplomatic correspondence."[11] Evert Duyckinck, keeping his brother George (who was in Paris) abreast of American attitudes in the spring of 1848, reported that "People look at this Revolution with recollections of the Era of Robespierre and suspect every revival of the old political phraseology of that period. An article attributed to Alison is going the rounds from Blackwoods in which he sets Satan grinning over the shoulders of Lamartine."[12] The *Blackwood's* article referred to had echoed the theme of "Earth's Holocaust" as it declared, "Experience will prove whether, by discarding all former institutions, we have cast off at the same time the slough of corruption which has descended to all from our first parents. We shall see whether the effects of the fall can be shaken off by changing the institutions of society; whether the devil cannot find as many agents among the Socialists as the Jacobins; whether he cannot mount on the shoulders of Lamartine and Arago as well as he did on those of Robespierre and Marat."[13]

The bloody June Days of 1848 seemed to confirm such scepticism, and even George Duyckinck, an ardent supporter of the French people, was reminded of the Reign of Terror and the role women played in it as he reflected upon recent events. "Human nature," he wrote his brother, "seems to be the same it was sixty years ago. Heads were stuck on pikes or swords and women danced about them as they did then and who can doubt but that if the insurgents had succeeded the guillotine would have been as busily at work today as it was then."[14] Although use of the guillotine had been discontinued (General Cavaignac used the firing

[11] Rpt. *Boston Post*, 29 June 1849, p. 1, col. 6.
[12] Letter to George Duyckinck, 18 April 1848; Duyckinck Family Papers, New York Public Library.
[13] "Fall of the Throne of the Barricades," *Blackwood's*, 63 (1848), 399.
[14] Letter to Evert Duyckinck, 30 June 1848; Duyckinck Family Papers, New York Public Library.

squad during the June Days, when an estimated 10,000 died), the shadow of that instrument loomed over all, and after Louis Napoleon came to power, it became unwise even to mention this symbol of revolution. Under Napoleon's administration in 1849, the owner of a Paris newspaper called *Le Peuple*, for an article entitled "The Restoration of the Guillotine," was fined and sentenced to five years imprisonment, while the proprietor of *La Revolution Democratique et Sociale*, for an article entitled "The Political Scaffold," was fined and sentenced to three years imprisonment.[15] In America, the guillotine and the scaffold carried not quite so much import, except, of course, in the mind of one decapitated surveyor.

Predictably, the American press drew careless comparisons between the European revolutions and the American political scene. When Zachary Taylor began his series of political appointments in the spring and summer of 1849, they were reported in the Democratic papers as revolutionary acts, as symbolic beheadings of Democratic party members. Some seven times in May and June, for example, the *Boston Post* printed, in conjunction with the announcement of a political appointment and removal, a small drawing presumably of General Taylor standing beside a guillotine, puffing a cigar, surrounded by heads (presumably of Democrats) at his feet. One of these drawings appeared on 11 June and on the following day, a letter to the editor appeared objecting to Hawthorne's removal from the Salem Custom House. "This is one of the most heartless acts of this heartless administration," the anonymous writer declared. "The head of the poet and the scholar is stricken off to gratify and reward some greedy partizan! ... There stands, at the guillotine, beside the headless trunk of a pure minded, faithful and well deserving officer, sacrificed to the worth of party proscription, Gen. Zachary Taylor, now President." As Arlin Turner has pointed out, this letter was probably a source of Hawthorne's "beheading" metaphor;[16] however, behind the reference were two years of revolutionary events in Europe, two years of revolutionary rhetoric and imagery.

[15] See the review "Lamartine's Histoire des Girondins," *Southern Quarterly Review*, 16 (1849), 58.
[16] *Nathaniel Hawthorne: A Biography* (New York: Oxford Univ. Press, 1980), p. 181.

II

Such rhetoric and imagery appeared not only in the newspapers, of course, but also in contemporary books, some of which dealt with revolution in a serious historical manner. Although *The Scarlet Letter* has often been praised for its fidelity to New England history, the central setting of the novel, the scaffold, is, I believe, an historical inaccuracy intentionally used by Hawthorne to develop the theme of revolution. The Puritans occasionally sentenced a malefactor to stand upon a shoulder-high block or upon the ladder of the gallows (at times with a halter about the neck),[17] but in none of the New England histories Hawthorne used as sources (viz., Felt, Snow, Mather, Hutchinson, and Winthrop) are these structures called scaffolds. In fact, I have been unable to find the word "scaffold" in them. The common instruments of punishment in the Massachusetts Bay Colony were, as Hawthorne shows in "Endicott and the Red Cross," the whipping post, the stocks, and the pillory. (The gallows, located in Boston at the end of town,[18] was used for hangings and serious public humiliations.) Although Hawthorne in his romance identifies the scaffold as part of the pillory, his narrator and his characters refer to it by the former term alone some twenty-six times, calling it the scaffold of the pillory only four times and the pillory only once.[19]

As early as 1557 and then later with increasing frequency during the first French Revolution, the word "scaffold" served as a synecdoche for a public beheading—by the executioner's axe or the guillotine. And, because of its role in the regicides of overthrown kings, the word acquired powerful political associations, which it still retains.[20] When King Charles I was beheaded with

---

[17] See Joseph B. Felt, *The Annals of Salem, from Its First Settlement* (Salem: W. & S. B. Ives, 1827), pp. 176, 317.

[18] See Caleb H. Snow, *A History of Boston, the Metropolis of Massachusetts* (Boston: A. Bowen, 1825), p. 169.

[19] See John R. Byers, Jr., and James J. Owen, *A Concordance to the Five Novels of Nathaniel Hawthorne*, II (New York: Garland, 1979), 667, 579.

[20] *Oxford English Dictionary*, IX (Oxford: Clarendon Press, 1933), 159. Beheading was not a common form of punishment in the Massachusetts Bay Colony. The only mention I have found of it involved the punishment of an Indian found guilty of theft and of striking a settler's wife in the head with a hammer, causing her to lose her senses. Neither a block nor a scaffold was used in his execution, however. "The executioner would strike off his head with a falchion," John Winthrop reported, "but he had eight blows at it before he could effect it, and the Indian sat upright and stirred not all the

an axe following the successful rebellion led by Cromwell, Andrew Marvell in his "An Horation Ode" used the word in the following tribute to his king:

> ... thence the royal actor born
> The tragic scaffold might adorn:
>   While round the armed bands
>   Did clap their bloody hands.
>   *He* nothing common did or mean
> Upon that memorable scene:
>   But bowed his comely head
>   Down, as upon a bed.[21]

One hundred and forty-four years later, when Louis XVI became a liability to the new French republic, he too, of course, mounted what was termed the "scaffold" and there became one of the victims of the new device being advocated by Dr. Guillotin. The association of a scaffold with revolution and beheading, particularly the beheading of Charles I and Louis XVI, explains, I think, why Hawthorne uses it as his central and dominant setting. It links the narrator of "The Custom-House" sketch with the two main characters in the romance proper, and it raises their common predicaments above the plane of the personal into the helix of history.

Hawthorne's desire to connect his narrative with historic revolutions abroad is further shown by the time frame he uses. The opening scenes of the novel take place in May 1642 and the closing ones in May 1649.[22] These dates coincide almost exactly with those of the English Civil War fought between King Charles I and his Puritan Parliament. Hawthorne was familiar with histories of this subject and had recently (June 1848) checked out of the Salem Atheneum Francois Guizot's *History of the English Revolution of 1640, Commonly Called the Great Rebellion*.[23] Guizot, Professor of Modern History of the Sorbonne when he wrote

---

time," *The History of New England from 1630 to 1649*, ed. James Savage, 2 vols. (1825–1826; rpt. New York: Arno Press, 1972), II, 189.

[21] *The Complete English Poems*, ed. Elizabeth Story Donno (New York: St. Martin's Press, 1972), p. 56.

[22] See Edward Dawson, *Hawthorne's Knowledge and Use of New England History: A Study of Sources* (Nashville: Joint Univ. Libraries, 1939), p. 17.

[23] Marion L. Kesselring, *Hawthorne's Reading, 1828–1850* (1949; rpt. New York: Norwood, 1976), p. 52.

this work, became, of course, Louis Philippe's Prime Minister whose policies provoked the French Revolution of 1848. During the spring of 1848 Guizot's name became familiar to Americans, and probably the man's recent notoriety led Hawthorne to a reading of his work in the summer of 1848.

Examination of the simultaneity between fictional events in *The Scarlet Letter* and historical events in America and England verifies that the 1642–1649 time frame for events in the romance was carefully chosen to enhance the treatment of revolutionary themes. When Hester Prynne is led from the prison by the beadle who cries, "Make way, good people, make way, in the King's name," less than a month has passed since Charles's Puritan Parliament had sent him what amounted to a declaration of war. Five months later, in October, 1642, the first battle between Roundheads and Cavaliers was fought at Edgehill, and word of the open hostilities reached America in December.[24] Then and in the years that followed, the Bay Colony fasted and prayed for victory by Parliament, but these became times of political anxiety and stress in America as well as England. According to one of Hawthorne's sources, Felt's *Annals of Salem*, in November 1646 the General Court (presided over by Messrs. Bartholomew and Hathorne) ordered "a fast on Dec. 24th, for the hazardous state of England ... and difficulties of Church and State among themselves, both of which, say they, some strive to undermine."[25] By the final scenes of the novel, when Arthur is deciding to die as a martyr, Charles I has just been beheaded (on 30 January 1649); thus, when Chillingworth sarcastically thanks Arthur for his prayers, calling them "golden recompense" and "the current gold coin of the New Jerusalem, with the King's own mint-mark on them" (p. 224), Hawthorne adds to Chillingworth's irony with his own. Furthermore, given the novel's time frame, the tableau of Arthur bowing "his head forward on the cushions of the pulpit, at the close of his Election Sermon" (p. 250), while Hester stands waiting beside the scaffold, radiates with ominous import, particularly when one recalls that Arthur is not a graduate of Cambridge, as most of the Puritan ministers of New England were,[26] but rather

---

[24] See Winthrop, II, 85.
[25] Felt, p. 175.
[26] See Frederick Newberry, "Tradition and Disinheritance in *The Scarlet Letter*," *ESQ*, 23, No. 1 (1977), 13.

of Oxford, the center of Laudian and Royalist sympathies and the place of refuge for King Charles during the Revolution.

By thus setting events in an age when "men of the sword had overthrown nobles and kings" (p. 164), Hawthorne provides a potent historical backdrop for the revolutionary and counter-revolutionary battles fought, with shifting allegiances, among the four main characters and the Puritan leadership. Furthermore, his battle imagery, such as Governor Bellingham's armor and Pearl's simulated slaying of the Puritan children, draws upon and reflects the actual warfare abroad and thus illuminates the struggles being fought on social, moral, and metaphysical grounds in Boston.

Bearing upon the novel perhaps even more than its connections with the English "Rebellion" and its attendant regicide are its connections with the first French Revolution and the execution of Louis XVI. In the romance itself, Hawthorne first alludes to one tie when he describes the scaffold in the opening scenes; "it constituted," he writes, "a portion of a penal machine, which ... was held, in the old time, to be as effectual an agent in the promotion of good citizenship, as ever was the guillotine among the terrorists of France" (p. 55). This allusion may be derived from the imagery appearing, as discussed above, in the contemporary press; but it is also shaped, in a more profound way, by an overlooked source of *The Scarlet Letter*, Alphonse de Lamartine's *History of the Girondists*, a history of the first French Revolution published in France in 1847, translated into English by H. T. Ryde and published in the United States in three volumes in 1847–48.[27]

Lamartine, the poet-statesman who had risen to the head of the Provisional Government in Paris following the February 1848 Revolution, became a well-known figure in America during 1848–49 and was widely admired for his idealism, courage, and eloquence. Numerous Americans expressed high regard for him;[28]

---

[27] The relationship between the French and English revolutions is one point emphasized in Lamartine's work; he points out that "Louis XVI had read much history, especially the history of England.... The portrait of Charles I., by Van Dyck, was constantly before his eyes in the closet in the Tuileries; his history continually open on his table. He had been struck by two circumstances; that James II. had lost his throne because he had left his kingdom, and that Charles I. had been beheaded for having made war against his parliament and his people," (New York: Harper, 1847–48) I, 52. (This edition of Lamartine will hereafter be cited parenthetically in the text.)

[28] Evert Duyckinck in a letter to his brother George, reported that from the point of view of Americans "Lamartine stands out nobly" and speculated that if the new

the *New York Herald,* deviating from its usual format, ran an engraving of him on its front page;[29] and one New York City speculator, trying to dignify a venture, even named a street of sixpenny shanties "Lamartine's Row."[30] After he had fallen from power due to his unwillingness to align himself with the radical republicans or the right-wing Bonapartists, Lamartine was treated as a noble martyr in the American press. The *New York Evening Post* on 23 June 1849, the day after Bryant's editorial on Hawthorne's behalf appeared there, devoted two and a half front-page columns to a glowing summary of Lamartine's literary and political career. "[His] brief administration," the article concluded, "born of the barricades of February, expired amidst the roar of the cannon of June," proved "that Lamartine is too righteous a man to be a politician." "He was no demagogue; he appreciated the crisis, approved the revolution, but dreaded its excess. To save his country from terrorism and communism, he cheerfully laid down his popularity, as he would have laid down his life."

Before this political martyrdom, which would have engaged Hawthorne's sympathy, Lamartine's career had been advanced by his writings; his *Histoire des Girondins* established his credentials as a republican leader, helped inspire the Revolution of 1848 that he struggled to lead and moderate, and acquired much international renown. "We doubt whether this is not already the most popular *book*, as its author is the most popular *man* of the day," a reviewer for the *New York Courier and Enquirer* proclaimed,[31] when the English translation appeared. Unlike Guizot, Lamartine was not a scholarly historian, and his account of the first French Revolution is an imaginative and dramatic construct that gains much of its power from its sympathetic treatment of Louis XVI and its suspenseful narrative structure, which includes a tableau

---

republic progressed well then Lamartine "will be the Washington of France" (3 April 1848, Duyckinck Family Papers, New York Public Library). Emerson, while in Paris, attended a session of the National Assembly and heard Lamartine's speech on Poland. "He did not speak ... with much energy," Emerson wrote his wife, "but is a manly handsome greyhaired gentleman with nothing of the rust of the man of letters, and delivers himself with great ease & superiority (*Letters*, IV, 77).

[29] On 29 March 1848.

[30] See *The Diary of George Templeton Strong*, eds. Allan Nevins and Milton Halsey Thomas, I (New York: Macmillan, 1952), 344.

[31] 17 May 1848, p. 2, c. 3.

at the scaffold as its climactic scene. Throughout the first volume and a half of his history, Lamartine, while detailing the political infighting of the National Assembly and their struggle with the king for power, generates sympathy for Louis. He and his family are seldom free from danger, and the two high points of Volume I are their unsuccessful attempt to flee the country and their confrontation with a mob of thousands at the Chateau of the Tuileries. In Volume II, Lamartine shows the situation of the royal family becoming more desperate and the king acquiring strength and character as his fate unfolds. In terms a decapitated surveyor could appreciate, Lamartine observes that "all the faults of preceding administrations, all the vices of kings, all the shame of courts, all the griefs of the people, were accumulated on his head and marked his innocent brow for the expiation of many ages" (I, 27). "He was the scape-goat of olden time, that bore the sins of all" (II, 323).

Lamartine shifts from third-person omniscient narration to third-person limited after the National Assembly renders its verdict of guilty and its judgment of death. Thus, unlike Carlyle's clipped, brusque, and almost sarcastic account of the regicide, Lamartine's treatment generates sympathy; the reader is beside the king for some thirty intensely moving pages—as he parts with his family, as he rides in the carriage with his priest, who hears his confession, and as he sees and enters the Place de la Révolution to be beheaded. "There," Lamartine writes, "a ray of the winter's sun ... showed the place filled by 100,000 heads, the regiments of the garrison of Paris drawn up round all sides of the scaffold, the executioners, awaiting the victim, and the instrument of death prominent above the mob, with its beams and posts painted blood-color. It was the guillotine!" (II, 370). Stationed around the scaffold are "unscrupulous and pitiless ruffians," who desire "the punishment should be consummated and applauded" (II, 371). In contrast, the king steps forward composed and aloof. Humiliated by being bound, he regains his composure, mounts the scaffold, faces the multitude, casts a farewell glance on his priest, and meets his death. "The plank sunk, the blade glided, the head fell" (II, 373), Lamartine writes, as this chilling and memorable scene comes to an end. Appearing in almost the exact center of the narrative, on the 867th page of 1578, the scene dominates the history; all that goes before anticipates it; all that follows refers back to it. The rest of Volume II and all of III detail the excesses of the Revolution: the assassination of Marat, the Reign of Terror, the wave upon wave of bloodletting, and so on, all of which become horrifyingly repetitive.

Lamartine's stirring treatment of revolutionary events and political martyrdom and especially his unprecedented use of the scaffold as both a dramatic setting and a unifying structural device lead one to speculate that Hawthorne may have read this work before he wrote *The Scarlet Letter*; however, speculation is unnecessary. He did. The records of the Salem Atheneum reveal that on 13 September 1849, he checked out the first two volumes of Lamartine's *History*.[32] Moreover, Sophia Hawthorne's letters to her sister and mother, combined with Hawthorne's notebook entries, reveal, as no biographer has yet pointed out, that it was about ten days later, most likely between 21 September and 25 September, that Hawthorne began work in earnest on *The Scarlet Letter*.[33] On 27 September he checked out the third volume of Lamartine's *History*, and on that date Sophia, in an often-quoted letter, informed her mother, "Mr. Hawthorne is writing morning & afternoon.... He writes immensely—I am almost frightened about it—But he is well now & looks very shining."[34] (He returned the first two volumes of the *History* 6 November and the third volume 12 November.) This correlation in dates plus Hawthorne's allusions to the terrorists of France suggests that what has become one of the most celebrated settings in American literature, the scaffold of *The Scarlet Letter*, was taken from the Place de la Révolution of eighteenth-century Paris, as described by Lamar-

---

[32] Kesselring, p. 42.

[33] Hawthorne and his wife spent much of the last half of August and the first part of September househunting, first on the Atlantic shore near Kittery Point, and then in the Berkshires near Lenox. Hawthorne may have worked on *The Scarlet Letter* during the second week in September after Sophia returned from Lenox, but if he did, it was not with the commitment he later displayed, for on 17 September he set out with his friend Ephraim Miller on a leisurely three-day journey to Temple, New Hampshire. Assuming he rested on the 20th, the day after his return, and knowing it was the 27th when Sophia first said he was writing "immensely" mornings and afternoons, it seems likely that between 21 September and 25 September he became absorbed in the writing of his romance. All of the letters from Sophia Hawthorne to her mother Elizabeth P. Peabody and her sister Mary Mann are quoted with the kind permission of the Henry W. and Albert A. Berg Collection, The New York Public Library, Astor, Lenox and Tilden Foundation.

[34] Letter to Elizabeth P. Peabody (mother); Berg Collection, New York Public Library.

tine, and transported to the Marketplace of seventeenth-century Boston, where it became the focal point of Hawthorne's narrative. Along with it came, most likely, a reinforced scepticism about violent reform.

III

Recognition that revolutionary struggle stirred at the front of Hawthorne's consciousness as he wrote *The Scarlet Letter* not only accounts for many structural and thematic details in the novel but also explains some of the apparent inconsistencies in his treatment of his characters, especially Hester and Arthur. The issue of the degree and nature of Hawthorne's sympathies in the novel has been debated for years, at times heatedly, and I have no hope of resolving the debate here; however, I think the revolutionary context of events provides a key for sorting out Hawthorne's sympathies, or more accurately those of his narrator (whose biases closely resemble Hawthorne's). The narrator, as a member of a toppled established order, an *ancien régime* so to speak, possesses instincts that are conservative and antirevolutionary, consistently so, but the individuals he regards undergo considerable change, thus evoking inconsistent attitudes on his part. Specifically, when Hester or Arthur battle to maintain or regain their rightful place in the social or spiritual order, the narrator sympathizes with them; when they become revolutionary instead and attempt to overthrow an established order, he becomes unsympathetic.[35] The scaffold serves to clarify the political and spiritual issues raised by events in the novel, and the decapitated surveyor of the Custom House, not surprisingly, identifies with whoever becomes a martyr upon it.

Hawthorne's use of the scaffold as a structural device has long been recognized; in 1944 Leland Schubert pointed out that the novel "is built around the scaffold. At the beginning, in the middle and at the end of the story the scaffold is the dominating

[35] Nina Baym in her discussion of "The Custom-House" sketch posits that "like Hester, [Hawthorne] becomes a rebel because he is thrown out of society, by society.... The direct attack of 'The Custom-House' on some of the citizens of Salem adds a fillip of personal revenge to the theoretical rebellion that it dramatizes," *The Shape of Hawthorne's Career* (Ithaca: Cornell Univ. Press, 1976), pp. 148–49. Hawthorne's attack, I think, can be more accurately termed a counterattack and seen as dramatizing not a rebellion but his reaction to a rebellion.

point."[36] The way in which the scaffold serves as a touchstone for the narrator's sympathies, however, has not been fully explored, particularly with reference to the matter of revolution.

As every reader notices, at the beginning of the story, Hester is accorded much sympathy. Her beauty, her courage, her pride, all receive emphasis; and the scaffold, meant to degrade her, elevates her, figuratively as well as literally. The narrator presents her as an image of Divine Maternity, and more importantly, as a member of the old order of nobility suffering at the hands of a vulgar mob. Her recollection of her paternal home, "poverty-stricken," but "retaining a half-obliterated shield of arms over the portal" (pp. 53, 58) establishes her link to aristocracy. Furthermore, although she has been sentenced by the Puritan magistrates, her worst enemies are the coarse, beefy, pitiless "gossips" who surround the scaffold and argue that she should be hanged or at least branded on the forehead. The magistrates, whom Hawthorne characterizes as "good men, just, and sage" have shown clemency in their sentence, and that clemency is unpopular with the chorus of matrons who apparently speak for the people.

Through the first twelve chapters, half of the book, the narrator's sympathies remain with Hester, for she continues to represent, like Charles I, Louis XVI, and Surveyor Hawthorne, a fallen aristocratic order struggling in defense of her rights against an antagonistic populace. The poor, the well-to-do, adults, children, laymen, clergy, all torment her in various ways; but she, the narrator tells us, "was patient,—a martyr, indeed" (p. 85). It is Pearl, of course, who anticipates what Hester will become—a revolutionary—and reveals the combative streak her mother possesses. "The warfare of Hester's spirit," Hawthorne writes, "was perpetuated in Pearl" (p. 91), and this is shown by Pearl's throwing stones at the Puritan children ("the most intolerant brood that ever lived" [p. 94]), her smiting and uprooting the weeds that represent these children, and her splashing the Governor himself with water. "She never created a friend, but seemed always to be sowing broadcast the dragon's teeth, whence sprung a harvest of armed enemies, against whom she rushed to battle" (p. 95). (The echo

---

[36] *Hawthorne the Artist* (Chapel Hill: Univ. of North Carolina Press, 1944), pp. 137-38.

here of Margaret Fuller's dispatch from Rome is probably not coincidental.)

Hester's own martial spirit comes to the fore in the confrontation with Bellingham, but here she fights only to maintain the *status quo* and thus keeps the narrator's sympathies. She visits the Governor not to attack him in any way but to defend her right to raise Pearl. Undaunted by Bellingham's shining armor, which "was not meant for mere idle show," Hester triumphs, because she has the natural order upon her side and because Arthur comes to her aid. Drawing Pearl forcibly into her arms, she confronts "the old Puritan magistrate with almost a fierce expression"; and Arthur, prompted into action by Hester's veiled threats, responds like a valiant Cavalier. His voice, as he speaks on her behalf, is "sweet, tremulous, but powerful, insomuch that the hall reechoed, and the hollow armour rang with it" (p. 114).

In the central chapters of the novel, when the narrator turns his attention toward Arthur and evidences antipathy toward him, it is not only because of the minister's obvious hypocrisy but also because of the intellectual change that he has undergone at Chillingworth's hands. Subtly, Arthur becomes radicalized and anticipates Hester's ventures into the realm of speculative and revolutionary thought. "There was a fascination for the minister," Hawthorne writes, "in the company of the man of science, in whom he recognized an intellectual cultivation of no moderate depth or scope; together with a range and freedom of ideas, that he would have vainly looked for among the members of his own profession" (p. 123). And if Arthur is the victim of the leech's herbs and poisons, he is also a victim of more deadly intellectual brews as well. The central scene of the novel, Arthur's "vigil" on the scaffold, is inspired, apparently, by the "liberal views" he has begun to entertain. "On one of those ugly nights," we are told, "the minister started from his chair. A new thought had struck him" (p. 146). This thought is to stand on the scaffold in the middle of the night, but by so doing he joins the ranks of Satan's rebellious legions. As he indulges in "the mockery of penitence" upon the scaffold, his guilt becomes "heaven-defying" and reprehensible, in the narrator's eyes. Rather than seeking to reestablish his moral force, which has been "abased into more than childish weakness," Arthur, in his imagination, mocks the Reverend Wilson, the people of Boston, and God himself. Furthermore, as

Henry Nash Smith has pointed out, the "lurid playfulness" Arthur indulges in upon the scaffold, calls into question "the very idea of a solid, orderly universe existing independently of consciousness."[37] The questioning remains Arthur's, however, not the narrator's, and the scene itself, with the scaffold as its setting, serves to reveal the cowardice and licentiousness Arthur has been reduced to. The blazing A in the sky, which Arthur sees "addressed to himself alone," marks Governor Winthrop's death, according to the townspeople, and thus further emphasizes (by its reference to Winthrop's famous leadership and integrity) the nadir Arthur has reached by his indulgence in defiant thought and behavior.

The transformation Hester undergoes in the middle of the novel (which only appears to be from sinner to saint) is a stronger version of that which Arthur has undergone at her husband's hands; she too becomes, like the French revolutionaries of 1789 and the Italian revolutionaries of 1849, a radical thinker engaged in a revolutionary struggle against an established political-religious order. And as such, she loses the narrator's sympathies (while gaining those of most readers). The transformation begins with her regaining, over the course of seven years, the goodwill of the public, which "was inclined to show its former victim a more benign countenance than she cared to be favored with, or, perchance, than she deserved" (p. 162). The rulers of the community, who "were longer in acknowledging the influence of Hester's good qualities than the people," become, as time passes, not her antagonists but rather the objects of her antagonism. We first see her impulse to challenge their authority when Chillingworth tells her that the magistrates have discussed allowing her to remove the scarlet letter from her bosom. "It lies not in the pleasure of the magistrates to take off this badge" (p. 169), she tells him. Similarly, when she meets Arthur in the forest several days later, she subversively asks, "What hast thou to do with all these iron men and their opinions? They have kept thy better part in bondage too long already!" (p. 197).

The new direction Hester's combativeness has taken is political in nature and flows from her isolation and indulgence in specu-

---

[37] *Democracy and the Novel: Popular Resistance to Classic American Writers* (New York: Oxford Univ. Press, 1978), p. 25.

lation. In a passage often quoted, but seldom viewed as consistent with the rest of the novel, because of its unsympathetic tone, the narrator explains that Hester Prynne "had wandered, without rule or guidance, in a moral wilderness.... Shame, Despair, Solitude! These had been her teachers,—stern and wild ones,—and they had made her strong, but taught her much amiss" (pp. 199–200). Hester's ventures into new areas of thought link her, significantly, with the overthrow of governments and the overthrow of "ancient prejudice, wherewith was linked much of ancient principle." "She assumed," the narrator points out, "a freedom of speculation, then common enough on the other side of the Atlantic, but which our forefathers, had they known of it, would have held to be a deadlier crime than that stigmatized by the scarlet letter" (p. 164). Referring for the second time to the antinomian Anne Hutchinson, whom Hawthorne in another work had treated with little sympathy, the narrator speculates that if Pearl had not become the object of her mother's devotion, Hester "might, and not improbably would, have suffered death from the stern tribunals of the period, for attempting to undermine the foundations of the Puritan establishment" (p. 165).[38]

Although Hester does not lead a political-religious revolt against the Puritan leadership, these speculations are quite relevant to the action which follows, for Hawthorne shows her radicalism finding an outlet in her renewed relationship with Arthur, which assumes revolutionary form. When they hold their colloquy in the forest, during which she reenacts her role as Eve the subversive temptress, we learn that "the whole seven years of outlaw and ignominy had been little other than a preparation for this very hour" (p. 200). What Hester accomplishes during this hour (other than raising the reader's hopes) is once again to overthrow Arthur's system and undermine his loyalty to the Puritan community and the Puritan God. She establishes a temporary provisional government within him, so to speak, which fails to sustain itself. Although Hester obviously loves Arthur and seeks only their happiness together, her plan, which most readers heartily endorse,

---

[38] For excellent discussions of Hawthorne's attitudes toward women activists, see Neal F. Doubleday, "Hawthorne's Hester and Feminism," *PMLA*, 54 (1939), 825–28; Morton Cronin, "Hawthorne on Romantic Love and the Status of Women," *PMLA*, 69 (1954), 89–98; and Darrel Abel, "Hawthorne on the Strong Dividing Lines of Nature," *American Transcendental Quarterly*, No. 14 (1972), 23–31.

challenges, in the narrator's eyes, the social order of the community and the spiritual order of the universe, and thus earns his explicit disapproval.

When Hester tells Arthur that the magistrates have kept his better part in bondage, the narrator makes it clear that it is Arthur's better part that has actually kept his worse and lawless self imprisoned. For some time the prison has proved sound, but "the breach which guilt has once made into the human soul is never, in this mortal state, repaired," the narrator declares. "It may be watched and guarded; so that the enemy shall not force his way again into the citadel. . . . But there is still the ruined wall" (pp. 200–01). Thus, as Hawthorne draws upon the popular revolutionary imagery of 1848–49 to present Hester as a goddess of Liberty leading a military assault, she prevails; however, her victory, like that of the first Bastille day, sets loose forces of anarchy and wickedness. Arthur experiences "a glow of strange enjoyment" after he agrees to flee with her, but to clarify the moral dimensions of this freedom, Hawthorne adds, "It was the exhilarating effect—upon a prisoner just escaped from the dungeon of his own heart—of breathing the wild, free atmosphere of an unredeemed, unchristianized, lawless region" (p. 201).

Unlike the earlier struggle that Hester and Arthur had fought together to maintain the *status quo*—the traditional relationship between mother and child—this struggle accomplishes something far more pernicious: "a revolution in the sphere of thought and feeling." And because it does, it receives unsympathetic treatment. "In truth," Hawthorne writes, "nothing short of a total change of dynasty and moral code, in that interior kingdom, was adequate to account for the impulses now communicated to the unfortunate and startled minister. At every step he was incited to do some strange, wild, wicked thing or other, with a sense that it would be at once involuntary and intentional" (p. 217).

Donald A. Ringe among others has suggested that this abrupt change in Arthur's system is beneficent, a fortunate fall, in other words, that gives him insight and powers of expression;[39] however, the narrative emphasizes that it is unfortunate and unholy. Arthur's impulses to blaspheme, curse, and lead innocence astray are a stronger version of those seen during his vigil, and they confirm

---

[39] "Hawthorne's Psychology of the Head and Heart," *PMLA*, 65 (1950), 129.

the narrator's assertion that the minister has acquired "sympathy and fellowship with wicked mortals and the world of perverted spirits" (p. 222). It is important to notice also that the success of Arthur's sermon, which is so eloquent, so filled with compassion and wisdom, depends ultimately not upon his new revolutionary impulses but upon older counter-revolutionary sources that are spiritually conservative. He draws upon the "energy—or say, rather, the inspiration which had held him up, until he should have delivered the sacred message that brought its own strength along with it from heaven" (p. 251).

The final change of heart and spirit that Arthur undergoes and that leads him to his death on the scaffold is foreshadowed by events in the marketplace prior to his sermon. There the exhibition of broadswords upon the scaffold plus Pearl's sense of "impending revolution" suggests that while the minister's better self has been overthrown, it will reassert itself shortly. The procession in which Arthur appears dramatizes the alternative to the lawless freedom Hester has offered. Here, as Michael Davitt Bell has observed, we have "the greatest tribute in all of Hawthorne's writing to the nobility of the founders."[40] The people, we are told, had bestowed their reverence "on the white hair and venerable brow of age; on long-tried integrity; on solid wisdom and sad-colored experience; on endowments of that grave and weighty order, which gives the idea of permanence, and comes under the general definition of respectability" (pp. 237–38). These are the qualities that distinguish Bradstreet, Endicott, Dudley, Bellingham, and their compeers. And, although we are not told who the new governor is (it was Endicott), we know that his election represents orderly change, in contrast to the rebellion and regicide that has recently occurred in England. "Today," Hester tells Pearl, "a new man is beginning to rule over them," and, in harmony with this event, Arthur acts to reestablish his place within the order of the community and within the order of the kingdom of God.

During the sermon Arthur seems to regain some of his spiritual stature and is described as an angel, who, "in his passage to the skies, had shaken his bright wings over the people for an instant,—at once a shadow and a splendor." Because Arthur is still

---

[40] *Hawthorne and the Historical Romance of New England* (Princeton: Princeton Univ. Press, 1971), p. 140.

a hypocrite, considerable irony exists within this description; however, when the minister walks to and mounts the scaffold, the narrator's irony turns to sincerity. Arthur attempts, before he dies, to regain God's favor, and as he nears the scaffold, where Hester and Chillingworth will both oppose his effort to confess, we are told that "it was hardly a man with life in him, that tottered on his path so nervelessly, yet tottered, and did not fall!" The exclamation mark indicates the double sense of "fall" Hawthorne wishes to suggest, and at the end Arthur seems to escape from the provisional control over him that both Chillingworth and Hester have had.

"Is not this better than what we dreamed of in the forest?" he asks Hester, and although she replies "I know not! I know not!" the revolutionary context of the novel, the bias toward restoration and order, indicate we are supposed to agree that it is.[41] Arthur's final scene upon the scaffold mirrors Hester's first scene there, even though he proceeds from the church whereas she had proceeded from the prison. But, unlike Hester, Arthur through humility and faith seems to achieve peace, whereas she, through "the combative energy of her character," had achieved only "a kind of lurid triumph" (p. 78). In the final scaffold scene, Pearl acts as an ethical agent once again and emphasizes Hawthorne's themes about peace and battle, order and revolt. At the moment of his death, Arthur kisses Pearl, and the tears she then sheds are "the pledge that she would grow up amid human joy and sorrow, nor for ever do battle with the world, but be a woman in it." In what seems to be a reward for her docility, she marries into European nobility (thereby accomplishing a restoration of the ties with aristocracy her maternal relatives once enjoyed); similarly, Hester at last, we are told in a summary, forsakes her radicalism and recognizes that the woman who would lead the reform movements of the future and establish women's rights must be less "stained with sin," less "bowed down with shame" than she. This woman must be "lofty, pure, and beautiful, and wise, moreover, not through dusky grief, but the ethereal medium of joy" (p. 263).

[41] A number of critics have read this scene as ironic and seen Dimmesdale as deluded or damned; however, the *Pietà* tableau, Arthur's Christlike forgiveness of Chillingworth, and Hawthorne's own emotional response to the scene (when he read it to Sophia) make it difficult to agree with such a reading.

More than one reader has correctly surmised that this ending to the novel constitutes a veiled compliment to Hawthorne's little Dove, Sophia, and a veiled criticism of Margaret Fuller, America's foremost advocate of women's rights and, at the time, one suffering from a sullied reputation due to gossip about her child and questionable marriage. Hawthorne's long and ambivalent relationship with Fuller and his response to her activities as a radical and revolutionary in 1849 had a decided effect upon the novel. There are several parallels which indicate Fuller served as a model for Hester: both had the problem of facing a Puritan society encumbered by a child of questionable legitimacy; both were concerned with social reform and the role of woman in society; both functioned as counsellor and comforter to women; and both had children entitled to use the armorial seals of a non-English noble family. All of these Francis E. Kearns has pointed out;[42] however, a more important parallel Kearns fails to mention is that for Hawthorne both women were associated with the ideas of temptation and revolution, with the figures of Eve and Liberty. Fuller was not only the most intelligent, articulate, and passionate woman Hawthorne had ever spent so many hours alone with,[43] she was also, as he began *The Scarlet Letter*, an ardent revolutionary supporting the overthrow of the most prominent political-religious leader in the world.

Certainly Hawthorne's knowledge of and interest in the New England past were considerable; however, as Thomas Woodson has pointed out, his interest in his contemporary world was far greater than the critical emphases of recent decades would indicate.[44] In his writing of *The Scarlet Letter* he drew upon the issues and rhetoric he was encountering in the present, especially those relating to himself as a public figure. Moreover, he responded strongly and creatively to accounts of foreign revolutions and revolutionaries that he found in the newspapers, the periodicals, and books new to the libraries. Although to most of his coun-

---

[42] "Margaret Fuller as a Model for Hester Prynne," *Jahrbuch für Amerikastudien*, 10 (1965), 191–97.

[43] The most revealing information about the Hawthorne-Fuller relationship is contained in Margaret Fuller's 1844 Commonplace Book, which deserves to be edited and published. The manuscript is on deposit by Mrs. Lewis F. Perry at the Massachusetts Historical Society.

[44] "Hawthorne's Interest in the Contemporary," *Nathaniel Hawthorne Society Newsletter*, 7 (1981), 1.

trymen the overthrow of kings and the triumph of republicanism were exhilarating events, to a man of Hawthorne's temperament, the violence, the bloodshed, the extended chaos that accompanied the revolutions of 1848–49 were deeply disturbing. Associated in his own mind with his personal plight, they, along with his reading in Guizot and Lamartine, shaped *The Scarlet Letter* in Burkean ways the reader of today finds difficult to accept. We value too highly Thomas Paine and the rights of woman.

Nature and Frontier in "Roger Malvin's Burial"
James McIntosh

I

"ROGER Malvin's Burial" has been much studied as a moral and psychological fable, a tale of hidden motives unconsciously acted out; and as a historical romance, a tale of an Indian-fighter who begins by defending the frontier against the savage but ends by carrying on a war within himself. One key feature of the tale that has received remarkably little attention is Hawthorne's treatment of the wilderness landscape, the natural setting in which the main action of the story occurs. There are reasons enough for this neglect. The action itself is so psychologically suggestive that some critics in recent decades have been drawn to it to the exclusion of other elements. Other critics have been intrigued by the historical account of "Lovell's Fight" that begins the tale, and have explained the tale as the enactment of a problem in New England's moral history.[1] Hawthorne's treatment of landscape, by contrast, has rarely been a subject of debate in this or any of his work.[2] In general, it is assumed,

---

[1] For readings of the psychological and moral action of "Roger Malvin's Burial," see especially Hyatt Waggoner, *Hawthorne* (Cambridge: Harvard Univ. Press, 1955), pp. 78–86; Frederick C. Crews, "The Logic of Compulsion in 'Roger Malvin's Burial,'" *PMLA*, 79 (1964), 457–65, and *The Sins of the Fathers: Hawthorne's Psychological Themes* (New York: Oxford Univ. Press, 1966), pp. 80–95; and Sharon Cameron, *The Corporeal Self: Allegories of the Body in Melville and Hawthorne* (Baltimore: Johns Hopkins Univ. Press, 1981), pp. 137–44. For historicist readings, see especially Robert S. Daly, "History and Chivalric Myth in 'Roger Malvin's Burial,'" *Essex Institute Historical Collections*, 109 (1973), 99–115; and Michael J. Colacurcio, *The Province of Piety: Moral History in Hawthorne's Early Tales* (Cambridge: Harvard Univ. Press, 1984), pp. 107–30.

[2] William J. Scheick suggests the central importance of the unknowableness of nature in the tale in "The Hieroglyphic Rock in Hawthorne's 'Roger Malvin's Burial,'" *Emerson Society Quarterly*, 24 (1978), 72–76. An excellent brief commentary on Hawthorne's

Hawthorne's descriptions are either factual and journalistic, as in "Sketches from Memory" and, more subtly, *The Blithedale Romance*, or allegorical, as in "The Man of Adamant" and, more elaborately, *The Scarlet Letter*. Moreover, conventional opinion has it that Hawthorne had little disposition toward Romanticism, and hence little use for the idea of "Nature." As a result of this neglect, readers have tended to absorb the landscape in "Roger Malvin's Burial" without realizing what it has meant to them.

"Roger Malvin's Burial" is a very early work by Hawthorne. As we know from his correspondence, he had ready a version of it by late 1829 that he submitted to Samuel Goodrich; and two years later it was published in Goodrich's *Token* along with those other early masterpieces, "My Kinsman, Major Molineux" and "The Gentle Boy." As he launched himself as a writer of historical romance, then, Hawthorne explored three strains of New England history, the matter of the Puritans in "The Gentle Boy," the matter of the Revolution in "My Kinsman, Major Molineux," and the matter of the frontier in "Roger Malvin's Burial." Yet while he was to return to the Puritans again and again and to the Revolution in ample measure in the late 1830s, "Roger Malvin's Burial" is his only significant attempt to dramatize the frontier. It is unique also in the ways it presents a frontier landscape. Hawthorne's interest in frontier psychology led him, it seems, to work out a special relation between his frontiersmen and their wilderness environment. Granted, Hawthorne takes his characters into the wilderness elsewhere, in "Young Goodman Brown" and *The Scarlet Letter*, for instance, but in those fictions the landscape tends to be used as an arena for the allegorical projection of character when it is not used as scenic background. In "Roger Malvin's Burial" the relation between character and setting is more continuously central to the effect of the story because the setting has an interest in itself unusual for Hawthorne. "Nature" has its own unknowable character that develops in the course of the tale. At the same time, those hunters and pilgrims Roger Malvin and Reuben, Dorcas, and Cyrus Bourne project a variety of human attributes onto

---

treatment of the frontier in "Roger Malvin's Burial" appears in Edwin Fussell, *Frontier* (Princeton: Princeton Univ. Press, 1965), pp. 75–77.

the forest as they make their way through it. Such a treatment of landscape is unusually shifting and varied for Hawthorne. It is one of those early experiments in imagination and technique that he will not precisely repeat.

"Roger Malvin's Burial" belongs to the first phase of Hawthorne's career as a short-story writer. We can date this phase approximately from 1829 to 1832, comprising his writings after *Fanshawe* and before "The Story-Teller." It should be conceived as a distinct phase rather than only as a time of anticipations.[3] One reason it has not usually been so conceived is that Hawthorne's efforts during these years are so experimental and heterogeneous. He tries his hand at a host of new literary ventures, not only "provincial tales" but ghost stories, personal essays like "Sights from a Steeple," and the four "biographical sketches" of figures from New England history. In the three major historical tales, moreover, not only is his invention fertile and diverse, but his designs are inordinately ambitious. He has not yet chosen to limit the scope of his tales or learned to give them ready generic boundaries. Never again will he write such an overdetermined tale as "My Kinsman," which is at once Robin's personal midsummer night's nightmare and a condensed political allegory, a ritual communal comedy and the poignant tragedy of a persecuted old man. Nor, at least in his other short fiction, will he present such a detailed picture of seventeenth-century New England manners as he does in the 1831 "Gentle Boy," as if he were preparing himself for a career as a historical novelist rather than that of an elliptical romancer. Thus it should not surprise us that "Roger Malvin's Burial" also reflects Hawthorne's many-sided ambition and contains unrepeated experiments, in its treatment of landscape and narrative as well as in its celebrated treatment of Reuben Bourne's "logic of compulsion."[4]

As we shall see, Hawthorne's experiment with the representation of landscape in the story is inextricably involved with his experiment with narration. The variety of stances his characters take toward the wilderness requires a flexible control of point

---

[3] A satisfactory account of this phase remains to be written. Nina Baym's in *The Shape of Hawthorne's Career* (Ithaca: Cornell Univ. Press, 1976), pp. 29–39, is, as we might expect, the best we have, but is more cursory than her treatment of other periods.

[4] See Crews, "The Logic of Compulsion in 'Roger Malvin's Burial.'"

of view. Hawthorne dramatizes his narrator in a varying, yet pointed manner, so as both to enter his characters' minds and to pass ironic judgment on them. Descriptive writing within this drama offers him a suitable medium for his changeable tentativeness, and also a means by which to exercise his moral authority.

Another ambitious impulse that enlivens "Roger Malvin's Burial" as well as the other two major tales is Hawthorne's proclivity to rewrite New England history in his own new way. He casts himself in these tales as a discreet revisionist historian. The three tales take a subversive approach to New England historical pieties and treat ironically the attempts of nineteenth-century New Englanders to gloss over the cruelty of the Puritan community at the time of Endicott, the violence of the Sons of Liberty during the Stamp Act Crisis, and the aroused spirit of vengeance of Captain Lovewell's band of frontier warriors. Hawthorne knew that Lovewell and his men ventured into the wilderness not only to defend the settlements but also to murder and scalp Indian warriors for large rewards. Hence in the historical account that begins "Roger Malvin's Burial" he implies that the 1825 commemorations of "Lovell's Fight" in Maine, New Hampshire, and Massachusetts amounted in part to a wishful refusal to face disagreeable facts, which "imagination" had "cast ... judiciously into the shade."[5] I would not oversimplify. Here as elsewhere Hawthorne is engaged in a moral balancing act; and he backhandedly justifies the use Providence made of this frontier violence, which brought peace to New England for a time. Nevertheless, the reader misses one of the chief assumptions underlying the tale if he or she fails to notice that in the opening paragraph the frontiersmen are made morally equivalent to the Indians.[6] Both parties display the same "open bravery," which,

---

[5] *Mosses from an Old Manse* (Columbus: Ohio State Univ. Press, 1974), p. 337 (vol. 10 of *The Centenary Edition of the Works of Nathaniel Hawthorne*). Further references to "Roger Malvin's Burial" will be to this edition.

[6] I agree with Daly and Colacurcio, and differ respectfully with David Levin, in that I think Hawthorne's intent ironic in his account of Lovell's Fight. See Levin, "Modern Misjudgements of Racial Imperialism in Hawthorne and Parkman," *Yearbook of English Studies*, 13 (1983), 145–58. The vital barbarism of New England frontiersmen is treated ironically also in Hawthorne's very early historical sketches, "Sir William Phips" and "Sir William Pepperel." See especially in "Sir William Phips" the description of the "man clad in a hunting-shirt and Indian stockings" whose clothes are covered with leaves from "the tangled wilderness" and who wears on his head "a wig made of the long and

the narrator remarks ironically, is "in accordance with civilized ideas of valor." (As Hawthorne knew, both parties slaughtered their enemies with wanton cruelty in incidents before the battle. Rather than following "civilized ideals," whites and Indians alike behaved like savages, first in their cruelty and then in their bravery.) Likewise, the battle was "so fatal to those who fought" on both sides. The dead of one hundred years ago do not share in any self-congratulatory commemorations but are simply and fatally dead. Indians and whites are joined in death, untouched by the wishful "imagination" of later generations.

This subversive implication that frontiersmen and Indians resemble each other persists in the ensuing tale of Roger Malvin and Reuben Bourne. A historical question the tale asks is how could these men maintain their inherited Puritan ways of thinking and at the same time share attitudes and habits of behavior with their neighbors, the Indians, and what does this combination make them as representatives of their place and time? For representative frontiersmen they surely are, responsive to the long period of savage conflict with French and Indian on the northern frontier that lasted from King Philip's War till the defeat of the French in 1763. One way Hawthorne manages this question is by setting his tale in a wild, or as he calls it "savage," landscape. This is the home of the Indian, yet the frontiersman has begun unconsciously to make it his home as well. He is intermittently attracted to it, while at the same time as a Puritan he finds it inscrutable and desolate and wishes to protect himself from it. His ambivalence toward the landscape mirrors the division in his cultural and psychological make-up. He is at war to the death with the Indian, yet has made himself akin to him in order to survive.

Reuben and his family define themselves consciously as opposed to the Indians and different from them. Late in the tale, when Dorcas prepares supper in the wilderness for her husband and son, she sings an anonymous song "descriptive of a winter evening in a frontier-cottage, when, secured from savage inroad by the high-piled snow-drifts, the family rejoiced by their own fireside." The song calls up a picture of New England innocence;

---

straight black hair of his slain savage enemies"—*Tales, Sketches, and Other Papers* (Boston: Houghton Mifflin, 1883), p. 231 (vol. 12 in the 1883 *Works of Nathaniel Hawthorne*).

in "simple words," Hawthorne writes, "the poet had instilled the very essence of domestic love and household happiness." The narrative commemorates this innocence, but also implies that domestic bliss and household happiness can only be preserved through fierce hostility to the native inhabitants. Similarly, when Reuben leads Dorcas and Cyrus back toward Roger Malvin's rock, they are described as traveling "into a region, of which savage beasts and savage men were as yet the sole possessors." Opposed to the Indian, they intrude in his accustomed home, the undomesticated wilderness.

In this passage Hawthorne, I am sure, remembers William Bradford's (or as he knew it Nathaniel Morton's) description of the landscape that greeted the pilgrims of the Plymouth colony in 1620: "What could they see but a hideous and desolate Wilderness full of wilde Beasts and wilde Men?"[7] Indeed, as Michael J. Colacurcio has argued, the narrative implies throughout that men and women on the frontier think of themselves as pilgrims.[8] When Reuben, Dorcas, and Cyrus take their leave of the settlements they become "pilgrims" venturing into "the untrodden forest." Earlier, both Roger's life on the frontier and Reuben's journey through the woods to the settlements are called "pilgrimages." Thus the persons of the story are linked with Bradford, and with New England's conception of itself as a place of Christian pilgrimage. Yet these eighteenth-century frontiersmen differ from the Plymouth brethren in a way that brings them closer to the Indians they oppose. They identify themselves not only as pilgrims but also and more often as hunters —indeed it is as "a hunter and a warrior" that Roger wishes to

---

[7] Nathaniel Morton, *New England's Memorial* (1669; rpt. Boston: Club of Odd Volumes, 1903), p. 13. Bradford's *Of Plimouth Plantation* was as yet unpublished in 1829, but Morton's transcription of parts of it was readily available. Hawthorne had borrowed a recently published new edition of *New England's Memorial* (Boston, 1826) from the Salem Athenaeum on 26 April 1828. (See Marion L. Kesselring, "Hawthorne's Reading, 1828–1850," *Bulletin of the New York Public Library*, 53 [1949], 71, 187.) In *Grandfather's Chair*, Hawthorne refers to this same passage explicitly when he has Grandfather describe Lady Arbella Johnson's unhappy exile in New England: "Poor Lady Arbella watches all these sights, and feels that this new world is fit only for rough and hardy people. None should be here, but those who can can struggle with wild beasts and wild men, and can toil in the heat or cold, and can keep their hearts firm against all difficulties and dangers" —*True Stories from History and Biography* (Columbus: Ohio State Univ. Press, 1972), pp. 16–17 (vol. 6 of *The Centenary Edition of the Works of Nathaniel Hawthorne*).

[8] *The Province of Piety*, p. 124.

be remembered on his tombstone. He implies unwittingly that he has partly taken on the character of an Indian hunter and warrior in order to give his life meaning. He has lived by this Indian calling and now after Lovell's Fight he will die by it. As Hawthorne read the history of the Fight, then, he saw the kinship between the hunters on both sides, and partly for that reason he made the motif of frontiersmen-as-hunters crucial to the drama of "Roger Malvin's Burial."

The likeness of frontiersmen and Indians is hinted at several times in the course of the tale. The frontier inhabitants are said to pay "an almost superstitious regard . . . to the rites of sepulture" "arising perhaps from the customs of the Indians." Elsewhere the narrative speaks of Reuben's "superstitious fears, of which none were more susceptible than the people of the outward settlements." The implication is that as a man living on the edge of the wilderness Reuben partly thinks like an Indian. A signal irony in the action is that Reuben leaves Roger sitting upright in the posture of Freneau's Indian hunter and warrior dressed for burial;[9] in effect he has buried him alive as if he were an Indian. The intimation throughout the tale that "the people of the outward settlements" are primitive as well as Christian in feeling helps ground the ending, when Reuben trusts that Heaven will afford him an opportunity of expiating his sin, but then restores his heart only by killing his son. Tragically, he deludes himself that regeneration comes through violence.[10] Reuben is impelled to his final act both by the trust of a pilgrim and "the instinct of a hunter." In his final misery he is a savage as well as a Puritan. The tale shows that Hawthorne is well aware of the moral confusion implicit in this combination.

II

"Roger Malvin's Burial," then, quietly dramatizes the proto-

[9] Freneau's own note to his well known poem, "The Indian Burial Ground," explains: "The North American Indians bury their dead in a sitting posture; decorating the corpse with wampum, the images of birds, quadrupeds, &: And (if that of a warrior) with bows, arrows, tomhawks and other military weapons." *The Poems of Philip Freneau*, ed. F. L. Pattee (1903; rpt. New York: Russell & Russell, 1963), II, 369.

[10] I allude to Richard Slotkin's *Regeneration Through Violence: The Mythology of the American Frontier* (Middletown, Conn.: Wesleyan Univ. Press, 1973). Slotkin's own treatment of "Roger Malvin's Burial" is brief, but he studies in great detail the tendencies of white settlers to imagine themselves partly as Indians.

Melvillean point that, despite their Christian upbringing, frontiersmen have the propensity to act like savages. It also questions the New England chauvinism that helped justify the violence accompanying the opening of the frontier. Yet in its tonal elaboration the tale is Hawthorne's, not Melville's. Its ironies are quiet, its subversiveness suffused with lyricism. Its author pursues his research in the hearts of the frontiersmen "as well by the tact of sympathy as by the light of [ironic] observation."[11]

At the start of the tale proper, after the account of Lovell's Fight, Hawthorne moves sympathetically into the hearts and minds of his characters. He manages this movement initially by means of a description of the landscape surrounding the rock where Roger Malvin sits dying. Intermittently throughout the tale, this landscape, or a variation of it, is evoked to modify and mediate our responses to the characters. The wilderness seems to solicit different responses at different times, depending on the occasion. Like other settings in Hawthorne, it reflects the minds of the characters within it. Reuben especially is a complex and conflict-ridden character. Since he is both a hunter and a pilgrim he colors what he sees with the eyes of both these disparate types, and this partly accounts for the wide variety of responses to the wilderness the text expresses. Yet in this tale the wilderness is more than just a means to characterization. The treatment of landscape has another dimension, owing partly to the fact that Lovell's Fight took place in southwestern Maine near Raymond, a region with which Hawthorne was deeply familiar. It is where he "ran quite wild"[12] as a boy, and also heard tales of wilderness strife between frontiersmen and Indians. It came naturally to him to use this familiar landscape not only as a place to reenact the past but also as an authentic emblem of wild Nature itself. The landscape in the tale seems more closely and affectionately observed than elsewhere in his work. This helps him give the wilderness something of a fictional character of its own. It plays a role not always fully controlled by the conscious or unconscious imaginations of the merely human characters.

---

[11] *The Snow-Image and Uncollected Tales* (Columbus: Ohio State Univ. Press, 1974), p. 4 (vol. 11 of *The Centenary Edition of the Works of Nathaniel Hawthorne*).

[12] From Hawthorne's 1853 account of his early life, quoted in Julian Hawthorne, *Nathaniel Hawthorne and His Wife* (Boston: Houghton Mifflin, 1884), I, 95. For a valuable treatment of his early experience in Maine, see Melinda Ponder, "Hawthorne and Raymond, Maine," *Nathaniel Hawthorne Review*, 12, No. 2 (1986), 4–10.

This partly independent role is immediately apparent in the opening description.

> The early sunbeams hovered cheerfully upon the tree-tops, beneath which two weary and wounded men had stretched their limbs the night before. Their bed of withered oak-leaves was strewn upon the small level space, at the foot of a rock, situated near the summit of one of the gentle swells, by which the face of the country is there diversified. The mass of granite, rearing its smooth, flat surface, fifteen or twenty feet above their heads, was not unlike a gigantic gravestone, upon which the veins seemed to form a description in forgotten characters. On a tract of several acres around this rock, oaks and other hard-wood trees had supplied the place of the pines, which were the usual growth of the land; and a young and vigorous sapling stood close beside the travellers.

I would call attention to several features of this description. To begin with, it conveys an illusion of objectivity. It contains facts about the contours of the land and the local species of trees, even about what Thoreau would call "the succession of forest trees."[13] The narrator knows the country and is ready to inform the reader about it. Yet at the same time there is something unknowable about the scene. The inscription "in forgotten characters" on the rock is a natural mystery that is never explained in the course of the story. It points to an aspect of the wilderness which the frontiersmen cannot understand and which they fear. However much it may seem human at times, the wilderness is also enigmatically itself. Finally, even with its mystery, this is a congenial landscape, with cheerful sunbeams, gentle swells of countryside, and a bed of leaves for Roger to rest on. In itself such an image of Nature has no hostility to man—if anything it seems his nurse and comforter.

This initial description engages us with its sensuous detail and its tone of sympathy, and registers an impression against which we measure other views of the wilderness proffered later by the persons of the story as well as by other narrative voices within it. Of course, our first impression has no fixed validity. The significance of the landscape is fluid in the text and evolves with our reading of it. For example, the narrator gives a different

---

[13] "The Succession of Forest Trees," in *The Writings of Henry David Thoreau* (Boston: Houghton Mifflin, 1906), V, 184–204, especially 189.

impression of the wilderness when he explains Roger's change of countenance as he thinks of dying in it: "after all, it was a ghastly fate, to be left expiring in the wilderness." The narrative reflects Roger's mind here, voicing his secret doubts about his advice to Reuben, but it also implies that after all this is not such a comforting place as it first appeared. Nevertheless, the effect of the opening description is powerfully with us during the whole first scene. It ought, for example, to influence our reading of Roger's comment on the landscape as he seeks to persuade Reuben to abandon him. "There is many and many a long mile of howling wilderness before us yet." Far from convincingly characterizing the wilderness itself, this assertion typecasts Malvin. As we know, he is drawing on the remembered language of his particular culture, the language of Bradford and Endicott. "Howling wilderness" is the early settlers' customary label for undomesticated nature in New England. Roger betrays his conditioned anxiety as an embattled pilgrim, sharing with Reuben his emotional bias as well as his knowledge of the territory.

This changing perspective toward the wilderness is a feature of the narrative throughout. By the juxtaposition of the congenial opening description with Malvin's contrary assessment, we should be trained to read everything that is voiced about the wilderness as partial, whether it comes in the speech of the characters or in the narrative. The "real" wilderness remains untouched by all these partial assessments, beyond the scope of language to articulate definitively. Yet it remains as a fictive presence in the tale. The opening description has made the presence of the wilderness both trustworthy and mysterious, and we read on partly to see the mystery deepened or varied or clarified.

The multitude of perspectives taken toward the wilderness is nowhere more evident than at that point when Reuben and his family quit the settlements to pursue their fortunes elsewhere. Reuben, a ruined man, decides that only one course is open to him. "He was to throw sunlight into some deep recess of the forest, and seek subsistence from the virgin bosom of the wilderness." So the howling wilderness has a virgin bosom! Hawthorne shows how well he understands the cognitive dissonance inherent in the Puritan Errand and the particular confusion of one poor hunter-pilgrim. When provoked by fear at the end of the tale Reuben too will speak of "this howling wilderness." As he proposes to journey into the forest, however, he shows that he also shares with his culture the image of a virgin wilderness, the notion that one can encroach on wild Nature without her resisting. Three paragraphs later the text dilates rhapsodically on this partial perspective. "Oh! who, in the enthusiasm of a day-dream, has not wished that he were a wanderer in a world of summer wilderness, with one fair and gentle being hanging lightly on his arm?" The voice Hawthorne ironically projects is that of a wishfully innocent reader all too ready to imagine a Reuben or Cyrus purified of conflict.[14] The narrator expatiates on the prospects of this imagined early American as pilgrim-hunter. He is to found a family, become a patriarch, be remembered in afterlife as a father of the frontier. But of course such a notion of an effortless appropriation of Nature is drastically undercut. None of the Bournes is to claim such an inheritance. More explicitly than any image of the wilderness in the whole tale the image of its virginal availability is a falsification, a dreamer's "fantasy," as the chameleon narrator suggests less ironically in his next picture: "The tangled and gloomy forest, through which the personages of my tale were wandering, differed widely from the dreamer's Land of Fantasie; yet there was something in their way of life that Nature asserted as her own; and the gnawing cares, which went with them from the world, were all that now obstructed their happiness."

Hawthorne burrows deeply here, suggests hidden feelings in the hearts of these frontier explorers of which they are scarcely aware. "The tangled and gloomy forest" corresponds with the family's gnawing cares and thus expresses their mind more accurately than the fantasy of summer wilderness. Yet at the same time there is something else in "Nature" that stimulates and empowers them. Nature is making them into more natural men. They may be losing touch with the social "world," but they feel a primitive pleasure in the way of life the forest enjoins and have intimations of a primitive, natural happiness. Though Hawthorne does not spell out the idea except by association, the Bournes have become more like savages, with savage advantages

---

[14] I follow Fussell and Colacurcio in my reading of this passage. See *Frontier*, p. 76, and *The Province of Piety*, pp. 121–23.

as well as limitations. The passage momentarily lends a heathen hope to their errand while at the same time obliquely portending the disaster that will strike these hunters at the end of the tale. They are now arriving in a region of savage beasts and savage men and will be more disposed in the depths of their hearts to act on savage instincts.

This evocation of "the tangled and gloomy forest" does more than illustrate how perspectives on the wilderness change in keeping with the changing moods of the characters and the voice of the narrative. It also raises the question of the meaning of "Nature." If all perspectives on the landscape are partial, are either culturally or psychologically determined, does Nature have any meaning in itself, or is it only a stage set for human responses and projections? Hawthorne certainly uses the word diversely in the tale to fit the dramatic needs of his characters. Earlier, when Reuben gloomily watches Roger praying in solitude, Hawthorne writes, "there seemed a gloom on Nature's face, as if she sympathized with mortal pain and sorrow." Later Dorcas, left alone by her husband and son, lays out her snow-white tablecloth "in the desolate heart of Nature." In these three contexts Nature is by turns a figure for secret natural energies, a figure for maternal sympathy, and a figure for the howling wilderness.

Yet as readers of the tale we never believe that Nature is incoherent—it impresses us as having one character, however diverse. This is partly because Nature, dramatically considered, is simply a personification for the wilderness. The method of the tale allows us to think of the wilderness, and hence of Nature, both as persistently the same and as varying to suit the needs of the fictive occasion. Conceptually, these diverse ideas of Nature are conventional in 1829–31. They are part of the equipment with which a young writer of the period would be likely to imagine the wilderness. Moreover, as a writer emerging in the immediate aftermath of English Romanticism (and while American Romanticism is gathering strength), Hawthorne treats all these ideas of Nature as one idea. In this tale he deploys an American Romantic conception, which he will later regard more skeptically, of wild Nature as an all-encompassing other, connected to human nature yet apart from it, sympathetic to the plight of sufferers but also mysterious and potentially threatening. This other corresponds with the minds of the characters from time to time but also asserts its own difference. Of course, Hawthorne does not endorse such a Romantic conception of Nature. Now as later his mind is too fine to be suited to didacticism. Rather, he uses the conception to give the wilderness meaning, wholeness, attractiveness, and power as a fictive presence.

No doubt Hawthorne plays with this conception and puts it through as many variations as it will take. Yet one of the reasons the tale works as an integrated fiction is that wilderness Nature captivates the reader throughout. Even in the opening description several ideas of the wilderness—as a comforting mother, as a vital source, and as a self-assertive stranger—are all more or less implicit. This opening description imparts a poetic faith in wilderness Nature as an independent entity, a faith nothing else in the tale will shake. Through all the permutations of the setting, the character of the wilderness keeps evolving in itself as well as illustrating human fear and desire. This character is large and flexible enough to include all the disparate significances that human voices in the text attribute to the wilderness, because the dramatic illusion is maintained that it remains itself.

Overall, Hawthorne carefully balances the impression of congeniality he creates in the opening with an impression of threatening power he invokes on other occasions. The impression of Nature's power increases dramatically when Reuben and his family arrive back in the vicinity of Roger Malvin's rock. The narrative echoes the opening description, but with a telling difference: "On the afternoon of the fifth day, they halted and made their simple encampment, nearly an hour before sunset. The face of the country, for the last few miles, had been diversified by swells of land, resembling huge waves of a petrified sea." We recall "the gentle swells, by which the face of the country is there diversified." These are now likened to "huge waves of a petrified sea." With this change in the image the same wild place is no longer so congenial but has become sublime, its sublimity portending an unnamed crisis. Such a tone is displaced by others as the tale moves to its climax. Yet this is a key moment, suggesting that the landscape has a power of its own to be what it will, that it can play a role in directing Reuben's fate.

In the course of the tale, the landscape increasingly takes on the role of a surrogate for fate. The wilderness throughout has seemed a large and shadowy other to the frontiersmen. They keep guessing its meaning but they fail to understand it. One effect of all their misreadings is to build up its shadowy power. At the end the wilderness exercises its power and draws Reuben back to the scene of his imagined crime. The landscape in the final episode is presented more allegorically than at the start of the tale, when Hawthorne took pains to create an illusion of factuality. The details of the final scene conspire to exert a quasi-magical hold on Reuben and his family. When the branches of the trees rustle and their trunks creak, it seems to the narrator and to Reuben (we are in his mind) "as if the forest were waking from slumber." Even seemingly neutral details such as the "dense and bushy undergrowth" take on an obscure imagined life and support an emerging psychological allegory. More centrally to the story, the rock becomes a palpable image of internal as well as external fate, a metonym for Reuben's projected inner necessities as well as a synechdoche for the wilderness' magnetic power.

Yet at the same time, the scene has a more complex effect because it remains more than merely allegorical.[15] The wilderness landscape continues to play another role, that of a natural world apart that frontier man will never know. From the start it has had a mysterious objective presence that perforce eludes human definitions; and even at the end the text makes clear that all readings of the landscape are human and partial. The narrator's own readings are manifestly conjectural. Before he imagines the forest waking from slumber, he interprets the sounds that it makes and that humans hear quite differently. The Bournes have lit their campfire, and the narrator comments: "The dark and gloomy pines looked down upon them, and, as the wind swept through their tops, a pitying sound was heard in the forest; or did those old trees groan, in fear that men were come to lay the axe to their roots at last?" The narrator's question reminds us that we do not know what the trees feel. Despite our illusory

---

[15] However valuable Crews's Freudian reading of the story's plot and symbols continues to be, when he writes that the forest into which Reuben travels is simply "his own mind," and when he calls Hawthorne's region of savage beasts and savage men only "the mental region of Hawthorne's best insight and highest art," he oversimplifies the story's partially naturalistic treatment of the wilderness and neglects its historical dimension. (*Sins of the Fathers*, pp. 94, 95.)

conjectures the forest keeps its own counsel and remains itself. Similarly, the rock at the end may well stand for the internal and external power that dictates Reuben's destiny, but at the same time it is still a rock somewhere in the uncharted territory north of the settlements. Even the oak tree is imagined as a natural tree as well as a metonym for Reuben as a ruined older man. It sheds "real" leaves that physically cover the bones of the dead as well as the metonymic tears of a natural double. As in later Hawthorne, "Nature seems to love us,"[16] but continues to carry out its own operations. Yet Hawthorne uses the unknowableness and the inhumanity of the landscape to good fictional effect here. It helps keep the ending from seeming hermetically psychological. After he kills his son, Reuben must go on with his life in the actual and unfathomable forest.

III

Hawthorne has made the meaning of "Nature" elusive and varied yet central in "Roger Malvin's Burial." He wishes to do justice to the confused complexity of a representative frontiersman's perspective on the wilderness in the era when the settlements in northern New England were still the frontier. The wilderness is not only the home of the hostile savage, a boundless region with a desolate heart, but is also a place where a frontiersman can hunt and grow wild, a source of comfort and delight. Both these views are in play in the depiction of the frontier mind. Both also are comprehended in the idea that Nature is a living whole which the frontiersmen do not understand, which nourishes them but may overpower them and even enact a judgment on them. Nature as a living whole is of course a nineteenth-century idea. Yet, Hawthorne suggests, the Malvins and the Bournes must have sensed the presence of such a Nature when they found themselves surrounded by the wild unknown and felt drawn to it as well as in awe of it. The frontiersmen were not just invading the lands of the Indian but also dimly discovering who they were in the mirror of the new world wilderness.

---

[16] *The Blithedale Romance* and *Fanshawe* (Columbus: Ohio State Univ. Press, 1964), p. 244 (vol. 3 of *The Centenary Edition of the Works of Nathaniel Hawthorne*).

The reader too is implicated in Reuben's invasion and discovery. Because landscape has a powerful subliminal effect on reading, it helps the reader to integrate the tale and respond to both its historical and its personal tragedy. An important esthetic function of the landscape is to make it possible for one to read the cultural-historical and the psychological-moral dimensions of the tale as if they were aspects of a single whole. The wilderness in "Roger Malvin's Burial" is an obscure and comprehensive enough mirror to reflect disparate human desires as if they belonged together in one undifferentiated mass of desire. Reuben's feelings as a pilgrim-hunter who would seek his fortune on Indian lands are reflected in his responses to the wilderness, but so also are his feelings as an errant foster-son who has failed to heed his adopted father's call to bury him in his place of death. The landscape's persistent presence mediates in our reading between the tale as an historical representation of a culture and the tale as a "timeless" psychological drama. Through landscape, Hawthorne is able to take up his different stories, including the story of Lovell's Fight, and transform them into one story.

In addition, the changing relation between man and the landscape in "Roger Malvin's Burial" is its own submerged alternative story that runs slightly counter emotionally to the drama of a ruined frontiersman and the murder of his son that is the main subject of the tale. Because this alternative story is conveyed through description, the reader takes it in less directly and continuously, more as a series of intermittent impressions. The reader is sensitive to its being in a different generic mode, as if "Roger Malvin's Burial" in one of its dimensions were a Romantic narrative of the conflicted relation between man and Nature, not just a tale of guilt and expiation. The landscape in this alternative story is a sort of wild card that from time to time unpredictably alters the rules of the game Hawthorne plays with us. On occasion, the reader feels a measure of identity with the characters because he or she too faces Hawthorne's imagined wilderness with somewhat similar emotions, with excitement and awe before an unknown. In other words, Hawthorne's use of landscape creates a hidden fraternity between characters and readers.

It is not just that the lyrical early descriptions induce sympathy with the wounded warriors. The reader is also brought close to Reuben and his son when they feel by turns excited and estranged in the forest toward the end. Such a connection between reader and characters is of course kept tentative and intermittent by the thematic and tonal ironies that mark the tale throughout. In its course, Reuben is inescapably judged and found wanting while the laws of his psychological and historical being are anatomized and dramatized. It is essential to the tragic effect of the whole that one recognizes and judges Reuben's archetypal failure from a moral and esthetic distance. Nevertheless, the landscape helps engender an equally essential sense of identity with him. Such a use of landscape, in which a morally equivocal character takes on a new dimension because he or she is cast in a Romantic relation with Nature, is significant in other fictional texts of the period, such as Brown's *Edgar Huntly*, or Goethe's *Elective Affinities*, or Brontë's *Wuthering Heights*. In these texts too the landscape is a means for creating a bond of identity between readers and characters as well as a device for probing the impulses of the unconscious. Because landscape has these unpredictable but central effects on the reading experience, Hawthorne uses it from beginning to end of "Roger Malvin's Burial" to make his tale resonate with the voice of the reader's own feeling.

Nathaniel Hawthorne's Intention in
"Chiefly About War Matters"

James Bense

DESPITE its notoriety among Hawthorne specialists, "Chiefly About War Matters" remains one of the author's least known and appreciated writings published during his lifetime. Hawthorne's motive in what is alleged to have been an act of authorial self-censorship has not been clearly understood. Neither has evidence to the contrary been fully examined. Traditionally, an imprecise account of disagreements that arose between Hawthorne and his publishers has beclouded the genesis of the text, confusing elements of Hawthorne's intentional satire with reported last-minute concessions to suppress and nullify parts of the original version.

The following analysis of what happened brings the essay into its proper light and takes a first step toward a critical appreciation of its true character. Although expurgations did occur, the facts derived from the evidence as a whole indicate that Hawthorne had originally devised his essay in great part as a censorship hoax. As a result of constraints he felt while trying to write honestly about the war, he created a satirical dialectic between his narrator and an imaginary editor. Through this ventriloquism, which has been misapprehended as self-censorship, Hawthorne's essay communicates the importance of maintaining freedom of speech while it is most severely tested, when the passions of a nation in turmoil threaten to suppress it.

I

After following the early events of the Civil War from a distance, Hawthorne resolved to approach the crisis more closely. In March 1862, accordingly, he traveled from New England to Washington, observed General George McClellan reviewing

Union troops, met President Lincoln, and toured Union military installations along the Virginia border. "Chiefly About War Matters," later published in the July 1862 *Atlantic* under the pseudonymous appellation of "A Peaceable Man," presents a narrative of firsthand impressions gathered during the trip and reflects Hawthorne's dissent from the social idealism of the Northern public.

Hawthorne intended his essay to be provocative. Its probing observations sustain a sharp focus and immediacy; as a result, the essay's narrative consciousness is dynamic and complex. The discursive movement of the text registers candid, humorous, and heartfelt reflections, far-flung in their implications and unsettling to the North's moral vision of the war. This persona is countered by the defensive reactions of a censorious editor, apparently of the *Atlantic*, whose objections to parts of the text represent the prevailing mood and opinion of Northern readers.

Hawthorne's contemporary readers were disturbed by the essay's broad range of disconcerting viewpoints about the war crisis. Many were fooled by the pseudo-authenticity of the editorial notes.[1] Subsequently, neither Hawthorne's intention nor achievement has been accurately recognized. To some extent, the confusion surrounding the text has been symptomatic of the fervid atmosphere of political crisis in which he wrote. Even so, the later failure of eminently competent readers to perceive the essay's notes as the author's own is surprising.[2] More importantly, an apocryphal tradition has grown up among Hawthorne's twentieth-century biographers and critics, who acknowledge that the notes are Hawthorne's but maintain that they were his reluctant concession to self-censorship.[3]

---

[1] For evidence of the contemporary response, see Julian Hawthorne, *Nathaniel Hawthorne and His Wife* (Boston: Houghton Mifflin, 1884, 1893), II, 311–14; Moncure D. Conway, *Life of Nathaniel Hawthorne* (1890; rpt. New York: Haskell House, 1968), pp. 203–06; and Daniel Aaron, *The Unwritten War: American Writers and the Civil War* (New York: Knopf, 1973), p. 51.

[2] Henry James and historian George M. Fredrickson have taken Hawthorne's footnotes to be authentic reactions of the *Atlantic* management, thus exemplifying the extent of the irony that has resulted historically from Hawthorne's Swiftian intention. See, respectively, *Hawthorne*, ed. Tony Tanner (1879; rpt. New York: St. Martin's, 1967), p. 159; and *The Inner Civil War: Northern Intellectuals and the Crisis of the Union* (New York: Harper & Row, 1965), pp. 2–3.

[3] The misleading information in the Riverside Edition and Fields's reminiscence of Hawthorne (both cited below) evidently led Randall Stewart to infer that Fields had

Hawthorne's plan to publish a satirical hoax was obscured initially by unanticipated censoring on the part of his friend and editor James T. Fields and, later, by subsequent historical accounts of the matter. A manuscript written in Hawthorne's hand and bearing the signatures of typesetters (presumably those who produced the proof sheets for the July 1862 *Atlantic*) still survives; nonetheless, a complete text of the essay as originally submitted has never appeared in print.[4] In both the first published version, edited for the *Atlantic* in 1862, and the partially-restored version first printed in the 1883 Riverside Edition of Hawthorne's collected works, footnotes written by Hawthorne but implicitly attributed to the *Atlantic* editor raise objections to remarks in the text. When Hawthorne as narrator asserts, for instance, that "Man's accidents are God's purposes. We miss the good we sought, and do the good we little cared for," Hawthorne as pseudo-editor replies in an anonymous footnote: "The author seems to imagine that he has compressed a great deal of meaning into these little, hard, dry pellets of aphoristic wisdom. We disagree with him. The councils of wise and good men are often coincident with the purposes of Providence; and the present war promises to illustrate our remark."[5]

Moreover, as revealed by Hawthorne's manuscript, he also devised textual disjunctions creating the illusion of missing pas-

---

deleted the passages about Lincoln and "certain Cabinet-members and Congressmen." Not able "to locate the original manuscript," Stewart concluded that this material "would seem to be irrecoverable" ("Hawthorne and the Civil War," *Studies in Philology*, 34 [1937], 96n). Apparently basing his remarks on the same sources as Stewart, Matthiessen inferred that Hawthorne had written the notes at the insistence of the *Atlantic* (*American Renaissance: Art and Expression in the Age of Emerson and Whitman* [New York: Oxford Univ. Press, 1941], p. 317). Similarly, Nina Baym, *The Shape of Hawthorne's Career* (Ithaca: Cornell Univ. Press, 1976), p. 267, speaks of the actual removal of "paragraphs pertaining to Washington officials"; and Raymona E. Hull has Hawthorne promising Fields to add the notes (*Nathaniel Hawthorne: The English Experience, 1853–1864* [Pittsburgh: Univ. of Pittsburgh Press, 1980], pp. 209–10). Arlin Turner concludes correctly that the essay "remained thoroughly Hawthornean." But his reference to "deleted passages" later published by Fields suggests that Turner was still not sure exactly what Fields had done to Hawthorne's text (*Nathaniel Hawthorne: A Biography* [New York: Oxford Univ. Press, 1980], p. 366).

[4] Nathaniel Hawthorne Collection 6249-g, the Clifton Waller Barrett Library, University of Virginia.

[5] "Chiefly About War Matters," *The Complete Works of Nathaniel Hawthorne*, Riverside Edition, ed. George Parsons Lathrop (Boston: Houghton Mifflin, 1883, 1891), XII, 332. All subsequent references are cited as *R*. The essay was originally printed in *Atlantic Monthly*, 10 (1862), 43–61.

sages regarding the Congress and President Lincoln's Cabinet. Each purported suppression, indicated by a sudden breaking-off of the narrator's discourse, is highlighted by an explanatory note. The editor's comment, however, has the humorous effect of stimulating reader interest in the missing passage while characterizing the freedom of description that has made its removal necessary. This element of his hoax seems to have established a precedent within the essay's text, apparently unintended by Hawthorne, for an unexpected excision of an interview with Lincoln. Fields's insistence that details of Lincoln's appearance would have to be modified brought about Hawthorne's last-minute decision to remove the interview passage altogether. This modification of the manuscript text was certainly the most notable, though other deletions and alterations were made as well.

Much of the confusion that has grown up around the genesis and publication of Hawthorne's essay is traceable to the influence of Fields. His account of the matter, including the text of the essay's deleted Lincoln interview, first appeared in 1871 in the *Atlantic*'s "Our Whispering Gallery" and later in *Yesterdays with Authors* (1872). Fields's comments on the censor's role he had exercised nine years earlier have been the source of misleading inferences: "If any one will turn to the paper in the Atlantic Monthly (it is in the number for July, 1862), it will be observed there are several notes; all of these were written by Hawthorne himself. He complied with my request without a murmur, but he always thought I was wrong in my decision." These remarks suggest that Hawthorne wrote the footnotes to the essay at Fields's request. Fields's comments as a whole invite the inference that other deleted passages, most likely those others indicated in the essay by footnotes, along with the Lincoln interview, resulted from his insistence on "alterations."[6] In fact, as will be shown further on, the textual changes brought about by Fields, in the interest of propriety, stripped the essay's manuscript text of Hawthorne's most revealing satirical humor,

---

[6] *Yesterdays with Authors* (Boston: Osgood, 1872), p. 98; these remarks appeared earlier in epistolary form as part of a shorter version of Fields's recollections of Hawthorne in "Our Whispering Gallery," *Atlantic Monthly*, 27 (1871), 510; and subsequently in expository form as part of a revised and expanded chapter of Fields's memoirs in *Yesterdays with Authors*.

particularly unmistakable signals of mock-seriousness within the footnotes. Fields did not, however, alter the fundamental nature of Hawthorne's intentional hoax.

The editorial gloss in the Riverside Edition was almost certainly derived from Fields's account of the matter. George Parsons Lathrop, editor of the Riverside whose initials are appended to the headnote to the text of "Chiefly About War Matters," was so unaware that the footnotes were a part of Hawthorne's authorial intention that he states, "It has seemed best to retain them in the present reproduction" (*R*, XII, 299). Most likely, Lathrop did not know of Hawthorne's manuscript and used Fields's article as the source of the Lincoln interview passage, which he restored in the Riverside text. Lathrop's apparent reliance on Fields's published account (probably after Fields's death in 1881) very likely explains why the Riverside text presents only a partial restoration of Hawthorne's original essay, rather than a faithful representation of the manuscript.

Other comments in the Riverside gloss, evidently based upon Fields's account, have perpetuated further misunderstandings. Lathrop's headnote, which was retained with slight alterations in later collected editions of Hawthorne's works, states that when the article first appeared, "the editor of the magazine objected to sundry paragraphs in the manuscript, and these were cancelled with the consent of the author, who himself supplied all the foot-notes that accompanied the article when it was published" (*R*, XII, 299). Moreover, in the Riverside and later editions, an explanation appended to the Lincoln interview states that the restored passage "was one of those omitted from the article as originally published" (*R*, XII, 312), reiterating the implication that others had been omitted as well. Accordingly, current readers are still presented with the erroneous impression that the missing passages of the essay's text, which were to have satirized the Congress and Lincoln's Cabinet, were deleted from the essay, at Fields's request, before its first publication. Scholars, as well, have been continually misled into assuming that not only were these apparent "cancellations" once included in the text, but that the footnotes were part of an overall author-editor agreement to make the article acceptable for the *Atlantic* in 1862.

For reasons of his own, Fields in 1871 obscured much that he might have elucidated. In view of what seems to have occurred, his circumspect account does not explicitly falsify the facts. On the other hand, his confusing shift of focus between matters regarding the article as a whole and the tenuous resolution of the issue of the Lincoln interview does suggest that Hawthorne's manuscript text was unadulterated by editorial interventions and was therefore fundamentally different from the *Atlantic* version.

The impact of this erroneous impression has been pernicious and long-lived. If Hawthorne had violated his text only as a concession to Fields's conditions for publishing it, the surviving version would seem to nullify Hawthorne's original intention. Questions relating to the restoration of Hawthorne's text have not been pursued, perhaps in part because the author has been thought to be unsure of his purpose. What might be construed as malice, however, seems entirely inconsistent with Fields's generous nature. His motivation, as discussed further on, is not easily determined.

Hawthorne's own motivation in producing a satirical hoax and the final form it was to have taken *are* clear, however, from his correspondence with his publishers, the surviving manuscript of "Chiefly About War Matters," and the historical context in which he wrote. Initially, he had written much more than he could include in the space limit of the article. As he told Fields in his letter of 7 May 1862 accompanying the manuscript, he "had to leave out a great deal; else it would have grown into a book."[7] But the necessity of being selective by itself would not have inspired him to invent the censored version of his essay that his manuscript presents. More importantly, he anticipated that much of his material would be objectionable to Northern readers of the *Atlantic*. This fact and his response to it explain why he was led to contrive the satirical form that his essay assumed.

The extent of Hawthorne's sociopolitical estrangement from his Northern world, though well-known in general, was more extreme than can be readily imagined. In his biography, Moncure D. Conway observed that in the early days of the war

---

[7] *The Centenary Edition of the Works of Nathaniel Hawthorne*, ed. William Charvat et al. (Columbus: Ohio State Univ. Press, 1962-). All subsequent references are cited as *C*. Subsequent quotations from *The Letters, 1857–1864* (C, XVIII) are identified in the text, e.g., Hawthorne to Fields, 7 May 1862. I am indebted to Centenary editors Thomas Woodson and James A. Rubino for generously sending me computer file copies of Hawthorne's correspondence before this volume was published.

Hawthorne "had no party,—then nearly equivalent to having no country. Probably," Conway went on to speculate, "there was not an individual in the United States who would have subscribed his article [sic], 'Chiefly About War Matters.' "[8] Conway's abolitionist allegiance, which was a radical revolt against his own Southern heritage, may have led him to exaggerate Hawthorne's estrangement. Nevertheless, Fields's explanation of Hawthorne's notoriety during the same period corroborates the propriety of Conway's assessment: "Those were troublous days, full of war gloom and general despondency. The North was naturally suspicious of all public men, who did not bear a conspicuous part in helping to put down the Rebellion."[9]

Ironically, the politics of the war had flung Hawthorne back into an earlier predicament, despite his lifelong attempt "to open an intercourse with the world" (*C*, IX, 6). The problem of audience he encountered in 1862, though more intense and acutely focused, produced an effect reminiscent of the authorial isolation he had experienced for more than a decade, until the publication of *The Scarlet Letter* (1850). Hawthorne had humored himself in 1851 by observing that prior to this recognition he could hardly "regard himself as addressing the American Public, or, indeed, any Public at all" (*C*, IX, 5).

The same could be said of Hawthorne's situation as a commentator on the Civil War, though for very different reasons. An article on the subject uppermost in the national consciousness would come to the attention of the *Atlantic*'s 30,000 or more subscribers. But Hawthorne certainly knew that a magazine with Republican sympathies (whose semiannual title pages in the collected volumes bear the Union flag in glorious sunlight above somber clouds) would have few readers prone to appreciate the narrator's examination of the crisis from a Southerner's point of view. Few could be expected to reflect calmly on the implications of a Swiftian proposal to allow only men of "fifty-five or sixty" to be "eligible for most kinds of military duty and exposure." Most would probably be somewhat puzzled and annoyed at the sardonic tone beneath the veil of lyricism, particularly as the

---

[8] Conway, p. 206.
[9] Fields, p. 107.

narrator's argument proceeds from a lament over the tragic loss of youthful lives to a poeticized reflection upon the prospect of an elderly combatant's death—the bullet wound "a pretty little orifice, through which the weary spirit might seize the opportunity to be exhaled!" (R, XII, 334). Readers holding to patriotic illusions would not be predisposed to recognize the cool anger with which the author seems here to have dwelt upon the evil of language appropriated to glorify sentimental heroics and obscure the brutal facts of the battlefield. Though the essay might reach the hands of a multitude, the unsettling illuminations of "A Peaceable Man" would have few understanding listeners.

Some realization of this irony must have occurred to Hawthorne. The derisive humor in his two letters to Fields, though private, is very much in consonance with the essay itself. Taken together, the public and private record serve as an index of the unsparing satirical spirit in which Hawthorne devised his literary hoax. There were strong currents of public opinion that he intended to play upon, and provocatively undercut, for which he could expect little sympathy even from his friends. His attempt to humor Fields in what seems to have been the first disclosure of a plan to foist an editorial pose on Fields himself reveals the extent to which Hawthorne's problem of audience had complicated his intention. After informing Fields that he had left out "a great deal," his letter of 7 May continued: "You will see that I have affixed some editorial foot-notes, which I hope you will have no hesitation in adopting, they being very loyal. For my own part, I found it quite difficult not to lapse into treason continually; but I made manful resistance to the temptation. I am afraid it will prove a stupid affair."

Circumstances during the next week or so would cause Hawthorne to become increasingly troubled over the possibility of creating "a stupid affair." On 17 May, ten days after submitting the article, he wrote to William D. Ticknor, senior partner of Ticknor and Fields. He had learned that Fields had trustingly "transmitted" his manuscript "to the printer unread" and had departed for New York "without looking it over in the proof-sheet." Evidently, Hawthorne had been hoping Fields's reaction would allay his own apprehensions; now the article was on its way to final production. Not wishing to cause a disaster for the

Atlantic's circulation (as in fact, Harriet Beecher Stowe brought about seven years later with her Byron article), he thought it time to alert Ticknor.

Despite its genial tone, the letter reveals a sharply divided impulse. After discussing the financial plight of his sister Elizabeth, Hawthorne shifts incidentally to Fields's departure: "This is somewhat to be regretted; because I wanted the benefit of somebody's opinion besides my own as to the expediency of publishing two or three passages in the article. I have already half-spoilt it by leaving out a great deal of spicy description and remark, and whole pages of freely expressed opinion, which seemed to me as good as anything I ever wrote, but which I doubted whether the public would bear."

The ambivalent effect of the assertions that follow belies the casual approach in the letter as a whole: what remains of the article "is tame enough in all conscience, and I don't think it will bear any more castration; but still, I don't wish to foist an article upon you that might anywise damage the Magazine." On this point, Hawthorne tries a reverse argument: "I think the political complexion of the Magazine has been getting too deep a black Republican tinge, and that there is a time pretty near at hand when you will be sorry for it. . . . After all, I think I left out almost everything that could possibly be objectionable (that is to say, everything in the least worth retaining,) . . . so that I need not have mentioned it to you at all. Nevertheless, my advice about the Magazine may be worth considering."

These concerns for the magazine notwithstanding, his determination to publish his opposition to popular views, regardless of the consequences to his reputation, shows the strength of his convictions about the war. Although contributors to the 1862 *Atlantic* were not identified, except in the alphabetical listings of the semiannual, library volumes, authorship was no secret among the magazine's readers around Boston where most of the contributors resided. Hawthorne presented Ticknor with this mitigating factor alongside his intention to upset reader expectations: "On the other hand, I shall be known as the author, and should be willing to take the responsibility of much worse things than I have written here. . . ."

Ticknor did not reply to Hawthorne's alert but was soon to confer with Fields. On 21 May, four days after Hawthorne had written, the putative censor replied: "I have just returned from New York and at once went to the Printing Office of the A.M. as a loyal Editor should do. I found yr. article all ready to send to you in proof and sat down to read it." Though he had expected to "like it hugely" and said he did, he specified changes he and Ticknor had agreed would have to be made. All references to *"Uncle Abe"* should be changed to "the President," and "the description of his awkwardness & general uncouth aspect" should be left out.[10] Fields referred to other troublesome passages, but did so by indicating pages of the proof where he had made markings.[11] At one point, he explicitly touched upon a remark regarding the Southerners that may have resulted in the noticeable strengthening of the narrator's Northern allegiance in the penultimate paragraph of the essay.[12] Moreover, Fields's other markings most likely brought about the deletion of a footnote (in the manuscript text) that follows the portrait of General McClellan.[13] This passage and other alterations of the manuscript were not restored after 1871.[14]

On 23 May, two days after Fields had written his instructions, Hawthorne was ready to return the page proofs. His response shows none of the earlier uncertainty he had expressed to Ticknor. Though he thinks Fields is "wrong," he is "going to comply." It was Hawthorne's decision to omit "the whole description of the interview with Uncle Abe, and his personal appearance," because he did "not find it possible to alter them." Fields had merely requested that he take out irreverent details of Lincoln's awkwardness. Hawthorne "likewise modified the other passage" to which Fields had referred, most likely the

[10] Fields to Hawthorne, 21 May 1862 (*C*, XVIII, 458n).

[11] These numbers do not match those pages the essay came to occupy in the final printing of the issue.

[12] The manuscript states that "Very excellent people, hereabouts, remember the many dynasties in which the Southern character has been predominant, and contrast the genial courtesy, the warm and graceful freedom of that region, with the awkward frigidity of our Northern manners, and the uncouthness of Uncle Abe"; the printed essay was amended to read, "with what they call (though I utterly disagree with them) the frigidity of our Northern manners, and the Western plainness of the President" (*R*, XII, 344).

[13] "Apparently with the idea of balancing his gracious treatment of the Commander-in-chief, the author had here inserted some idle sarcasms about other officers whom he happened to see at the review; one of whom (a distinguished general,) he says, 'sat his horse like a meal-bag, and was the stupidest looking man he ever saw.' Such license is not creditable to the Peaceable Man, and we do him a kindness in crossing out the passage."

[14] Other alterations to the manuscript are noted in *Letters* (*C*, XVIII, 462n; 464n).

comparison of Northern and Southern manners near the end (as noted above).

In connection with the removal of the Lincoln interview, Hawthorne also states that he has "altered and transferred one of the notes," indicating that he performed what would have been a quick operation, due to the pseudo-censorship already established elsewhere in the text. Apart from the interview, the discussion of Lincoln includes a paragraph in which the Peaceable Man "deem[ed] it proper to say a word or two in regard to him, of unfeigned respect and measurable confidence" (*R*, XII, 313). These remarks remained in the *Atlantic* version. Following the longer passage on Lincoln in the manuscript text, however, a footnote that survives in modified form originally began: "We hesitated to admit the above sketch, and shall probably regret our decision in its favor." This humorous signal of satirical intent must have taken on a new semblance of dramatic irony for Hawthorne as he deleted it, moved the rest of the note to the juncture where the interview passage would be taken out, and substituted a new beginning: "We are compelled to omit two or three pages, in which the author describes the interview, and gives his idea of the personal appearance and deportment of the President" (*R*, XII, 312).

While going along with his publishers, Hawthorne distanced himself from their decision. His patronizing reply to Fields as he claimed to be "the most good-natured man, and the most amenable to good advice (or bad advice either, for that matter)," followed by the complete withdrawal of the Lincoln interview, must have struck Fields forcibly. After asserting that the passage "must be omitted," Hawthorne immediately reversed the responsibility, laying the action on Fields: "and in so doing, I really think you omit the only part of the article really worth publishing. Upon my honor, it seems to me to have a historical value—but let it go."

The close friendship between Hawthorne and Fields seems to have been unaffected by their differences of opinion about the article. Evidently, both could remove themselves as private individuals from their public roles. Three months after the publication of "Chiefly About War Matters," Hawthorne displayed the depth of their trust in a letter which appeared as a headnote with his next sketch in the October 1862 *Atlantic*. This letter from the "Peaceable Man" opens with a mock-heroic threat of a gentleman's challenge to duel, including a near pun on Fields's name:

> My Dear Editor,—
> You can hardly have expected to hear from me again, (unless by invitation to the field of honor,) after those cruel and terrible notes upon my harmless article in the July Number.[15]

Hawthorne probably felt that the character of his intention in "Chiefly About War Matters" had been somewhat obscured by the last-minute changes. The note as a whole offers a public clarification. The tone throughout, like that in the opening remarks above, is highhandedly playful. The grievances expressed *do* contain an unescapable germ of private truth, though they are exaggerated with fictitious license. To the public, on the other hand, this "sendup" was sufficiently obvious to have cleared Fields of any serious involvement as "the Editor" in the previous article. Moreover, by explicitly connecting the pseudonymous authorship of "Chiefly About War Matters" with the English travel pieces to follow, Hawthorne leaves no doubt that he meant to take full authorial responsibility for what was, after all, a censorship hoax.

Fields's apparent exaggeration of his influence in changing the essay remains very curious. Evidently, his profound respect for Hawthorne produced an unresolvable conflict between his role as a guardian of the faith during the national upheaval and his obeisance to Hawthorne's artistic integrity. In his 1871 reminiscence, he summed up his earlier feelings by remarking that "the office of an editor is a disagreeable one sometimes, and the case of Hawthorne on Lincoln disturbed me not a little." Seven years after Hawthorne's death, and six years after the South's surrender, the war's outcome and the apotheosis of Lincoln as savior of the Union no doubt seemed to vindicate his earlier judgment. Thus, he prefaced his disclosure of the suppressed passage on Lincoln with the assurance that "I will copy here verbatim what I advised my friend, both on his own account and the President's, not to print nine years ago."[16]

---

[15] "Leamington Spa," *Atlantic Monthly*, 10 (1862), 451. Fields carefully distinguished between the personal and professional in reply to Hawthorne's essay. Appended to "I don't like* the way you speak of the Southerners. . ." is a qualifying note: "*as an Editor and Publisher" (C, XVIII, 458n).

[16] Fields, p. 98.

But this forthrightness and his candor following the Lincoln sketch are belied by the misleading impression of his other remarks, regarding the genesis of the footnotes. Despite his defense of his earlier judgment, Fields's distaste over his role as censor may have led him to the false conclusion that he had prevented Hawthorne from writing the work that the author had originally intended. This hypothetical work was probably of the same order as others, which Hawthorne said, belonged "on a certain ideal shelf, where are reposited many other shadowy volumes of mine, more in number, and very much superior in quality, to those which I have succeeded in rendering actual" (*C*, V, 4).

Hawthorne's own clarification of the matter along similar lines should have led Fields to quite a different conclusion. Here are his final comments in the reply he made to Fields with the proof sheets of his article:

What a terrible thing it is to try to let off a little bit of truth into this miserable humbug of a world! If I had sent you the article as I first conceived it, I should not so much have wondered.

I want you to send me a proof-sheet of the article in its present state, before making any alterations; for, if ever I collect these sketches into a volume, I shall insert it in all its original beauty.
(Hawthorne to Fields, 23 May 1862)

Explicit are two conclusive points: first, the public taste and opinion of the Northern establishment for which Hawthorne wrote had compelled him to abandon an original conception, something closer to his own ideal; second, he fully endorsed the text he had actually produced. His strategy of truncating the text was prompted in part by anger at the vehement public mood. As he told Fields, the last-minute alterations necessitated by the omission of the Lincoln passage were "to indicate to the unfortunate public that it here loses something very nice."

II

It would be a mistake, however, to characterize Hawthorne's achievement in the essay as the product of a makeshift plan. His own estrangement from contemporaries evidently heightened his awareness of the danger of self-censorship during the crisis. This concern informs his ironic framework as a whole. While he was primarily determined to give full expression to his critical detachment from the politics of the war, he accomplished this purpose and more. By incorporating the voice of opposition into his essay, Hawthorne enlarged its critical scope and necessarily detached himself from his own skeptical attitudes. Thus, he not only objectified his vision of the crisis, but also displayed the passionate tensions of the historical moment.

The notes as a whole serve two radically different functions. On the one hand, there is the conspicuous representation of censorship. The voice of the imaginary censor—alternately acute, strident, or unwittingly humorous—sustains Hawthorne's ironic vision with powerful economy. As mentioned earlier, some of the humor that arises from the editor in the manuscript text has yet to be restored to the essay. A deleted footnote describing a general on horseback concludes: "Such license is not creditable to the Peaceable Man, and we do him a kindness in crossing out the passage." Not an unkindly figure, the editor here takes the form of a dangerous oppressor, the benign authoritarian. With good reason, perhaps, Fields may have thought the image of the general who "sat his horse like a meal-bag, and was the stupidest looking man" the narrator had ever seen, too offensive. If so, his reaction corroborates the narrator's judgment elsewhere in the text that Lincoln's stories, which "smack of the frontier freedom," might not bear repeating "on the immaculate page of the Atlantic" (R, XII, 312). Clearly, Hawthorne devised the humor in this passage—with the editor's disclosure of material he means to suppress—as a signal that the editorial intrusions should be understood as satire.

On the other hand, the footnotes raised in protest against the text dramatically illustrate the dialectic of freedom of speech. As Walter Lippmann once explained, freedom of speech is not simply the expression of opinions, it is "the confrontation of opinions in debate."[17] Although the full range of Hawthorne's intention in the essay as a whole cannot be reduced to one didactic effect, the footnotes demonstrate this important lesson. Thus, it is precisely because "the freedom of opinion which causes opposing opinions to be debated" is, as Lippmann argues, "indispensable" that some of the editorial remarks stand up forcibly against the views expressed in Hawthorne's text. His application of this principle may have contributed to the impression that

---

[17] "The Indispensable Opposition," *Atlantic Monthly*, 164 (1939), 188.

he was confused during the war. But the opposition within the essay is a corollary to the dialectical habit that probes for truth in much of his writing. Unlike the Hegelian dialectic, his was most penetrating when it remained unresolved.[18] The value of his analysis in the midst of crisis has little to do with the outcome of events. It was the discrepancy between the ideological faith necessary to win a war and the particular truths as he observed them that engaged him as a critic of history itself.

Finding himself at odds with the American world, Hawthorne could not accept the solution of silence. As he wrote at the beginning of the essay, "there is a kind of treason in insulating one's self from the universal fear and sorrow . . . in the dread time of civil war" (R, XII, 300). Self-isolation, a recurrent theme of his life and work, was here recast as a form of "treason." His daring appropriation of this term, denoting the most heinous of crimes during the crisis of the war, raises its significance beyond the causes of the moment, to the ultimate level of forsaking involvement with the rest of humanity. This quintessential "treason" had always been a capital offense in Hawthorne's moral universe. Hawthorne's detachment from the popular support of the Northern cause in the Civil War has been criticized, but his engagement with the tragic drama itself should be praised. As an artist and public figure, Hawthorne fulfilled a moral imperative by making his views of the war a matter of public and historical record. To do so without compromising his integrity, he incorporated the voice of opposition into his overall intention, both for the expediency of the moment and with the full realization that what he wished to convey could only be achieved through a unique demonstration of his impersonality as an artist.

---

[18] I am indebted to Professor Brom Weber for this description of Hawthorne's dialectic, and for other very helpful advice in the preparation of this article.

Index

Aaron, Daniel, 263n.
Abel, Darrel, 52n., 239n.
allegory, 52–64, 100, 106–113, 124–126, 129–131, 134, 137
ambiguity, 24–32
Andros, Sir Edmond, 3
Arthur, William, 141–142n., 143n.
Arvin, Newton, 89n., 112, 134n.
Auchincloss, Louis, 166n.

Baym, Nina, 166n., 180n., 194–220, 235n., 247n., 264n.
Bell, Michael D., 241
Bense, James, 262–276
Bewley, Marius, 123n., 124n.
Bible, the, 27, 77, 137
Blake, William, 52, 184
Bowdoin College, 141
Boyton, Jeremy, 142n.
Bradford, William, 250
Brattle, Thomas, 114
Bridge, Horatio, 141
Brodkin, Stanley, 180n., 191
Brontë, Emily, 261
Brooks, Van Wyck, 52
Brown, Charles Brockden, 261
Brownell, W. C., 2
Browning, Robert, 82
Bryant, William Cullen, 6n., 232
Burhans, Clifton, 180n.
Byers, John B., 228n.
Byron, Lord, 270

Cameron, Sharon, 245n.
Canaday, Nicholas, 179n.
Cantwell, Robert, 196
Carlyle, Thomas, 36
Champollion, Jean-Françoise, 123
Chandler, E. L., 13n.
Charles I, 229, 231n., 236
Choate, Rufus, 3–5
Chrétien, L. E., 11

Civil War (American), 262–276
Clark, C. E. Fraser, 180n.
Colacurcio, Michael J., 245n., 248n., 250, 255n.
Conway, Moncure D., 263n., 267–268
Cooper, James Fenimore, 2, 6n.
Cowley, Malcolm, 52n., 53
Crane, J. T., 142n.
Crews, Frederick C., 82–105, 164n., 166n., 180n., 245n., 247, 258n.
Cronin, Morton, 239n.
Curti, Merle, 141n.

Daly, Robert S., 245n., 248n.
Dauber, Kenneth, 180n.
Dauner, Louise, 24–32, 49n.
Davidson, Frank, 82, 89
Dawson, Edward, 229n.
Degler, Carl N., 202
Doubleday, Neal, 1–7, 239n.
Downing, David, 180–192
Duyckinck, Evert, 223, 226n., 231–232n.
Duyckinck, George, 223n., 226, 231–232n.

Ehrlich, Gloria, 196
Eisinger, Chester, 111n.
Eliot, T. S., 178
Emerson, Ralph Waldo, 166, 223, 232n.
England, 152–163
epic, 54, 64
Eyck, Frank, 222n.

Fejto, François, 222n.
Felt, Joseph B., 228n., 230
feminism, 165, 171, 172
Fiedler, Leslie, 133n.
Fields, James T., 1n., 152, 262–276
Finney, Charles G., 142, 144
Fitzgerald, F. Scott, 178

Fogle, Richard H., 52n., 53, 106n., 112n., 120, 123n.
Foster, R. S., 142n.
Franzosa, John, 195n.
Frederickson, George M., 263n.
Freneau, Phillip, 251
Freud, Sigmund, 10–11, 12n., 15–16, 89, 197, 258
Fuller, Margaret, 223–224, 237, 243
Fussell, Edwin, 246n., 255n.

Gardiner, W. H., 2
Garibaldi, Giuseppe, 224
Gerber, John C., 52, 222
Goethe, Johann Wolfgang von, 261
Goodrich, Samuel B., 39, 223, 246
Gorman, Herbert, 196
Griffith, Kelley, 166n.
Griswold, Rufus W., 173
Gross, Seymour, 39–51
Guizot, François, 222, 229–230, 232, 244
Gwynn, F. L., 106n.

Hart, James D., 222
Hathorne, Elizabeth ("Ebe"), 198, 201–202, 207, 208–212, 270
Hathorne, Elizabeth Manning, 194–220
Hathorne, Louisa, 198–199, 202, 207
Hathorne, Nathaniel, 201
Hawthorne, Julian, 1n., 83, 195n., 198–200, 207n., 208, 210, 211, 224n., 252n., 263n.
Hawthorne, Manning, 196, 205n.
Hawthorne, Nathaniel: Writings by,
    "Alice Doane's Appeal," 116, 185–193
    "Chiefly About War Matters," 262–276
    Dr. Grimshawe's Secret, 163
    "Endicott and the Red Cross," 3, 4, 5, 40, 228
    Fanshawe, 2, 207, 247
    French and Italian Notebooks, 206n.
    "Grandfather's Chair," 250n.
    "Graves and Goblins," 135–136
    "Howe's Masquerade," 2n., 3
    "Leamington Spa," 273n.
    "Liberty Tree," 225n.
    "Main Street," 40, 157, 160, 217
    Mosses from an Old Manse, 116n.
    "Mrs. Hutchinson," 3, 5
    "My Kinsman, Major Molineux," 39n., 193, 204, 225, 246, 247
    "Old Esther Dudley," 2n.
    Our Old Home, 153–154, 157, 159, 162
    "Outside Glimpses of English Poverty," 219
    Passages from the French and Italian Note-Books, 11n., 19n.
    "P's Correspondence," 7
    "Rappaccini's Daughter," 106–113, 123, 174
    "Roger Malvin's Burial," 2n., 39n., 245–261
    Septimius Felton, 2n., 13n., 19–20, 225n.
    "Sights from a Steeple," 247
    "Sir William Pepperel," 248n.
    "Sir William Phips," 248–249n.
    "The Ambitious Guest," 129n.
    The American Notebooks, 20n., 83n., 102n., 113n., 133n.
    The Ancestral Footstep, 163
    "The Artist of the Beautiful," 89
    "The Birthmark," 156, 174
    The Blithedale Romance, 6n., 82–105, 149, 160, 164–179, 218–219, 246
    The Elixir of Life Manuscripts, 225n.
    The English Notebooks, 7, 152n., 153, 206n.
    "The Gentle Boy," 3, 5, 24–32, 39–51, 153, 157, 246
    "The Great Carbuncle," 2n.
    "The Grey Champion," 3, 4, 153
    "The Hall of Fantasy," 39n.
    "The Haunted Mind," 145
    "The Hollow of the Three Hills," 156, 180–185

The House of the Seven Gables,
    33–38, 64, 147, 160, 164, 218
"The Man of Adamant," 246
The Marble Faun, 6n., 8–23, 25,
    37, 89, 149–150, 153, 154–155,
    156, 158, 159–160, 161–162, 204,
    218–219
"The Maypole of Merry Mount," 3,
    5, 19
"The Old Tory," 225n.
"The Prophetic Pictures," 89
The Scarlet Letter, 6, 25, 29, 52–64,
    65–81, 123–140, 147, 156, 159,
    160–161, 163, 177, 194–220, 221–
    244, 246, 268
"The Story-Teller," 247
"The Wedding Knell," 139
"The Wives of the Dead," 39n.
True Stories from History and Biography, 152n.
Twice-Told Tales, 207
"Young Goodman Brown," 3, 5,
    29, 114–122, 160, 246
Hawthorne, Sophia. *See* Peabody,
    Sophia
Hawthorne, Una, 213
Hedges, William, 166n.
Hegel, Georg Wilhelm Friedrich, 276
Heilman, Robert B., 112n.
Hemingway, Ernest, 178
Hicks, Granville, 8
Hillard, 224
Hirsch, John C., 170n.
Hoeltje, Hubert, 194n., 196
Housman, A. E., 113
Howard, Leon, 141n.
Howells, W. D., 82, 164
Hull, Raymona, 264n.

Italy, 152–156, 162

James, Henry, 6n., 8, 9, 29, 30n., 31,
    52, 66, 82, 104, 111, 164, 178, 178–
    179n., 263n.
James II, 231n.
Johnson, Claudia D., 141–151

Joyce, James, 104
Justus, James H., 164–179

Kearns, Francis E., 243
Kesselring, Marion L., 229n., 234n.,
    250n.
King Philip's War, 249

Lamartine, Alphonse-Marie-Louis de,
    231–234, 244
Laser, Marvin, 141n.
Lathrop, George P., 1n., 40n., 116n.,
    123n., 266
Laud, William, 46
Lawrence, D. H., 9n.
Levin, David, 114–122, 248n.
Levin, Harry, 115n., 121n.
Levy, Leo B., 166n.
Lewisohn, Ludwig, 8–9
Lincoln, Abraham, 263, 264, 265, 266,
    267, 271, 272, 273, 275
Lippmann, Walter, 275
Liverpool, 152–159
London, 154–155, 162–163
Loughman, Celeste, 225n.
Louis Napoleon, 224
Louis Philippe, 230
Louis XVI, 229, 232, 236
"Lovell's Fight," 2n., 245–261
Lowell, J. R., 223

McCabe, Bernard, 107n.
McClellan, George, 262–263, 271
McIntosh, James, 245–261
McKeithan, D. M., 115
Maclean, Hugh N., 52–64
McNamara, Anne Marie, 65–81,
    124n., 131n.
McWilliams, John P., 225n.
Mahan, Asa, 142n., 144
Male, Roy R., 106n., 112n., 124n.,
    133n., 178n.
Mann, Thomas, 8–9, 15, 20, 21–22
Manning, Elizabeth Clarke, 200–201
Manning, Richard, 201, 204, 205
Manning, Robert, 204
Manning, Samuel, 207

Marraro, Howard, 223n.
Martin, Terence, 152–163, 173n.
Marvell, Andrew, 229
Mather, Cotton, 116–117, 118n., 121n.
Mather, Increase, 114
Matthiessen, F. O., 52, 53, 64, 83, 120, 264n.
May, Arthur J., 223n.
Mazzini, Giuseppe, 223
Meek, Alexander, 5–6n.
Mellow, James, 196, 207n., 221n.
Melville, Herman, 28, 31, 32, 52, 64, 252
Michaud, Régis, 11n.
Michelangelo, 19
Miller, Harold P., 39n.
Miller, Paul W., 115n.
Morgan, Ellen E., 168n.
Morris, Lloyd, 9n., 19n., 196
Morton, Nathaniel, 250

nationalism, literary, 1–7
Neal, John, 3
Newberry, Frederick, 230n.
New England, 1–7, 155–156, 162–163, 165, 166, 246, 252
New-England Primer, The, 136
Nissenbaum, Stephen, 194n.
Normand, Jean, 195n.
Noyes, John Humphrey, 142, 143n.

O'Connor, W. V., 82
Orel, Harold, 33–38
Orians, G. H., 1, 3n., 4, 40n.
Osgood, James R., 207
Owen, James J., 228n.

Paine, Thomas, 244
Palmer, Phoebe, 142n.
Pandeya, Prabhat, 180n.
Pattee, F. L., 3n.
Peabody, Elizabeth, 198–199, 203
Peabody, Sophia [Hawthorne], 197–199, 207–212, 218, 224, 234
Pearce, Roy Harvey, 152
Pearson, Norman Holmes, 196, 199n., 203n.

perfectionism, 141–151
Pierce, Franklin, 152
Ponder, Melinda, 252n.
Praxiteles, 13
Price, S. R., 112n.
Puritanism, 2, 4, 5, 25–32, 39–51, 122, 142, 154, 156–157, 180–193, 229, 246, 248, 254

Quakers, 25–32, 39–51, 114

realism, 90, 100, 167
Republican Party, 268, 270
revolution, 221–244
Reynolds, Larry, 221–244
Ringe, Donald A., 240
Romance, the, 2, 52–64, 82, 85–86, 88, 90–96, 98–100, 102–103, 104, 153, 167, 173, 177, 256, 257, 260, 261
Rome, 154–156, 159–163, 224
Rosenberry, Edward H., 106–113
Rubino, James A., 267n.

Scheick, William J., 245n.
Schubert, Leland, 66, 235
science, 106–113
Scott, Sir Walter, 1–7
Sedgwick, W. E., 6n.
Shakespeare, William, 30, 42, 110
Simms, William Gilmore, 5–6
Slotkin, Richard, 251n.
Smith, Henry Nash, 238
Snow, Caleb H., 228
Sparks, Jared, 1n.
Spengemann, William, 213n.
Spiller, Robert, 6n.
Stewart, Randall, 6n., 20n., 113, 116n., 152n., 196, 207n., 263–264n.
Stock, Ely, 180n.
Stowe, Harriet Beecher, 270
Strong, George T., 232n.
Stubb, John C., 178n.
Swift, Jonathan, 104

Taylor, Edward, 78n., 118
Taylor, Zachary, 227
Tharp, Louise Hall, 212n.

Thoreau, Henry David, 253
Ticknor, William D., 269, 270, 271
tragedy, 28, 31, 42, 113
Trevor-Roper, H. P., 192n.
Trollope, Anthony, 164
Tudor, William, 2–3
Turner, Arlin, 13n., 83n., 164n., 195n., 196, 208n., 209n., 227, 264

Upham, Thomas C., 141–151

Van Doren, Carl, 2n.
Van Doren, Mark, 51n., 53n., 83, 106n., 195–196
von Abele, Rudolph, 83, 89, 165n.

Waggoner, Hyatt, 82, 89, 102n., 106n., 113, 123–124n., 183n., 245n.

Walsh, Thomas M., 115n.
Waples, Dorothy, 8–23
Ward, Nathaniel, 45
Warren, Austin, 33, 106n.
Warren, Robert Penn, 178n.
Weaver, Raymond, 31n.
Weber, Brom, 276n.
Westminster Catechism, 136, 137
Whelan, Robert E., 123–140
White, Elizabeth, 223n.
Whittier, John Greenleaf, 2n., 4n.
Williams, Roger, 5
Williams, Stanley, 33
Winters, Yvor, 82
Woodberry, George, 1, 4n., 196
Woodson, Thomas, 206n., 243, 267n.

Ziff, Larzer, 192n.

Notes on Contributors

Nina Baym (1936–). University of Illinois, 1963–. *The Shape of Hawthorne's Career* (1976); *Women's Fiction: A Guide to Novels by and about Women in America, 1820–1870* (1978); *Novels, Readers, and Reviewers: Responses to Fiction in Antebellum America* (1984); *The Scarlet Letter: A Reading* (1986).

James Bense (1948–). University of Maryland, 1978–1981; University of California, Davis, 1982–.

Frederick C. Crews (1933–). University of California, Berkeley, 1959–. *The Tragedy of Manners: Moral Drama in the Later Novels of Henry James,* (1962); *The Pooh Perplex* (1963); *The Sins of the Fathers: Hawthorne's Psychological Themes* (1966); *Out of My System: Psychoanalysis, Ideology, and Critical Method* (1975); *Skeptical Engagements* (1986).

Louise Dauner (1907–). University of Wisconsin, 1945–1946; Butler University, 1946–1947; Drake University, 1948–1963; Indiana University (IUPUI), 1963–1977.

Neal F. Doubleday (1905–1976). University of Wisconsin, 1936–1939; Montana State University, 1939–1940; University of Connecticut, 1940–1945; Milikin University, 1946–1970. *Mark Twain's Picture of His America* (1960); *Hawthorne's Tales of His Native Land* (1962); *Hawthorne's Early Tales: A Critical Study* (1971).

David Downing (1947–). Eastern Illinois University, 1979–1988; Indiana University of Pennsylvania, 1988.

Seymour L. Gross (1926–). Indiana University, South Bend, 1955–1957; University of Notre Dame, 1957–1969; University of Detroit, 1969–1987. *Images of the Negro in American Literature* (1966).

Claudia D. Johnson (1938–). University of Alabama, 1973–. *An Annotated Bibliography of Shakespearian Burlesques, Parodies, and Travesties* (with Henry Jacobs (1976); *The Productive Tension of Hawthorne's Art* (1981); *Memoirs of the Nineteenth-Century Theatre* (1982); *American Actresses: Perspective on the Nineteenth Century* (1984).

James H. Justus (1929–). University of Tennessee, 1956–1957; Indiana University, 1961–. *The Achievement of Robert Penn Warren* (1981); Editor, Baldwin, *The Flush Times of Alabama and Mississippi* (1987).

David Levin (1924–). Stanford University, 1952–1971; University of Virginia, 1971–. *What Happened in Salem?* (1952, 1960); *History as Romantic Art: Bancroft, Prescott, Motley, and Parkman* (1959); *Cotton Mather: The Young Life of the Lord's Remembrancer, 1663–1703* (1978); *Exemplary Elders* (1990).

Notes on Contributors

Hugh N. Maclean (1919–). University of Toronto, 1948–1950; Royal Military College of Canada, 1950–1956; University of Cincinnati, 1956–1960; York University (Canada), 1960–1963; SUNY-Albany, 1963–1986. *The Argyll and Sutherland Highlanders of Canada (Princess Louise's)* (1953); *Edmund Spenser's Poetry* (1969, 1982); *Ben Johnson and the Cavalier Poets* (1974).

Terence Martin (1925–). Indiana University 1954–. *The Instructed Vision: Scottish Common Sense Philosophy and the Origins of American Fiction* (1961); *Nathaniel Hawthorne* (1965, rev. ed., 1983).

James McIntosh (1934–). Tufts University, 1962–1967; Yale University, 1967–1975; University of Michigan, 1975–. *Thoreau as Romantic Naturalist: His Shifting Stance Toward Nature* (1974); *Nathaniel Hawthorne's Tales* (1987).

Anne Marie McNamara (1909–1961?). Catholic University, 1947–1957; Sacred Heart College (Newton, Mass.), 1957–1961?.

Harold Orel (1926–). University of Kansas, 1957–. *Thomas Hardy's Epic-Drama: A Study of "The Dynasts"* (1963); *The Development of William Butler Yeats, 1885–1900* (1968); *English Romantic Poets and the Enlightenment: Nine Essays on a Literary Relationship* (1973); *The Final Years of Thomas Hardy, 1912–1928* (1976).

Larry J. Reynolds (1942–). Texas A&M University, 1974–. *James Kirke Paulding* (1984); *European Revolutions and the American Literary Renaissance* (1988).

Edward H. Rosenberry (1916–). University of Delaware, 1952–1979. *Melville and the Comic Spirit* (1955); *Melville* (1979).

Dorothy Waples (1896–1948). University of Illinois, 1923–1927; Lawrence University, 1927–1948. *The Whig Myth of James Fenimore Cooper* (1938).

Robert E. Whelan (1924–). Saint John's University (N.Y.), 1961–.

Library of Congress Cataloging-in-Publication Data
On Hawthorne: the best from American literature/edited by Edwin H.
Cady and Louis J. Budd.
(The Best from American literature series)
ISBN 0-8223-1032-5
1. Hawthorne, Nathaniel, 1804–1864—Criticism and interpretation.
I. Cady, Edwin Harrison. II. Budd, Louis J. III. American
literature. IV. Series: Best from American literature.
PS1888.05   1990   813'.3—dc20   89-25696

EAST BATON ROUGE PARISH LIBRARY
BATON ROUGE, LOUISIANA

JONES CREEK REGIONAL